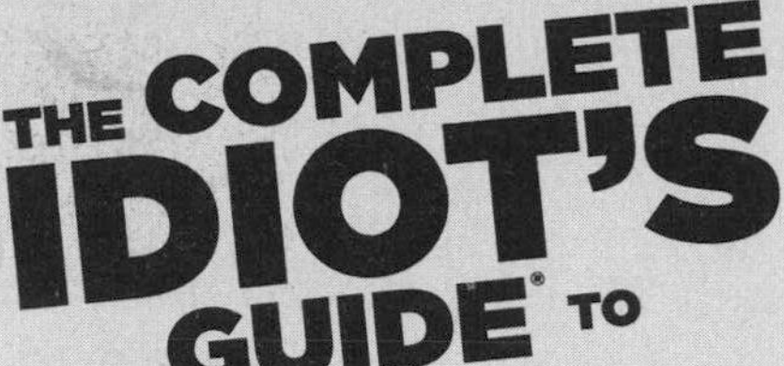

Pregnancy and Childbirth

Third Edition

Michele Isaacs Gliksman, M.D, with Theresa Foy DiGeronimo

ALPHA
A member of Penguin Group (USA) Inc.

I dedicate this book to my four children: Matthew, Erica, Keith, and David, who taught me what pregnancy and childbirth are really all about.—M. G.

ALPHA BOOKS

Published by the Penguin Group

Penguin Group (USA) Inc., 375 Hudson Street, New York, New York 10014, USA

Penguin Group (Canada), 90 Eglinton Avenue East, Suite 700, Toronto, Ontario M4P 2Y3, Canada (a division of Pearson Penguin Canada Inc.)

Penguin Books Ltd., 80 Strand, London WC2R 0RL, England

Penguin Ireland, 25 St. Stephen's Green, Dublin 2, Ireland (a division of Penguin Books Ltd.)

Penguin Group (Australia), 250 Camberwell Road, Camberwell, Victoria 3124, Australia (a division of Pearson Australia Group Pty. Ltd.)

Penguin Books India Pvt. Ltd., 11 Community Centre, Panchsheel Park, New Delhi—110 017, India

Penguin Group (NZ), 67 Apollo Drive, Rosedale, North Shore, Auckland 1311, New Zealand (a division of Pearson New Zealand Ltd.)

Penguin Books (South Africa) (Pty.) Ltd., 24 Sturdee Avenue, Rosebank, Johannesburg 2196, South Africa

Penguin Books Ltd., Registered Offices: 80 Strand, London WC2R 0RL, England

International Standard Book Number: 978-1-61564-030-0
Library of Congress Catalog Card Number: 2010920430

12 11 10 8 7 6 5 4 3 2 1

Interpretation of the printing code: The rightmost number of the first series of numbers is the year of the book's printing; the rightmost number of the second series of numbers is the number of the book's printing. For example, a printing code of 10-1 shows that the first printing occurred in 2010.

Printed in the United States of America

Most Alpha books are available at special quantity discounts for bulk purchases for sales promotions, premiums, fund-raising, or educational use. Special books, or book excerpts, can also be created to fit specific needs.

For details, write: Special Markets, Alpha Books, 375 Hudson Street, New York, NY 10014.

Publisher: *Marie Butler-Knight*
Associate Publisher: *Mike Sanders*
Executive Editor: *Randy Ladenheim-Gil*
Senior Managing Editor: *Billy Fields*
Development Editor: *Ginny Bess Munroe*
Senior Production Editor: *Janette Lynn*
Copy Editor: *Andy Saff*

Cover Designer: *Rebecca Batchelor*
Book Designers: *William Thomas, Rebecca Batchelor*
Indexer: *Tonya Heard*
Layout: *Brian Massey*
Proofreader: *Laura Caddell*
Illustrators: *Dana Chapman, Joe DiGeronimo*

Contents

Appendixes

Foreword

You're pregnant! This simple phrase introduces the most profound changes imaginable in a woman's life. Producing a new life is both thrilling and terrifying at the same time. How will I feel? How will I look? What will happen to my body? What will happen to my relationship with my partner? How am I going to deal with labor? What can I do to be sure my baby is healthy? These are questions that every woman addresses as pregnancy progresses.

The Complete Idiot's Guide to Pregnancy and Childbirth, Third Edition, is a wonderful reference for pregnant women and their partners. Dr. Michele Gliksman blends her unique point of view with wit, humor, a tremendous fund of knowledge, and many years of practical experience dealing with both normal and complicated pregnancies. The insights she shares are invaluable to all women as they approach pregnancy and childbirth.

The book is intended as a guide to all aspects of pregnancy and birth: how to follow a healthful diet, how to choose appropriate clothing, how to exercise safely and stay healthy. Dr. Gliksman encourages women to take an active role in their pregnancy and involve their partners in the process as well. She has a wonderful ability to communicate with women and educate them about the incredible journey they will experience.

The most impressive aspect of this work is its ability to allay the fears and anxieties all women face as pregnancy progresses. It is intended to complement, not replace, the advice and counsel provided by each woman's health-care provider. As your pregnancy progresses, this reference will be there for you at each stage of your baby's development.

It is organized to allow you to quickly access the information you want at this very moment. The guidance and reassurance it provides make it a truly invaluable resource for you and your partner. As you travel through your pregnancy, you will be able to turn to Dr. Gliksman for advice every step of the way. Enjoy!

—James S. Dolgin, M.D.

Dr. James Dolgin is an OB/GYN in private practice in Fair Lawn, New Jersey.

Introduction

So you're having a baby! Congratulations! Now the questions start. Things you never wondered about before become the center of your world, and everything you used to take for granted now becomes a major concern: What should I eat? What should I wear? Can I stand in front of a microwave oven? Can I travel in an airplane? Is it all right to dye my hair? Is it safe to take an aspirin?

When you're pregnant, you have to remember that everything you do affects another human being: When you are exercising, extra blood and oxygen circulate to your tiny fetus. When you sip a cup of coffee in the morning, your little baby gets a kick of caffeine. When you get overstressed at work, your fatigue and anxiety are shared with an itsy-bitsy person. This is what makes pregnancy such a wonderful—and at the same time, such an anxious—experience. How nice it would be if every pregnant woman knew an experienced and knowledgeable person who would hold her hand and lead her step by step through each day of pregnancy, labor, and delivery. That's why I've written this book. I want to be that person for *you*.

I'm an obstetrician, and every day of my life is spent guiding women through the maze of pregnancy. I love what I do, and I work hard to teach my patients about what's going on in their bodies, how their babies are developing, and what they can expect from each month of pregnancy. At the same time, I know that many of my patients go home, after each appointment, with 100 questions they forgot to ask or didn't think to ask because they don't have the basic facts about pregnancy. In this book, I tell you everything you need to know. Of course, your own health-care provider should be the first line of information, but it's always valuable to have another easy-to-get-at source that can clarify, explain, and reinforce what you learn at each medical checkup. In this book, you'll find the answers to all the questions that pop into your head in the middle of the night, as well as the reassurance you need when you're feeling uncertain or lost. All the facts and advice you need to be an active participant in the development and birth of your baby are right here—in one place.

When it comes to the process of human creation, almost every pregnant woman puts herself in the category of "complete idiot." Until it happens to you, there's no way to understand what it means to be pregnant. There's no advanced training, special qualifications, or entrance exam for this position. One day the stick turns blue on the home pregnancy test and there you are—an expectant mom. So don't feel "stupid" because you don't know how long a pregnancy lasts or can't imagine how a full-grown baby can leave your body through such a little hole. Every pregnant woman before you has wondered the same thing. Use this book as your training course. You may turn to page one as a member of The Complete Idiot's Club, but by the end of the book, you will graduate as an expert.

How This Book Is Organized

This book presents information in five parts.

Part 1: In the Beginning This first part gives you the most immediate and practical information you will need as a pregnant woman. It helps you choose a health-care provider and reminds you to contact your insurance company. It gives you forewarnings about the first physical symptoms of pregnancy and outlines a group of moms who need special attention right from the start. It also gives you a peek at the prenatal tests that are ready and waiting for you.

Part 2: The Countdown Here is your guided tour through the nine months of pregnancy. You'll learn what happens to your baby and your body each step of the way.

Part 3: Food and Drugs: The Good and the Bad Food, medications, alcohol, caffeine, nicotine, illicit drugs, and the environment we live in all affect the growing fetus. This part tells you what to load up on and what to avoid.

Part 4: Day to Day Even the simplest things can get complicated during pregnancy. This part will explain how daily activities such as exercising, working, lovemaking, traveling, and even taking a bath affect the baby in your womb.

Part 5: The Big Day Labor, delivery, and recovery from childbirth are the highlights of this part—and of your pregnancy!

More Facts, Advice, and Serendipity

Throughout the book I've scattered boxes filled with more facts, advice, and just plain interesting stuff. You will see five different kinds of these special boxes in each chapter of the book:

HEY MOM!

Think of these boxes as little advice columns for moms and moms-to-be.

PREGNANCY FACTS

Here you'll find additional facts about conception, pregnancy, and childbirth.

BABY TALK!

Here you'll find definitions of words that might be unfamiliar to you. These words are also found in the Glossary in Appendix A.

DADDY ALERT!

Unfortunately, dads-to-be often feel left out in the cold during their partners' pregnancies. These boxes are intended to help all those confused daddies-to-be out there understand what's going on with their partner and her body so they can feel "pregnant," too!

GREEN FROM THE START

There are many ways to reduce the carbon footprint of being pregnant and at the same time protect the health of your body, your unborn child, and the planet we live on. The tips in these boxes will show you how.

You'll also notice that some words in this book appear in italics. That means you can find the definition of the word in the Glossary in Appendix A.

Acknowledgments

What an incredible experience it has been to write a book with the potential to help hundreds of women! I would like to acknowledge a few individuals who have made the journey possible. First, I would like to thank my mother, Glenda Isaacs. Having delivered and raised four children, she deserves top billing. Next, my husband, Jeff, is a constant source of love and encouragement. Without him I could not be the person I am today. I would also like to thank two practicing obstetric gynecologists: my father, Dr. Eli Isaacs, and my uncle, Dr. Martin Goldstein. Besides offering emotional support, they continue to be fine models of professionalism and caring. I will be forever grateful to them.

Theresa Foy DiGeronimo and I would also like to thank our editors Randy Ladenheim-Gil, Ginny Munroe, Janette Lynn, and Andy Saff for their dedicated help throughout the writing of this third edition.

Trademarks

Part 1

In the Beginning

From the moment you find out that you're pregnant, your life spins in so many different directions that you'll begin to wonder if it—or you—will ever be the same again. The answer is no. After you conceive and bear a child, you become a new person and your life changes forever.

You will soon start to notice that the person you call "me" is rapidly changing. You're tired and grumpy. Your breasts hurt and your waistline is disappearing. You may be spending a lot of time in the bathroom. Looking down the line, you find out that more changes are in store for you.

The first part of this book will bring you up to speed on all the things you can expect from your new body.

Meet the New You

Chapter 1

In This Chapter

- Breast changes and weight gain
- Fighting fatigue
- Morning sickness, frequent urination, and stuffy noses
- The facts about mood swings

So the stick turned blue. You've missed your period. All the signs point to one thing: You're pregnant. During the nine months of pregnancy, your body will do things you never thought it could (or should) do. Not only will you lose your waist, but also you'll see your hips, your arms, and maybe even your ankles expand. Other changes will be more subtle: Your hair might become thicker or thinner, curlier or straighter, and your skin might become drier or oilier. Your sleep patterns might change. Even your personality might take on a new dimension. So strap yourself in and get ready for some fun, some tears, and a whole lot of changes.

Breast Changes

One of the first signs of pregnancy is a change in breast size. Your breasts are changing now to prepare for your baby's arrival. From the moment of conception, your breasts become stimulated by the hormones of pregnancy. At first, blood vessels dilate and grow to nourish the breast tissue. Then the milk ducts branch out and expand.

Your breasts will continue to grow throughout the pregnancy, but after childbirth and then nursing, they will return to their prepregnancy size.

Most women find that, in addition to getting larger, their breasts become tender. This discomfort is similar to the way your breasts might feel just before you get your period. Your nipples, too, might react to the news. They might get hard and sensitive. This breast discomfort should ease after the first month or so.

DADDY ALERT!

There's good news and bad news about your partner's growing breasts. They look terrific—but you might not be allowed to touch. In the beginning, the breast and nipple can become very sensitive and will hurt if "manhandled."

You might also find that the area around the nipple (the areola) will get darker. And if you look closely, you'll see blue lines under the skin of the breast. In the second half of the pregnancy, many women begin to notice fluid leaking from their nipples. If this happens, there is no need for alarm. This fluid is called colostrum—a thick yellow fluid that is the earliest form of milk.

The Disappearing Waistline

Your breasts are not the only part of your body getting bigger right from the start. By the time you get a positive result on your pregnancy test, you might find the waist of your pants fitting a bit tighter. It's not that you're growing a pregnancy belly yet. It's just that as your insides start to shift around to make room for the soon-to-expand uterus, the waistline seems to be the first to go. Long before you begin to "show," you'll find you can't close the top button of your pants.

To protect the fetus, your body will then add layers of fat to your lower abdomen, hips, thighs, and buttocks. This insulates the womb and stores up a source of energy for the end of the pregnancy, when you begin to eat less (this will happen!).

Fatigue

Ask a pregnant woman (especially in the first and last *trimesters*) what is the one thing in the whole world she would like most at that exact moment, and she's likely to say, "To take a nap." The fatigue of early and late pregnancy can be overwhelming.

BABY TALK!

Your pregnancy can be broken into three **trimesters.** The first trimester of your pregnancy is months one, two, and three. The second trimester of your pregnancy is months four, five, and six. The third trimester is months seven, eight, and nine.

This tiredness is very natural and a good sign that your body is hard at work. In the beginning, you can't see the results of these efforts, but inside you is a construction crew that works around the clock to build your baby's life-support systems within the womb. Your body is also very actively adjusting to the many physical and emotional demands of pregnancy. At the same time that you're so tired, the fluctuating levels of hormones can disrupt sleep patterns and make it difficult to get continuous, sound sleep. When you finally do fall into bed at the end of the day, you might find that you wake several times during the night.

Fatigue and disrupted sleep are your body's way of sending a message that says: Rest! What a wonderful excuse for taking an afternoon nap, sleeping late, or turning in early. Of course, sleeping during a business meeting is still not part of the corporate culture, and sleeping while your other children are running wild won't do, either. But where there's a will (and eyelids that feel like bricks), there's a way.

Speak up and ask for help here. Can your mother watch the kids while you sneak in some ZZs? Can your husband do the grocery shopping on the weekend? Don't say, "I can't." Your feet are dragging and your eyes are closing because your body is demanding the rest it needs to do the job of creating a child. You've got to give it a break occasionally.

Because exhaustion might be a constant companion during this time of your life, make it your friend. Work with it, not against it. If you're feeling tired right now, close the book, put your feet up, pull up the covers, and take a snooze.

Fatigue Boosters and Zappers

- **Coffee.** Caffeine might give you a temporary boost, but the drop in energy that follows leaves you far worse off than before. See Chapter 15 for more reasons to stay away from coffee.
- **Sugar.** Sugar works a bit like caffeine. A Snickers bar might give you a quick perk, but the drop in blood sugar that follows is a double whammy to your body's efforts to stay alert. Try to avoid sugary products.
- **"Hidden" caffeine.** Don't forget the "hidden" sources of caffeine that can throw your body onto the perk-up-fall-down roller coaster. Colas, chocolate, and cocoa are all apt to aggravate your sleepy state.
- **Carbohydrates.** Carbohydrates can calm your body and promote a good night's sleep. Try a complex-carbohydrate snack (such as crackers, cereal, bread, or pasta) before bed.

- **Nutrasweet.** Before bedtime, avoid foods with the artificial sweetener Nutrasweet (watch those diet sodas!). It is a stimulant that keeps the brain active and will make it even more difficult to sleep soundly.
- **Cigarettes and booze.** Not only are these things bad for your developing baby (see Chapter 15), but they also add to your fatigue. Stay away.
- **Chamomile.** Go natural. Try a cup of chamomile tea before bed. Chamomile is an herb famous for its ability to help people sleep soundly.

Exhaustion Exterminators

- **Exercise.** In addition to all the physical benefits of exercise (see Chapter 18), exercise is also good for boosting energy levels and promoting sound sleep. If you aren't sleeping well at night and are tired during the day, the last thing you'll feel like doing is getting up to exercise. But that's exactly what you should do to get a better night's sleep and feel energized during the day.
- **Take a power nap.** A quick 15- to 20-minute nap each day can revitalize your energy level. It can also improve alertness, sharpen memory, and generally reduce the symptoms of fatigue.
- **Try relaxation exercises.** Things like meditation, prayer, and controlled deep-breathing exercises can all help you boost your energy level and improve sleep.
- **Check with your doctor to see if you are anemic.** Your body requires more iron now, without it, you'll feel fatigued.
- **Count your calories.** Your metabolism has increased due to the pregnancy and you might not be meeting your daily calorie requirements. This will make you tired.

Nausea

One of the annoying things about nausea in pregnancy is that it's just not the same for everybody. Some pregnant women have none—not one minute—of the queasy, stuck-on-a-merry-go-round feeling that just won't quit. Some have a gnawing uneasiness that makes them feel like they should be throwing up, but nothing happens. For others, daily vomiting is a constant occurrence in the first three months. Some women seem to develop "morning sickness" five minutes after conception; others feel fine until week eight or so and then they can't get their head out of the toilet bowl.

It is not completely clear why about one half of all pregnant women suffer from nausea. It might be because of rising hormone levels. Their highest peak is in the first three months of pregnancy, when nausea is usually most severe. There's also a theory that nausea might be the body's way of keeping you away from harmful foods. Your sense of smell is immensely improved during pregnancy, and the slightest spoilage on a piece of cheese or meat can throw your stomach into a cartwheel. In either case, take heart in knowing that nausea is a sign of a healthy pregnancy.

To manage the nausea of pregnancy, try to keep track of the smells that trigger the upchuck reflex. If you throw up in the sink every time you open a can of dog food, hand the duty over to your partner. What other smells set you off? Coffee? Fried foods? Cooked vegetables? Then steer clear. If you have to stay out of the kitchen for a while, hand the apron to your partner or order out.

PREGNANCY FACTS

If your "morning sickness" has nothing to do with the morning, don't panic. The term "morning sickness" is very misleading. Although nausea might be worse in the morning because the stomach is empty, any woman who has experienced nausea during her pregnancy will tell you that it's a morning, noon, and night occurrence.

You can also calm an upset stomach by keeping food in it. Sometimes women try to beat their nausea by staying away from food. But an empty stomach is much more apt to be upset because the stomach acids have nothing to digest and because blood sugar drops when there's a long stretch between meals. Start eating very small meals throughout the day. Keep nutritious snacks, such as dried fruits or whole grain crackers, with you at all times. Nibble even when you're not hungry.

Don't force yourself to eat anything. When you're throwing up every day, of course you'll worry that your baby might not be getting all the nutrients she needs. But what good is eating a bowl of steamed broccoli if you're going to flush it down the toilet a few minutes later? True, you might not gain much during the first few months, but most women put on only two to four pounds then anyway. Such a small increase doesn't have an impact on the baby's growth at that point. Most women who have morning sickness gain as much weight by the end of pregnancy as women who haven't had the problem. For now, eat whatever you can keep down.

The following tricks have helped many women who have suffered nausea in pregnancy and have lived to tell about it.

- To prevent the queasiness that comes from an empty stomach during the night, eat something (such as a sandwich) before going to bed.
- Graze on bland snacks. Try crackers, dry cereal, and pretzels.
- Don't let yourself get dehydrated. In addition to water and juices, don't forget things like ice pops, sorbet, gelatin desserts, bouillon, and frozen grapes.
- Before getting out of bed, prop yourself up a bit and eat a cracker or some raisins. Don't drink anything. Then wait 15 minutes or so before standing up. This bit of digested food might keep your stomach calm.
- Some women calm nausea by smelling or sucking on a fresh cut lemon.
- Eat complex carbohydrates, because they're easy to digest. These include fresh fruits and whole grains, such as wheat bread and pastas.
- If your symptoms are worse at a particular time of day, head them off by eating a small meal at least 30 minutes before they kick in.
- Try one of those pressure-point wristbands developed to ease the symptoms of motion sickness and seasickness. (Most pharmacies carry them.)
- Apply acupressure to the Neiguan point. With the thumb of one hand, press on the other lower arm (with palm up) three inches below the wrist. Do this four times a day for 5 to 10 minutes each time.
- Many women find relief through acupuncture.

If these home remedies don't work, talk to your doctor. She might advise you to try an antacid or a B_6 vitamin supplement. If you're still spending too much time with your head in the toilet bowl and there's risk of dehydration, she might prescribe medication to calm the stomach upset. But don't take any antinausea or motion sickness medications without talking to your doctor first. Also, let her know if you can't keep down your prenatal vitamins.

Frequent Urination

Have you noticed that you're spending more time in the bathroom lately? The need to urinate more often than usual is another common reminder of your pregnancy at about six weeks after conception. This happens because your very little baby is starting to grow inside the uterus, which during early pregnancy sits right on your bladder. This growth pushes against the bladder. Pressure on the bladder is often relieved when the uterus rises into the abdominal cavity around the fourth month. It might return when the baby "drops" back down into the pelvis in the ninth month. The kidneys also add to the problem by working overtime to flush out waste products from the blood at a faster-than-normal pace.

PREGNANCY FACTS

The urine leakage that occurs during pregnancy with coughing, laughing, and bouncing is called urinary stress incontinence. Don't be alarmed or surprised if this continues after pregnancy. It might take your body nine months to recover its normal bladder control after delivery. Be patient with yourself!

You might find this problem especially annoying during exercise, when urine might leak out as you bounce up and down. There are two things you can do: (1) Always wear a sanitary pad, and (2) add a new exercise to your list: Kegel whenever you can. The kegel exercise is every pregnant woman's secret. It's the way you keep the muscles around your vagina and anus strong and flexible. See Chapter 18 for details.

Some previously sound sleepers find that their bladders are now calling for relief several times each night. You can reduce some of this annoyance by limiting your fluid intake after 7 P.M.

If you notice a stinging, burning feeling when you urinate, this usually means you have developed an infection called *cystitis*. To avoid complications, tell your doctor right away; she will probably prescribe antibiotics and advise you to drink plenty of liquids. Juices such as cranberry, orange, lemon, or grapefruit are especially good for this condition.

To prevent cystitis, wear cotton, rather than synthetic, briefs. Also, if you wear panty-hose, buy the kind that has a cotton panel in the crotch.

Stuffy Nose

Many pregnant women complain of a head cold that just won't quit during their pregnancy. Actually, they don't have a cold; they have nasal congestion caused by the high levels of reproductive hormones that increase blood flow to the mucous membranes of the nose, causing them to soften and swell.

Sometimes this stuffiness is accompanied by nosebleeds, which are not dangerous, only annoying. If you do have this problem, you can expect it to last throughout the pregnancy.

When treating congestion during pregnancy, stay away from over-the-counter medications and nasal sprays (unless directed by your physician). Saline nose drops (which are a simple combination of purified water and salt) work well, and you might use a humidifier if the air is very dry (often caused by heating systems that blow hot, dry air into the house).

Mood Swings

Pregnancy is known to bring about the most wonderful, elated, joyous feelings known on Earth. It is also known to turn a kind, mild-mannered woman into a raging bull. So don't be surprised if you find yourself saying, "I'm not usually like this." You might find yourself feeling irritable for no reason. In fact, it would not be unheard of if you picked arguments with your partner that are completely irrational and baseless. But hey, you're a pregnant woman and entitled to bouts of moodiness.

When you feel like crying or yelling over the littlest thing, remind yourself that your hormones are giving you a hard time, and that you wouldn't feel this way if you weren't pregnant. Knowing how unpredictable your emotions are right now should keep you from making binding changes in your job status, housing arrangements, or marriage. If you do, it's very possible that you'll look back and wonder, "What was I thinking?"

The Least You Need to Know

- Your new firmer, larger breasts aren't permanent. They'll return to their pre-pregnancy size after childbirth and nursing.
- Even with a good night's sleep, you may still feel tired during the first and third trimesters.
- Morning sickness affects some women more than others.
- Nasal congestion and an excessive need to pee are both common.
- Get ready to feel some wild mood swings. One minute you'll be on top of the world and the next you might be crying into your pillow.

Common Discomforts and Problems

Chapter 2

In This Chapter

- What the reasons are for body swelling, food cravings (and aversions), and dental problems
- What to do about digestive problems, varicose veins, backaches, and leg pains
- When to be concerned about cramping and bleeding
- Where to get support

Pregnancy is a wonderful, rather short-lived, time in a woman's life. It is a time for dreaming and planning. It's a time for special attention and pampering. It's a time to savor and enjoy. On the flip side, however, is the reality that pregnancy often brings with it a whole bag of physical discomforts. You might experience only some of these problems or you might be one of the not-so-lucky ones who get to experience them all. You might be bothered for only a week or two here and there, or you might spend the entire nine months dealing with one annoyance or another. Every woman is different. What is comforting to know, however, is that all of the problems discussed in this chapter are typical, to-be-expected discomforts that will disappear into memory when the baby is born.

Edema

As if adding layers of fat all over your body weren't bad enough, your body might also begin to look bloated as it retains fluids during pregnancy. This excess water buildup can cause swelling called *edema*. It is most commonly noticeable in the ankles, feet, and legs, but you might also find that your rings are fitting tighter on your fingers.

Edema will be most obvious late in the day, in warm weather, or after standing or sitting for a long time. Remarkably, the swelling usually disappears overnight or after lying down for a few hours.

Try these tricks to help ease the discomfort and bloated appearance of edema:

- When sitting down, prop your feet up on some type of ottoman.
- Wear loose-fitting shoes. (If your feet really swell, stick to slippers.)
- Avoid knee-high stockings that cut into your calves.
- When you sit, don't cross your legs.
- Use support pantyhose. Put them on before you get out of bed in the morning when there is little swelling.
- Drink lots of water! This might seem like a contradiction because an excess of fluid is causing this problem, but it's true. Water will flush out the waste products that are sitting around your body and causing the swelling.
- Don't overdo it on the salt. Although it's not necessary to cut out salt completely, take it easy. Too much salt encourages fluid retention and can add to the problem. (Don't forget that there's plenty of salt hidden in foods and condiments, such as ketchup, bacon, pickles, chips, and fast foods.)

DADDY ALERT!

Study up on edema. Lots of expectant fathers before you have scolded their partners for gaining too much weight when they see their "fat" fingers and feet. This is not fat—it's fluid and will disappear after the baby is born.

Although some swelling is normal in pregnancy, you or your partner should call your health-care provider if your hands and/or face become puffy, or if the swelling doesn't go down after napping or sleeping through the night. This might be a sign of high blood pressure.

Food Cravings and Aversions

Feel like eating a jar of pickles? Need a quart of chocolate ice cream at 2 A.M.? These are favorite TV sitcom clichés that get us to laugh at the harried husband, as he combs the streets looking for food to satisfy his pregnant wife's cravings.

I doubt there are too many pregnant women out there who really crave pickles or ice cream in the middle of the night, but those wacky hormones that course through the body in the first three months of pregnancy can and do cause both food cravings (strong feelings that you must have certain foods) and aversions (feelings of complete revolt against certain foods and the inability to eat them). Suddenly, you just have to have a certain food, or, just as suddenly, you can't stand the sight of a food you used to love!

Although hormones are the chief culprit in these cravings and aversions, there is a theory that these are signals from your body telling you what it needs and what you should stay away from. If you suddenly can't stand even the smell of coffee or the thought of a cream doughnut, this aversion could be your body's way of keeping toxins away from your developing baby. If you find yourself craving fruit (as many women do), your body might be low in complex carbohydrates. If you feel a daily need for an ice-cream sundae, your body might actually be calling for more dairy products and calcium. (In this case, it's best to skip the sundae and have some yogurt or cottage cheese instead.)

Sometimes there's no explanation at all for a particular food craving or aversion. If you wake up one day and can no longer stand the smell of green vegetables, don't panic. Don't force yourself to eat foods that are "good" for you if they make you sick to your stomach. If an aversion to a nutritious food doesn't disappear in a few days, try something else that will give you the same nutrients. For example, if you can't eat broccoli anymore, make up for this loss of a good source of calcium by eating more dairy products.

If you get a craving for food that is not nutritious for you and your baby, try these two strategies:

- **Substitute.** If you absolutely must have a piece of candy, for example, substitute the craving for something that's sweet but nutritious, such as raisins or dried fruits. If you must have ice cream, switch to a frozen fruit bar or yogurt.
- **Distraction.** When you feel drawn to a food you shouldn't eat, get up and do something else. Take a walk, read a book, or call a friend. Keep your mind busy until the craving passes. Or, have a glass of water; some say this often satisfies the urge to eat!

Dental Care

The American Academy of Pediatric Dentistry (AAPD) has established oral health guidelines for expectant mothers. These guidelines suggest using fluoridated toothpaste approved by the American Dental Association and rinsing every night with an alcohol-free, over-the-counter mouth rinse containing 0.05 percent sodium fluoride to help reduce the plaque levels and gum infections that have been associated with preterm, low birth weight babies.

A visit to the dentist is especially important in the second or third month of pregnancy. At this time, you might experience increased swelling, tenderness, and bleeding in gum tissue. This is called gingivitis. Don't panic if you bite into a soft sandwich and see traces of blood on the bread, but do see your dentist. He or she can show you proper brushing and flossing techniques to help soothe this condition. You can also get helpful information on gum disease during pregnancy from the American Academy of Periodontology. Visit them at www.perio.org. Gingivitis is a temporary condition that will end after you deliver your baby.

Constipation, Hemorrhoids, Indigestion, Heartburn, Flatulence, and Belching

Constipation, hemorrhoids, indigestion, heartburn, flatulence, and belching are all part of the fun of pregnancy. There's nothing to be embarrassed about here—it's a fact of life.

Constipation

Most of the digestive problems of pregnancy begin with *constipation*. This condition, caused by hard stools that are difficult to pass, is universally common in pregnant women for many reasons:

- The high level of certain hormones during pregnancy relaxes the muscles of the bowels and makes it hard for them to work efficiently.
- The growing uterus presses on the bowel and disrupts normal function.
- The iron in your vitamin supplement is known to make stools dry and difficult to pass.

Just because constipation is common in pregnancy doesn't mean you have to accept it. You can do many things to avoid constipation, including the following:

- **Drink lots of fluids.** Water and fruit juices soften stools and keep digested waste passing through the bowel. (Prune juice is a powerful constipation zapper!)
- **Eat fiber-rich foods.** Certain foods are especially good at keeping stools soft and at making sure they pass easily through the bowels. These foods include many of the highly nutritious foods recommended for a healthy diet during pregnancy: fruits, vegetables, whole grains, and legumes (dried beans and peas).
- **Limit sugary, processed foods.** They are binding.
- **Exercise.** Not only does exercise keep your muscles in shape, it boosts blood circulation and brings more oxygen to all organs (including the bowels) to help them do their jobs more efficiently.

When you are constipated, don't take a laxative. Not only can it wash necessary nutrients out of your system, it might be harmful to your baby. Talk to your doctor before taking any medicated remedy for constipation. There are many over-the-counter stool softeners that your doctor may recommend.

Hemorrhoids

Straining during a bowel movement to pass hard stools can cause *hemorrhoids*—a mass of swollen tissue at the opening of the rectum. These are varicose veins of the rectum that are sometimes called "piles" because they look like piles of small peas (see "Varicose Veins" later in this chapter for a detailed explanation of varicose veins).

If you see blood on your tissue when you wipe after a bowel movement, or if you have pain or excessive itching at the opening of the rectum, ask your doctor to check for hemorrhoids. (This might seem embarrassing, but it's nothing he or she hasn't seen before.) If you have hemorrhoids, they will accompany you through the pregnancy and will probably get worse during the pushing stage of delivery. If you take good care of them, however, they might disappear after the birth.

The following tips should help keep these piles from piling up, and if you don't have them yet, these tips will help you prevent them.

- Avoid constipation. Use all the tips mentioned earlier in this chapter to keep your stools soft and moving easily through your bowel.
- Try not to strain during bowel movements.
- Put your feet up on a small stool during bowel movements to make the movement easier.
- Don't read on the toilet. If you get into a good story, you'll sit there longer than necessary; this puts unnecessary strain on the anus.
- Avoid standing still or sitting for very long periods of time. Move around and change positions.

If you are bothered by the pain or itching of hemorrhoids, take action. You can use topical creams that are sold in pharmacies to ease the pain and itching. You might also try applying a compress of witch hazel or ice to the hemorrhoids. If the pain is so bad you can't sit comfortably in a chair, go to your pharmacy and buy a doughnut pillow (this is an inflatable pillow with a hole in the middle so your buttocks don't touch the chair!). When all else fails, get off your feet and lie down; this relieves the pressure and the pain.

Flatulence and Belching

The problem of flatulence (also known as "passing gas" or "blowing wind") is caused by a buildup of gases in the large intestine. Belching (also called burping) is the sudden expulsion of gases from the stomach. These are common problems during pregnancy that cause more embarrassment than pain or discomfort. Constipation can cause these problems, and so can certain foods. If you've been clearing out the room lately with odorous flatulence or belching, avoid constipation and steer clear of known gas producers, such as beans, onions, fried foods, cabbage, broccoli, and Brussels sprouts.

Vaginal Infection

If you have a thick, white vaginal discharge and feel intense itchiness and irritation in your vaginal area, you might have a vaginal infection. This is very common during pregnancy, and it is very annoying. If you think you have a vaginal infection, tell your doctor. He will recommend one of the over-the-counter medicines that are both safe and effective during pregnancy. He might recommend Gyne-Lotrimin, Myclex G, Femstat, or Monistat. (Only Monistat is recommended during the first trimester.) Most of these medications come in both creams and *suppositories* (hard, pill-like medication that is inserted into the vagina, where it dissolves). Your doctor can tell you which one would be better for you.

Before you use a commercial product, try to use a natural remedy for your vaginal infection:

- Apply witch-hazel compresses or ice packs to the inflamed tissues.
- Add two cups of cornstarch, plus one-half cup of baking soda to a warm bath. Soak for 10 minutes.
- Eat a few cloves of garlic and a cup of yogurt containing active *Lactobacillus acidophilus* (check the label) culture every day (until the infection goes away).
- Wear loose clothes and cotton underwear.

Here's what you can do to help prevent vaginal infections:

- Avoid long, hot baths, which provide the warm, moist environment that yeast loves.
- Avoid tight-fitting pants, nylon underwear, and pantyhose. Always wear cotton underwear.
- After a bowel movement, always wipe from front to back, to avoid transferring bacteria from the anus to the vagina.
- Avoid foods that contain molds, fungus, yeast, sugar, or refined carbohydrates. The list of foods to avoid includes yeast breads, aged cheeses, vinegar, beer, cookies, cakes, dried fruits, sweetened fruit drinks, mushrooms, melons, commercial sauces, and aged or fermented foods.

A vaginal infection is uncomfortable for you, but it won't harm your baby. If you deliver while you have a vaginal infection, there is a chance it will be passed on to the newborn. He or she will have white patches called thrush in his mouth. This isn't serious and is easily treated.

Varicose Veins

Does your mom have large, bluish, bulging veins in her legs? If she does, you also might be prone to these leggy veins. If you are overweight or if you stand or sit for long periods each day, you might be another candidate for varicose veins. Passed on through the generations, varicose veins appear when the walls of the blood vessels stretch so much that their valves don't close properly, causing blood to pool. These veins pop out in pregnancy because the blood volume in the body is increased and the weight of the uterus affects lower-body circulation. Varicose veins are most often seen in the legs, but they might also appear in the vulva (the lips of the vagina). Technically, hemorrhoids are varicose veins.

To prevent varicose veins, or to keep the ones you have from getting out of hand, try these tips:

- Watch your posture. Don't sit with your legs crossed or with your thighs pressed against the edge of the chair.
- Don't stand in one place. Standing or sitting for too long lets the blood pool. Move around, wiggle your feet, and change positions often.
- Wear support hose, and put them on before you stand up in the morning.
- Avoid knee-highs that restrict circulation.
- Elevate your feet when you sit or lie down.
- Watch your weight. Excessive weight aggravates these veins.
- Quit smoking. Besides being a general health zapper, smoking is known to worsen the symptoms of varicose veins.
- Walk. Don't let varicose veins keep you from moving around. Walking improves circulation, which improves the health of your veins.

Varicose veins often disappear shortly after childbirth. If they remain and are painful or just too ugly to keep, they can be removed surgically after delivery.

Lower-Back Pain

Imagine trying to carry a very heavy backpack (say 20 pounds) on the front of your body. You would probably change your posture to balance the load. You would plant your feet farther apart, tilt your hips forward, and arch your back with your belly pushed forward. Well, even though your baby isn't quite 20 pounds, you still might change your posture to carry the extra weight up front. This change strains the back muscles and causes backache. As your pregnancy progresses, the ache might worsen because, not only is the weight getting heavier, but also near the end of pregnancy the baby's head might be in a position that pushes against the lower spine.

HEY MOM!

Sleeping on your left side is good for your health. This is the position that lets blood flow most easily from your heart to your legs and baby. This will often ease the discomfort of varicose veins, edema, and even backache.

To prevent backache and reduce back pain, give these strategies a try:

- **Stand correctly.** Imagine there is a string attached to the top of your head that some invisible puppeteer is pulling upward. Then stand with your feet apart (about even with your hips). Don't lock your knees; bend them slightly. Imagine your baby is sitting toward your spine (no need to push the baby out front).
- **Sit correctly.** Sitting (especially for long periods) puts a lot of stress on your spine. When you sit, sit up tall; don't slouch. Keep your feet elevated if possible. Don't cross your knees. Stay away from extra-soft and backless chairs. Put a pillow between you and the back of the chair. Don't sit too long; after a half hour, get up, walk, and stretch for a few minutes.
- **Forget your spiked heels.** Even under normal circumstances, high heels are bad for the back. For pregnant women, they're disastrous. Wide two-inch heels are okay, and you might find them even better than flats for keeping your posture straight.
- **Avoid standing still for too long.** If you must stand still, try to keep a small step stool nearby so that you can keep one foot elevated. This helps relieve some of the pressure on your spine.
- **Watch your weight.** Gaining more than necessary will strain your back.
- **Sleep on a firm mattress.** If yours is very soft, put a board underneath it to give you more support.
- **Exercise your back muscles.** See Chapter 18 for some exercises that will keep the lower-back muscles strong.

As your body gets ready for childbirth, you might feel a persistent dull backache (along with cramps sometimes). If this happens, call your doctor (even if you don't think you're ready to deliver).

Leg Cramps

The calf muscles in your legs might give you some trouble (especially at night) in the second and third trimesters. The muscles might cramp up on you or they might twitch and jump uncontrollably. Some research suggests this might be caused by a lack of calcium or magnesium, so you might talk to your health-care provider about increasing these nutrients, either in your diet or through supplements.

To prevent these cramps, give your legs a little extra attention. Get off your feet and put your legs up for at least a short time every day. Wear support hose to keep the blood circulating. Exercise your lower legs by flexing at the ankle and rotating your feet.

You can do things to calm your leg muscles when you get a cramp or twitching muscle. First, make sure you don't point your foot; keep your ankle flexed so your toes point up toward your face. Gently massage the muscle (or better yet, get your partner to massage the muscle while you keep your knee straight). To stop a cramp and avoid them in the future, try this exercise: Stand one foot away from a wall with your feet about 12 inches apart. Put the palms of your hands on the walls with your arms straight. Bend your elbows, bringing your face close to the wall and keeping your feet flat on the floor. Straighten your arms again. Do this 5 to 10 times before bedtime or when you have a cramp in your calf.

The First Alarm: Abdominal Cramps

If you feel cramps in your abdomen (the area around your stomach), don't panic right away. Sometimes cramping is nothing more than a gentle reminder to take it easy, and at other times it might be a sign of digestive problems. Occasionally, however, cramping can be an emergency signal that says you need medical attention.

Take It Easy

The muscles and ligaments that support your uterus are being pulled and stretched in all directions during pregnancy. This can cause occasional cramping. The pain might be mild or sharp. It might be particularly noticeable when you make a quick move, get up out of a chair, cough, or sneeze. This is nothing to worry about. Some women get cramps when they exercise and put additional stress on muscles and ligaments that are already strained. If you feel cramps while exercising, listen to your body. Stop and rest. This is not the time to work through pain.

Cramps can also remind you to watch what you eat. As in your prepregnancy days, poor digestion will cause cramps. If you overeat or eat the wrong foods, you might feel stomach cramps. If you are constipated, you will feel cramps that can be very painful. Follow the suggestions given earlier in this chapter to avoid this pain.

Warning

Sometimes cramps are a danger signal that shouldn't be ignored. There are three specific medical conditions that are usually accompanied by cramping:

- **Miscarriage.** About 20 percent of all pregnancies end in a miscarriage within the first three months of pregnancy. (Miscarriage is the delivery of a baby before it is developed enough to survive outside the womb.) Severe cramping in the first trimester (often accompanied by bleeding from the vagina) can signal trouble. If you feel constant abdominal pain (with or without bleeding), call your doctor right away.
- **Ectopic pregnancy.** When the fertilized egg settles somewhere outside the uterus, you will get a positive pregnancy test, but as the egg begins to grow, it cannot survive and will cause sharp abdominal pains and bleeding. See Chapter 22 for more details.
- **Preterm labor.** Each year, hundreds of thousands of babies are born long before they are due. These babies announce their plans for an early entrance with a variety of signals that include cramping. Chapter 23 will discuss all the facts of these early births.

If your cramps are severe and/or persistent, call your doctor immediately.

The Second Alarm: Vaginal Bleeding

Everyone knows that when your monthly bleeding stops, it's a common sign of pregnancy. So what does it mean when a pregnant woman starts to bleed? Well, it can mean a number of things, so don't automatically panic and assume your pregnancy is in danger.

Bleeding in Early Pregnancy

Bleeding in early pregnancy (the first three months) is a sure-fire way to upset a newly expectant mom. Red spots on your underwear can make you think you're going to lose your baby, almost as soon as you've gotten used to the idea of being pregnant. If this happens to you, take it easy. You should call your doctor and report the bleeding, but it's most likely nothing to worry about.

In early pregnancy, vaginal bleeding that is not a cause for worry can be the result of either of the following conditions:

- **Settling in.** There is occasional light bleeding when the fertilized egg attaches itself to the wall of your uterus.
- **Hormonal changes.** It's not all that unusual for a pregnant woman to bleed at the time she would normally menstruate. This bleeding is usually light and short-lived.

Although most bleeding is nothing to worry about, it's also true that bleeding in early pregnancy can, in some cases, signal a problem. It can be a sign of two dangers:

- **Miscarriage.** Heavy bleeding, along with abdominal pain, might mean that you are experiencing a miscarriage (birth of the baby before it is old enough to survive outside the womb). At this point, there is nothing you can do to stop the miscarriage, but you should call your doctor immediately to make sure you receive medical care.
- **Ectopic pregnancy.** Brown vaginal spotting or light bleeding accompanied by abdominal pain on one side can mean an ectopic pregnancy. This happens when the egg is implanted outside the uterus and can't grow to full term in that location. See Chapter 22 for more details.

In both of these cases, the *embryo* (the word used to refer to the developing baby before it is 12 weeks old) cannot be carried to full term and the pregnancy ends. The reasons for these problems are discussed in Chapter 22.

Bleeding in Middle or Late Pregnancy

Bleeding in middle or late pregnancy might be nothing more than a sign that your cervix (the opening to the uterus) has been rubbed too much during intercourse or an internal exam. In other cases, however, it might be a sign that you need quick medical attention.

The most common medical causes of bleeding in middle or late pregnancy are as follows:

- **Problems with the placenta.** If the placenta (the organ on the inner wall of the uterus that supplies the baby with everything it needs to grow) is situated in the wrong position or is beginning to separate from the wall of the uterus, you will begin to bleed. The amount of blood and pain will depend on the degree of the problem. See Chapter 21 for the details.
- **Miscarriage.** Although a miscarriage in middle or late pregnancy is not common, it does happen. A possible miscarriage (that might be stopped with medical help) is often signaled by a pink discharge for several days, or a small amount of brown discharge that appears on and off for several weeks. Heavy bleeding, along with cramps, usually means the miscarriage cannot be stopped. See Chapter 22 for more details.
- **Labor.** Heavy bleeding, especially when combined with abdominal or back pain, can be a sign of *labor.* If this occurs in midpregnancy, your doctor will rush to intervene in hopes of stopping the baby from arriving early. If this occurs in the last week or two of your pregnancy, your doctor will probably tell you to meet him in the delivery room.

What to Tell Your Doctor About Vaginal Bleeding

When you call your doctor to report vaginal bleeding, be prepared to answer these questions:

- When did it start?
- Does it stop and go, or is it steady?
- What color is it: red, brown, or pink?
- How much blood are you passing? (Just spotting a bit? Enough to soak a sanitary pad in one hour?)
- Are you also passing any clots? Pieces of tissue?
- Do you have any other symptoms (such as nausea, vomiting, cramps, or fever)?

Getting the Support You Need

Constipation, hemorrhoids, varicose veins, back pain, leg cramps, and on and on. The list of discomforts that can accompany pregnancy is a long one—one that your friends and family might get tired of hearing about really soon. Most women find that their husband's sympathetic handholding ends somewhere in the middle of the second week of the pregnancy. No matter how supportive your family might be, only someone who is also pregnant can reassure you with the words, "I know just what you mean." That's why some pregnant women join support groups.

Support groups offer a place not only for sharing mutual complaints, but also for sharing information. Members discuss conventional and alternative care and trade experiences about what works and what doesn't. The members exchange tips on diet, travel, family, work, and the like. Knowing that you are not alone in your concerns, fears, and discomforts makes it much easier to endure the wait.

The positive benefits of belonging to a support group during these nine months are immeasurable if you're the kind of person who likes to reach out both to gain and to give comfort. If your pregnancy is complicated or high risk, you might find special benefit in talking to other women who are dealing with the same uncertainties.

The Least You Need to Know

- Swelling of the face, fingers, ankles, and feet is not due to weight gain; it's caused by fluid retention.
- Food cravings might be telling you that your body needs additional nutrients.
- Bleeding gums are common in pregnancy and signal the need for a trip to the dentist.
- Constipation, hemorrhoids, flatulence, and belching are all normal digestive demons that are common in pregnancy.
- Varicose veins, backaches, and leg cramps are common, but often preventable, side effects of pregnancy.
- Abdominal cramps and vaginal bleeding can mean absolutely nothing, or they might signal a medical emergency. Contact your doctor immediately.

Chapter 3
Tests

In This Chapter

- Prenatal tests, both screening and diagnostic
- A look at routine tests
- The details on screening for diabetes and birth defects
- High-tech diagnostic techniques
- An overview of other tests

Childbirth is as old as human existence, but perhaps one of the most important changes has been in the area of prenatal testing. Today more than ever before, you have the opportunity to know vital facts about your baby before he or she is even born. Your own mother didn't have as many prenatal tests available to her as you now have.

Definites and Maybes

Tests fall into two different categories: diagnostic and screening. You should know the difference between these terms because each of them tells you something important about the results of your prenatal tests.

- **Diagnostic tests.** These tests are accurate and give you a yes or no answer. A pregnancy test, for example, is a diagnostic test—either you are or you aren't. Medical decisions are made on the definite results of these tests.
- **Screening tests.** These tests tell you the likelihood or risk of a problem—they tell you that "maybe" something is wrong, but they cannot give you a yes or no answer. A positive result puts you in a group of people who are more likely than others to have a particular problem. Let's say, for example, that your doctor tells you the results of your Alpha-fetoprotein (AFP) test indicate

the possibility that your baby has a disease called spina bifida. Of course, this is upsetting news. But because the AFP test is only a screening test, you have to remember that the results do not say your baby has this disease, only that there is a risk that he or she might have it. Further tests (usually the more accurate diagnostic type) are then prescribed to investigate this likelihood.

This is the good and the bad of screening tests: They can detect the possibility of trouble very early in a pregnancy so that couples can investigate further if they choose to do so. At the same time, these tests can cause a lot of stress and worry over nothing.

As you read about each test in this chapter, remember to note whether it is a diagnostic or screening test.

Routine Tests

Routine, run-of-the-mill tests are the ones your doctor will conduct almost every time you visit him or her for a checkup. These include an evaluation of weight, blood pressure, urine, and blood.

HEY MOM!

Fortunately, the weight you gain during pregnancy is not all from your baby. Only 6 to 8 pounds are from the baby; the other 14 to 27 pounds are from the placenta, uterus, amniotic fluid, breasts, blood, fat, tissue, and fluids. Of course, women who are carrying twins (or more) gain much more weight.

Weight

For this "test," you will probably want to put down your pocketbook and take off your shoes, rings, earrings, barrettes, clothing, and maybe even your makeup. Although you're expected to gain weight during pregnancy, you should try to keep the total gain between 25 and 35 pounds.

Although nobody can say exactly how much weight you will put on each month, a general guideline says you should gain a total of about three or four pounds in the first three months; one pound a week for the next five months; and, finally, one or two pounds (if you gain any at all) in the ninth month of pregnancy.

Your health-care provider will be watching carefully for a sudden weight gain, which, combined with excessive swelling, could mean trouble. He or she will also take note if you aren't gaining enough weight, which could be dangerous for the developing fetus.

Blood Pressure

Blood pressure is tested every month. The test is no big deal, but it is very important. A health-care provider will wrap a Velcro sleeve around your upper arm. He or she will then check the blood pressure at the bend of your inner elbow using a stethoscope (the instrument medical people always wear around their necks to make them look official). The first reading will be used as a base to compare with all the others every month. A sudden rise in blood pressure is a warning for a problem such as preeclampsia—a high-tech word for high blood pressure during pregnancy. (See Chapter 23 for details.)

Urine Tests

How good is your aim? By the end of your pregnancy, you will probably be very good at peeing into a little cup because you get to practice this skill at every medical visit. Urine is tested for three things: (1) infection; (2) protein, which can be a sign of high blood pressure; and (3) sugar, which can be a sign of diabetes.

Blood Tests

If your health-care provider doesn't already know the details about your blood, he or she will draw some blood early in the pregnancy. The blood will be taken from a vein on the inside bend of your elbow. This blood will tell a lot about …

- **Your blood group: A, B, or O.** This information is important in case a blood transfusion is ever necessary.
- **Your rhesus (Rh) blood group.** Your Rh factor may be negative or positive. The difference means nothing unless you are negative and the baby's father is positive. In this case, your baby may be incompatible with your rhesus blood group, which can cause problems with future pregnancies. Knowing your blood type in advance lets your doctor prevent any trouble from occurring. See Chapter 23 for more information about Rh incompatibility.
- **Hemoglobin levels.** Hemoglobin keeps red blood cells filled with oxygen. Hemoglobin levels often fall during pregnancy, causing anemia; your doctor will want to make sure your levels don't go too low.
- **Your immunity to rubella (German measles).** If you have not built up an immunity to this disease, you will be cautioned to avoid exposure, especially during the first trimester.
- **STDs.** Because sexually transmitted diseases can cause many problems for the developing fetus and newborn, your blood will be tested for hepatitis B, human immunodeficiency virus (HIV), and syphilis.

In addition to this routine blood work, your doctor may offer blood tests that identify markers for certain genetic disorders. For example, there is a blood test for cystic fibrosis (CF), which is one of the most common genetic disorders in the United States. This disorder affects the lungs and digestive system, causing unusually sticky thick mucus, which in turn causes infections and a lower life expectancy. It is now recommended that all couples are screened in early pregnancy for this condition. Also, if you or your husband are Eastern European or Ashkenazi Jewish, your doctor will offer screening tests for genetic disorders that commonly run in these populations.

Glucose Screening

Most expectant moms are given a glucose-screening test between Weeks 24 and 28 of the pregnancy to check for gestational diabetes (a high blood sugar condition that some women get during pregnancy). (See Chapter 4 for information about the effects of diabetes on a fetus.)

You are at risk for developing gestational diabetes if you fit into any of these categories:

- You have had gestational diabetes during an earlier pregnancy.
- You have previously delivered a very large baby.
- You are greatly overweight (approximately 20 percent over your ideal body weight).
- You are over 35.
- You have high blood pressure.
- You have a parent or sibling who is a diabetic.

The test for gestational diabetes is not painful. It is long, however. To take the glucose-screening test, you will drink a sugar solution (which tastes like a thick, flat cola—I'm not saying it's delicious, but it's not all that awful either). An hour later, a blood sample will be taken and the blood sugar level will be checked. If the reading is abnormal (which occurs about 20 percent of the time) you'll go home and come back at a later date for a diagnostic exam, called a three-hour glucose tolerance test, to verify the results. If you get a high sugar reading on the first test, don't get too worried. Approximately 85 percent of those with a positive result on this screening test show normal blood sugar levels in the glucose tolerance test.

If you have gestational diabetes, it's good to find out early. Your doctor can then help you create a diet and exercise program that will keep the problem in check and safeguard the health of your baby. He or she may also prescribe insulin if necessary. Finding out that you have diabetes is certainly upsetting, but it's not cause for great alarm. Most women who develop diabetes during pregnancy go on to have normal, healthy babies. Be aware, however, that although gestational diabetes will probably disappear after the birth of the baby, some women ultimately develop full-fledged diabetes within the next 20 years. This is something you'll have to watch out for at yearly follow-up tests.

Alpha-Fetoprotein Screening Test

Alpha-fetoprotein (AFP) is a type of protein produced only by a fetus—you do not produce it on your own. Sometime between Weeks 16 and 18, your doctor will take a blood sample from you to check the level of this protein, which can give an indication of the risk of certain birth defects. A high level of AFP might mean trouble; a low level might mean another kind of trouble.

HEY MOM!

Like all prenatal tests, the AFP test is an optional test—which means you don't have to take it. Your physician may strongly recommend it, but the final decision is yours alone.

High levels of AFP indicate the possibility of various things: It could mean twins, or that you have been pregnant longer than you thought. It could also mean that the baby has a neural tube defect, such as spina bifida (a deformity of the spinal column) or anencephaly (the absence of all or part of the brain). If the AFP test is elevated, your doctor will want to perform an ultrasound to check the anatomy of the fetus, check that the date of your last menstrual period is accurate, and rule out a twin pregnancy. If all this is normal, the doctor may recommend an amniocentesis (discussed later in the chapter) for a proper diagnosis.

A woman's risk of a chromosomal abnormality such as Down's syndrome increases with advanced maternal age (over 35 years old). Therefore, historically this population of women has been offered invasive testing (such as amniocentesis) to check for chromosomal abnormalities. Then in 2007, the American College of Obstetrics and Gynecology and the College of Medical Genetics issued guidelines stating that all women should be offered the option of invasive testing for these potential abnormalities. Because of the increased risk of pregnancy loss that goes along with invasive testing, more noninvasive ways of screening the fetus at risk have been developed and now are offered to all pregnant mothers.

Recent advances in prenatal screening have focused on first trimester noninvasive testing, which offers the advantage of earlier diagnosis. This testing involves a blood test from the mom that includes testing for levels of free beta HCG and a marker called PAPP-A, which are both proteins made in the placenta. A special sonogram is performed at the same time to look at the size of the back of the fetal neck. This is called nuchal translucency. The ultrasound is offered between 11 weeks and 1 day to 13 weeks and 6 days. The results of these tests combined, HCG, PAPP-A, and nuchal translucency give a Down's syndrome prediction rate of 79 percent. If the outcome is positive, the woman is then offered a chorionic villus sampling or CVS (discussed later in the chapter) for accurate diagnosis.

When the second trimester AFP is drawn and the results are combined with other markers in the maternal blood (estriol and free beta HCG), this is called a triple screen. This test identifies the estimated risk that the fetus may have Down's syndrome. When the factors of the triple screen are added to one more maternal serum marker (inhibin), this is called a quad screen, which further increases the accuracy of the test. The quad screen has a pickup rate of Down's syndrome of 79 percent, just like the first trimester blood testing. So if your doctor tells you that this test is positive, there is still a 21 percent chance that the test is wrong and your baby has normal chromosomes. You will be offered an amniocentesis for an accurate diagnosis.

The AFP test and the triple and quad screens are just like any other blood tests and they are not risky at all—they will not hurt or harm you or your baby. The real risk associated with these tests is the same one you'll find with all screening tests: The results are not absolute and can cause a lot of needless worry. The risks involved in taking the diagnostic tests add to the fear of miscarriage, as well. If the results come back flagging the fetus as having a potential chromosomal problem, deciding what to do next is the most difficult part of these prenatal tests. The decision is ultimately what to do with a defective fetus. Do you abort it or do you want to know early on what the challenges are that you'll be facing at birth? There are other choices, such as adoption for Down's syndrome infants. Parents need to think, before they take an AFP, what they'll do with the results. You may be advised to take the screening test again, seek a second opinion, and/or meet with a genetic counselor. Whatever your choice, you must always keep in mind that most women who get abnormal screening test results give birth to normal babies.

Ultrasound

It's a good bet you have no pictures of yourself while you were still in your mother's uterus. But many of today's young children have this first photo of themselves, framed and hung right next to their birth photo. The technology that makes it possible to take a peek at the growing fetus is called ultrasound. Sound waves are bounced off the baby to create a picture without any of the potentially harmful effects often associated with x-rays.

An ultrasound comes in handy for the following reasons:

- **To date the pregnancy.** Ultrasound lets the doctor see whether the size of the baby matches what would be expected if the calculated due date is on target.
- **To monitor growth.** With an ultrasound, the doctor can see whether a baby is too large or too small for his or her age, which could indicate a problem.
- **To check for multiples.** Ultrasound can confirm or cancel suspicions of twins, triplets, or more.
- **To assess health.** Ultrasound allows doctors to check the location of the placenta, the amount of amniotic fluid in the uterus, and the general health of the baby. It can also determine the reason for vaginal bleeding. Ultrasound is used to determine the health of a fetus when a heartbeat has not been detected by the 14th week or if there has been no fetal movement by the 22nd week.
- **To check for suspected abnormalities.** With ultrasound, doctors are actually able to see the baby's organs and central nervous system.
- **To safeguard other tests.** Without the use of ultrasound to guide the procedures, tests such as amniocentesis would be far too risky.
- **To safeguard delivery.** Ultrasound can show the position of the baby before birth. And if the baby is overdue, ultrasound can check its size.

The best part about an ultrasound is that it's so easy, quick, and painless. If you are in the early stages of pregnancy, you may be asked to drink several glasses of water before the procedure because sound waves travel more easily through the fluid in your bladder. To begin the ultrasound, you will lie on your back or side on the examination table and expose the lower part of your abdomen. Next, the doctor or sonographer (a skilled medical professional who has received specialized education in imaging techniques) will apply an odorless, water-soluble gel to your skin. The gel makes it easier for sound waves to travel through your body. The gel is sticky, but it wipes off easily at the end of the exam.

After the gel is applied, the doctor or sonographer will move the transducer over your abdomen. As the transducer sends out sound waves and receives echoes, they are relayed to a computer and displayed as a real-time picture on a screen that looks like a television monitor.

With some help, you will see the first images of your baby. In the early stages of pregnancy, you may be able to see the beating heart, the curve of the spine, and the head, arms, and legs. At a certain age, you might even catch your baby sucking his or her thumb. Sometimes the genitals can be seen and you'll get a good idea about the gender of your baby. Selected pictures can be saved on paper, film, videotape, or in a computerized format to be reviewed later by your physician. (A still shot may be printed out as a keepsake for your baby's photo album.)

Technologic advances in ultrasound have enabled images of the fetus to be seen in three-dimension, known as 3-D sonograms. Traditional ultrasound uses the same sound waves to display the images in two-dimension. In 3-D ultrasound, the sound waves are set at angles that give a different image than the one you see in a two-dimensional image. This will show you the height, width, and depth of the fetus. This newer technology allows a physician to see the fetal surface and the internal organs more clearly. Adding another dimension, 4-D, allows you to see the fetus in motion. The best time to perform a 3-D or 4-D ultrasound is between 20 to 32 weeks of pregnancy.

Not all health-care facilities offer the 3- or 4-D sonograms as part of routine prenatal care, and most insurance polices will not pay for them. Although these early photos can increase a sense of maternal bonding, as of now the medical community has found no direct medical benefit of this newer technology in terms of identifying problems in the fetus. If you are unable to see 3- or 4-D images of your baby in the womb, don't fret; you'll be holding your bundle of joy in real-life dimension soon enough!

Because ultrasound uses sound waves instead of radiation, it is a safe way to assess your baby's well-being.

In the last trimester, an ultrasound is used to perform a test of fetal health called a biophysical profile (BPP). This test measures and rates components considered important to healthy growth and development. These include breathing, body movement, fetal tone, and the amount of amniotic fluid. These factors, combined with an assessment of the fetal heart rate (see "Checking the Baby's Heart Rate: Nonstress Test" later in this chapter), give a clearer picture of fetal health.

There are no known side effects from ultrasound imaging, and it is not necessary to take any special precautions following your exam. For more information about ultrasounds, you can contact the American Society of Radiologic Technologists, 15000 Central Avenue SE, Albuquerque, New Mexico 87123. Or visit the society's website at www.asrt.org.

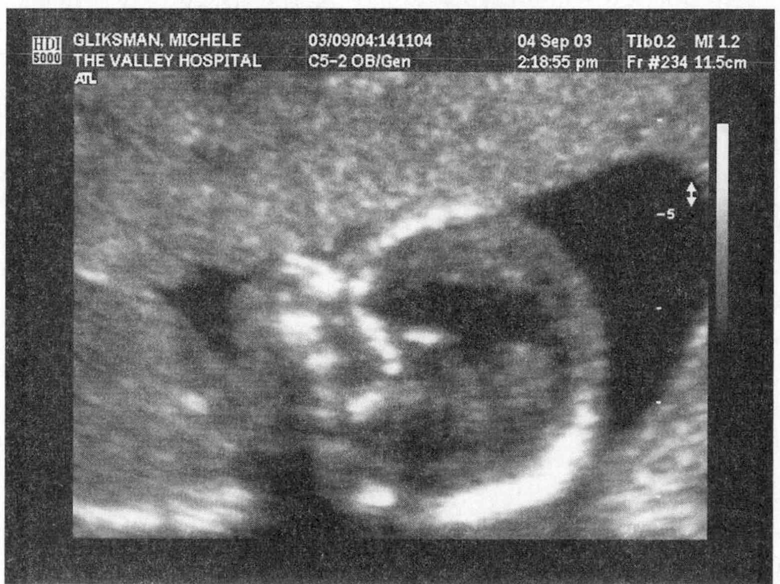

This ultrasound shows the profile of the head and shoulder of Dr. Gliksman's baby during her 13th week of pregnancy.

PREGNANCY FACTS

Some doctors now use 3-D/4-D ultrasound imaging equipment that gives a much clearer, photolike image of the fetus. These are thrilling to see, but be aware that they serve no medical need and are much more expensive than the standard ultrasound. In most cases, medical insurance companies have been refusing to pay the increased cost.

Amniocentesis

Amniocentesis is a procedure used to withdraw a small amount of amniotic fluid (the fluid in the sac surrounding the fetus). Analyzing this fluid can help diagnose a number of birth defects with approximately 99 percent accuracy. This diagnostic test offers the most remarkable advancement of this century in prenatal care.

Amniocentesis is usually performed between Weeks 15 and 18 of pregnancy. But it can be performed as early as Week 12 or as late as Week 20. It might also be performed toward the end of the pregnancy to check the baby's lung maturity. Depending on the tests being performed on the fluid, it can take anywhere from one day to one month to get the results.

Why Bother?

Amniocentesis is most commonly used to determine two things:

- **Chromosomal abnormalities.** These are birth defects or genetic problems. The test can identify several hundred genetic disorders, including some of the most common ones, such as Down's syndrome, Tay-Sachs disease, or sickle-cell anemia. It can also identify neural tube defects, such as spina bifida (a deformity of the spinal column) or anencephaly (the absence of all or part of the brain).
- **The maturity of the baby's lungs.** If there is a chance the baby will need an emergency early delivery, it is important to know whether the lungs are mature enough to allow the baby to breathe or whether he or she will need medical attention to assist with breathing.

Although the test is not given for this specific purpose, it can also tell the gender of the baby with great accuracy.

To Have or Not to Have

No one is required to have this test. But an amniocentesis is generally offered to women in the following three categories:

- Older women. Women over the age of 35 are at higher risk of having a baby with chromosomal disorders.
- At-risk women. These are women who have received a positive result on their AFP test or the triple or quad screen (see details in the section "Alpha-Fetoprotein Screening Test" earlier in this chapter). These tests can identify women whose babies are at risk for certain chromosomal problems.

- Women who have a family history of certain birth defects (or women whose partners do).

DADDY ALERT!

Your family medical history is also very important in determining whether your partner should undergo amniocentesis. Your genes share an equal part in creating the baby your partner is carrying. If you're not sure whether you have a history of birth defects or inherited diseases, talk to other family members and get the facts.

Some women want to have an amniocentesis; others say no way. Those who have it want to know in advance if their baby has a birth defect; this gives them time to decide either to terminate the pregnancy or to learn more about the baby's future needs. Other women choose not to have this test because they will not consider having an abortion and prefer to learn about the baby's health at delivery. This is not always a wise decision; knowing in advance about a baby's medical problems allows the health-care team and the parents to plan the safest timing, location, and method of delivery, with the appropriate specialists available immediately after birth. But nobody knows what's best for you, except you. This is a personal decision you should make with the help of your family, your doctor, and (if necessary) a genetic counselor.

Forewarned Is Forearmed

Nobody likes the thought of how an amniocentesis is performed, because it involves a long needle. But don't faint away just yet. Millions of women have had this test and have lived to tell the tale.

An amniocentesis is usually performed in a hospital. Here you will lie down on an examining table and the doctor or technician will use an ultrasound to locate the fetus and decide on the best place, away from the baby and the placenta, to insert the needle. This is not always a quick process, so lie back and relax. It can take up to about 20 minutes to find just the right spot.

The rest of the test is much faster. The doctor will take about five minutes to insert a long, thin, hollow needle through the abdominal wall and into the sac of amniotic fluid around the baby. As she does this, you're allowed to yell "Ouch!" (or shout any other word that comes to mind). It is not terribly painful, but most women say the needle stings as it goes in. The needle withdraws about two tablespoons of amniotic fluid and the test is over.

After the test, you may have some cramping and/or spotting. Your doctor will probably tell you to take it easy for the rest of the day. You will also be told to watch for signs of infection. About one woman out of 200 gets an infection or some other complication that results in miscarriage after an amniocentesis. That's why it's so important to let your doctor know immediately if you experience fever, chills, contractions, irritability, watery discharge, and uterine tenderness after having this test.

Chorionic Villus Sampling (CVS)

Chorionic villus sampling (CVS) is a diagnostic test that can identify or rule out certain birth defects. It is similar to an amniocentesis, with one major advantage: It can be done as early as the ninth week of pregnancy. This difference becomes important if the test reports the presence of a birth defect and the parents wish to have an abortion. It is always best to have an abortion as early in the pregnancy as possible.

An amniocentesis is rarely performed before the 12th week, and it can take several more weeks to learn the results. This long wait makes medically necessary abortions much more difficult both emotionally and physically.

CVS is not routinely offered to all pregnant women. Like amniocentesis, it carries the risk of miscarriage and possibly other complications such as limb abnormalities if performed before the 10th week. But it is an option for women who fit into one of these categories:

- Women over age 35. The risk of bearing a child with certain chromosomal birth defects increases as a woman ages.
- Women with a history of bearing a child (or children) with a birth defect.
- Women whose family medical history shows their children may be at risk for inheriting a genetic disorder.

CVS is generally performed in a hospital. Like an amniocentesis, ultrasound monitoring picks up the location and position of the fetus and placenta. A catheter (a small tube that's attached to a syringe) is used to extract the needed cells, but instead of taking amniotic fluid, the doctor will take a sampling of cells from the placenta.

The entry is first swabbed with an antiseptic solution to prevent infection. Then the doctor inserts either a catheter into the vagina through the cervix or a needle through the abdomen in order to obtain a tiny piece of chorionic villi (fetal cells of the placenta) for analysis. No anesthetic is given because this test is not painful. However, some women say they feel a pinch when the sample is taken.

After CVS, you may feel some cramping and have some spotting, but this should stop within a few days.

Checking the Baby's Heart Rate: Nonstress Test

In this test, the fetus does all the work. The *nonstress test* is given at any time during the last trimester when the health-care provider wants to evaluate the fetal heart rate (which usually ranges between 120 and 160 beats per minute). It may even be performed every day in the last month of particularly complicated and risky pregnancies.

To record fetal heart rate, an ultrasonic detector (called a Doppler transducer) is strapped to your abdomen over the area where the fetal heartbeat is most easily heard. The heartbeat is recorded on a strip of graph paper, which runs through a monitoring machine. A second detector (called a tocodynamometer) is strapped to the upper abdomen at a point over the top of the uterus. This detector records the frequency and strength of uterine contractions. The mother is asked to push a button to mark the monitor strip whenever she feels the baby move. It is expected that the fetal heart rate will increase in response to fetal movement. That's why this test generally lasts 20 to 40 minutes, in order to evaluate a number of fetal movements. If the fetus happens to be sleeping, this test can take even longer.

A new test can detect heartbeat irregularities in babies as early as 18 weeks. A report in *Circulation: Journal of the American Heart Association* says that researchers studied more than 30 fetuses with suspected heartbeat irregularities. Researchers used a new two-dimensional imaging technique, called tissue velocity imaging, that shows the heart's structure and gives information about the movement of the walls of the heart's four chambers. It took an average of four minutes to get a clear diagnosis, a much shorter time than is spent for conventional ultrasound testing.

Group B Strep and Umbilical Vein Sampling

Many other prenatal tests can be given in certain circumstances depending on the needs of the expectant mother and the wishes of the health-care provider. A few you might hear about include the following.

Group B Streptococcus (GBS)

Group B streptococcus is an infection carried in the vaginal or rectal areas of 10 to 35 percent of all adults. It is harmless and goes unnoticed, unless it is passed from mother to baby. Then it can cause meningitis (an inflammation of the brain or spinal cord), bacterial bloodstream infections, infant pneumonia, and even stillbirth.

PREGNANCY FACTS

Studies have found that engaging in oral sex may transmit GBS. Researchers found that among 120 college couples, fellatio increased the risk of transmitting the bacterial infection.

The risk of passing this infection on to a baby is greatest if the child is born prematurely, if the mother's water breaks early, or if there is a long delay between the time the water breaks and the baby's birth. The test for GBS (usually given during your 35th week) is simple: The doctor rubs cotton-tipped swabs against your vaginal and rectal area. These cells are sent to a lab for processing. If the results are positive, you will receive antibiotics during labor and delivery to prevent infecting the baby.

Umbilical Vein Sampling

Umbilical vein sampling (also called cordocentesis or percutaneous umbilical blood sampling) allows doctors to take a sample of fetal blood from the umbilical cord. This test is done by inserting a hollow needle through the maternal abdominal wall into a blood vessel in the *umbilical cord* (the tubelike cord that connects the baby at the navel to the placenta). Fetal blood is removed, which can then be evaluated for many things, including the following:

- Fetal anemia
- Infections such as rubella (German measles), toxoplasmosis (contracted from raw meat or cat feces), and herpes
- White cells that provide a chromosome count
- The amount of acidity, oxygen, carbon dioxide, and bicarbonate in the blood (such tests are especially important if the fetus is not growing as it should)

HEY MOM!

If you'd like more information about prenatal testing and birth defects, contact the March of Dimes Birth Defects Foundation. Call national headquarters at 914-997-4488 or visit www.marchofdimes.com.

The world of prenatal testing is growing and changing constantly. As new tests are introduced, others are being left behind. Ask your health-care providers to tell you more about any tests they recommend that are not listed here. It may be something outdated and unnecessary or it may be something new and very valuable. If you are unsure, do a little research: Check out the online sites listed in Appendix B and call the March of Dimes for the latest information.

Screening for Sexually Transmitted Diseases

There is a whole list of STDs that can be passed on from the mother to her baby and cause serious medical complications. Your doctor will need to know if you have an STD such as herpes, chlamydia, syphilis, hepatitis, or HIV. Women most at risk for these infections are those who have had multiple partners (or in the case of HIV, shoot drugs). If you fit into this category, get tested for STDs as soon as possible.

The U.S. Preventive Services Task Force now recommends that clinicians screen all sexually active women, including those who are pregnant, for gonorrhea infection if they are at increased risk for infection. Chlamydia is the most common infection passed from mother to fetus. This is probably because in most women, chlamydia has no symptoms. The Task Force notes that pregnant women with gonorrhea infection are at risk for preterm rupture of membranes, preterm labor, and infection of the amniotic fluid and the membranes that surround the fetus. Detection and treatment can cure gonorrhea infection, eliminating risks of delivery complications.

Also, the Institute of Medicine and the Centers for Disease Control and Prevention now recommend routine and voluntary HIV testing for all pregnant women. Given the new and effective interventions available to treat HIV-infected women and to reduce the risk of transmitting HIV to the baby at birth, such testing is a good idea for all pregnant women at risk for HIV.

Don't try to hide anything from your doctor—the secret will come back to haunt your child. If detected early, most effects of these illnesses can be treated and minimized, protecting your health and preventing transmission to the baby.

The Least You Need to Know

- Screening tests (which tell you maybe) are different from diagnostic tests (which tell you yes or no).
- You will get very used to having your health-care provider routinely evaluate your weight, blood pressure, urine, and blood.
- Common prenatal screening tests include glucose screening (for diabetes) and Alpha-fetoprotein screening (for birth defects).
- Diagnostic tests, such as ultrasound, amniocentesis, and CVS, can detect birth defects during pregnancy with great accuracy.
- There are many prenatal tests (including Group B strep test, umbilical vein sampling, and STD screening) that are available to women who might benefit from them.

Chapter

4

Special Moms

In This Chapter

- Defining a high-risk pregnancy
- Understanding the perils of pregnancy in women over age 35 and under age 20
- Doubling the fun (twins and more!)
- Becoming a mom through assisted reproductive techniques, surrogacy, or adoption
- Understanding the medical complications of asthma, DES, diabetes, epilepsy, heart disease, or high blood pressure

All expectant moms are special people. But some, because of their age or medical condition, require special care. If you fit into any of the categories explained in this chapter, you should expect a little more attention from your health-care provider.

Women who have a high-risk condition generally need top-level medical care. Family practitioners and midwives usually turn their high-risk patients over to an obstetrician. If the condition is especially risky, the obstetrician might bring in a specialist called a *perinatologist*. This is a medical doctor who specializes in taking care of high-risk pregnancies and deliveries. Most often, the perinatologist and the obstetrician or family practitioner work together. The obstetrician continues your routine care, and the perinatologist periodically checks for problems and does any specialized testing that's necessary.

Under 20

If you're a teenager and expecting a baby, let me congratulate you. Whether you planned this pregnancy or not, you're doing the right thing by reading books to find out what to expect and how to take care of yourself. You are not like other women. Your own body is still growing while your baby is growing inside of you. You have special needs that have to be considered during this time.

Statistics tell us that teenage girls are at risk for delivering a baby who weighs less than babies born to older women. These low-birthweight babies are at risk for medical complications and even death. The reason for this difference in birthweights is not known exactly, but we have a good idea. Many teens risk the health of their babies in these ways:

- They try to hide the pregnancy by dieting to keep their weight down.
- Even after the pregnancy is confirmed and known, they tend to eat poorly (definitely bad for the developing baby, which is called a *fetus*).
- Teens are less likely to quit smoking during pregnancy. Smoking definitely has an effect on the size of the growing baby.
- Pregnant teens continue to drink alcohol, often to excess.
- Teens with sexually transmitted diseases (STDs) often are so embarrassed by this medical problem that they don't get health care for themselves or their babies. They haven't gotten the message that the only thing shameful about having an STD is keeping it quiet and letting it affect the health of an unborn baby.

DADDY ALERT!

If you're a teen dad who wants to be involved in your partner's pregnancy—speak up! Too often, young fathers are left out in the cold because it's assumed that's what they want. Don't let everybody else tell you what you think.

Planning a Healthy Teen Pregnancy

As a pregnant teenager, you have a special responsibility to make sure your baby grows strong and healthy during your pregnancy. Take the following steps to help keep your baby safe:

- Get prenatal medical care right from the start. Do not put this off or skip any appointments.
- Eat a balanced diet with foods that will nourish your growing baby.
- Do not smoke during your pregnancy.
- Protect yourself during sex from getting a sexually transmitted disease. Make sure your partner wears a condom.
- It's time to give up nicotine, alcohol, and recreational drugs (such as marijuana and cocaine). If you have used these drugs in the past, they have to go during your pregnancy.
- Follow all the instructions of your health-care provider.

Over 35

The fact that you're over 35 and reading this book puts you ahead of the game already. The biggest reproductive problem faced by older women is getting pregnant in the first place, largely due to decreased fertility. So having cleared that hurdle, your next concern naturally turns to your own health during pregnancy and the health of your baby.

Getting pregnant at an older age doesn't automatically mean you will have problems with your pregnancy or childbirth. But statistically, older women do have more medical conditions that need to be closely monitored. For that reason, these women are usually bumped into a high-risk category.

Don't panic here, but it is true that older women are more likely than younger women to experience cesarean sections, miscarriages, and other complications. But many of the problems are not caused by age. Much more important than age is the state of a woman's health, along with family and genetic history. For example, if an older woman has high blood pressure or diabetes (two of the most common problems in older pregnant women), she's likely to need special attention during her pregnancy. This is not because she's old, but because she needs medical treatment for other conditions (the same treatment that young women with these same problems need). High blood pressure and diabetes can suddenly appear during the pregnancy of older women, making careful monitoring very important. But if a woman is healthy and has consistent prenatal care, she can expect a normal pregnancy.

Although the pregnancy might be uneventful, there are some problems during labor and delivery that are more commonly found in older women. For reasons no one completely understands, the babies of older women are more likely to move into a position that makes birth difficult (see "The Breech Delivery" in Chapter 24). Older women frequently have longer labors and a higher rate of cesarean sections. They also are more likely to have problems caused by early separation of the placenta because of a slightly increased risk of high blood pressure that occurs with age. (See Chapter 21 for the details on this condition called abruptio placenta.)

Even when the pregnancy, labor, and delivery run smoothly, the worrying is not over because there is an increased risk of birth defects as a woman gets older. The risk of Down's syndrome (one of several possible defects), for example, rises with age. At the age of 20, the risk is 1 in 10,000. It's about 3 in 1,000 for a 35-year-old mother, and 1 in 100 for a 40 year old. For this reason, women over the age of 35 are generally offered a test (called an amniocentesis) that removes fluid from the womb to test for abnormalities. Other tests (described in Chapter 3) might also be used to confirm and double-check all results.

The results of these tests let expectant parents know early in the pregnancy if the fetus is abnormal. If the results are positive, they can decide whether or not to continue with the pregnancy. This decision is made with the help and support of the doctor, genetic counselors, and pediatrician.

Medical advancements make childbearing for older women safer today than ever before. Prenatal screening for birth defects, medications that can put off an early birth, and fetal monitoring during labor that can detect problems with the baby (allowing quick response) all improve the likelihood of delivering a healthy baby.

Taking Charge

The good health and proactive attitudes of older women are positive factors in pregnancy. If you're over 35 and pregnant, take charge of your pregnancy by following this advice:

- **Get in shape physically.** See Chapter 18 and stick to an exercise routine that will help your body adjust to the changes it goes through each month.
- **Watch what you eat!** See Chapters 14 and 15 for the details on putting together a nutritional diet that will give both you and your growing baby what you need to stay healthy and strong.

- **Cut out risk factors such as cigarettes, coffee, and alcohol.** Chapter 17 will explain why these things are bad for both of you.
- **Get consistent prenatal health care.** Don't skip any appointments and do what your doctor says.

PREGNANCY FACTS

According to the National Center for Health statistics, the birthrate for women over age 40 has doubled in the past two decades.

Moms Through Assisted Reproductive Techniques

The American Society for Reproductive Medicine estimates that about 6.1 million American women and their partners are infertile—that's 10 percent of the reproductive age population! If you or your partner is a member of this group and are now reading this book because you or your partner is pregnant, congratulations! No doubt you have been through the ringer of assisted reproductive technologies (ART) that only those who have been there can truly understand.

Perhaps you've used fertility drugs, artificial insemination, or in vitro fertilization. Perhaps you've used frozen embryos, donor sperm or eggs, testicular sperm aspiration, transuterine fallopian transfer, tubal embryo transfer, gamete intrafallopian transfer, zygote intrafallopian transfer, or any of the other possible infertility treatments. By whatever methods you have tried, here you are pregnant and most likely wavering between euphoria and terror. Because you have been riding the emotional roller coaster of high hopes and disappointments for so long, it's understandable that you want to guard the health of your fetus to ensure a full-term pregnancy without complications. Well, here are the facts on your risk of miscarriage:

- If your pregnancy is the result of the use of fertility drugs (such as clomiphene citrate or human menopausal gonadotropin) with no other assisted reproductive procedure, your risk of miscarriage is not any higher than that of the general population—one in five. You are, however, more likely to have a multiple pregnancy (unless you used the fertility drugs bromocriptine or gonadotropin-releasing hormone [GnRH], in which case the risk of multiples is no higher than normal). It is estimated that 50 percent of twin pregnancies and 90 percent of triplet and greater multiple pregnancies are the result of ART.

- If you've had any kind of tubal repair surgery, your risk of an ectopic pregnancy is greater than that of the general population because your tubes might have scarred as a result of the repair procedure. (See Chapter 2 for information about ectopic pregnancies.)
- If you're pregnant as a result of artificial insemination, your pregnancy is no more risky than a routine pregnancy (except for the risks associated with multiple pregnancies resulting from the use of fertility drugs).
- If your pregnancy is the result of in vitro fertilization (IVF), gamete intrafallopian transfer (GIFT), intrauterine insemination (IUI), or any similar procedure (including microinjection), you do have a higher risk of miscarrying. Anything transferred directly into your fallopian tubes raises the risk of an ectopic pregnancy. But if your ART procedure transferred gametes or embryos directly into your uterus, there is only a slight risk of an ectopic pregnancy.

After the fertilized egg (or eggs!) implants itself securely in the lining of your uterus, your chances of a full-term pregnancy are just as good as those of any other expectant mom. But because of all you've been through to become pregnant and because of the risk of multiples, you should consider calling in a perinatologist to monitor your pregnancy. As noted previously, a perinatologist is a medical doctor who specializes in the complications of high-risk pregnancy, labor, and delivery.

Surrogate Moms

If a woman or her partner is infertile and all attempts at assisted reproductive technologies have failed, the only way to have a child and pass on the family genes is through a surrogacy arrangement. A surrogate mom offers her womb to nurture an embryo created from the egg of a woman (who cannot carry a baby full-term) and her partner's sperm. In this case, the baby is not genetically related to the surrogate mom at all. Or, the surrogate mom might be artificially inseminated with the sperm from the husband of a woman whose own eggs are defective in some way. In this case, the baby is genetically related to the surrogate and the intended father. The wife of the intended couple then adopts the child after its birth.

If you are a surrogate mom, this pregnancy will be especially exciting for you and the infertile couple as you all carefully follow the growth of this much-wanted baby. But because the health of someone else's baby depends on you, you might sometimes feel as if you're under a microscope. The intended parents will want to be sure that you're eating well, avoiding alcohol, and staying away from cigarettes and other drugs. They will monitor all your doctor appointments to follow the development of their baby, and they will want to keep in close touch throughout the pregnancy. This might get a little too close for comfort sometimes, but the close monitoring is well intended and will help you meet the ultimate goal of giving birth to a healthy child. The information in this book will help you better understand why your behavior and daily habits are now so closely linked to the well-being of another human being.

Intended Parents (Surrogacy and Adoption)

If you are the intended parent in a surrogate arrangement (like Sarah Jessica Parker) or an adoption in which you know the expectant woman, this book will help you feel involved in the process of pregnancy. Follow along each month so you can keep track of the baby's growth and development. Pay particular attention to the schedule of medical checkups and routine testing to make sure the pregnancy is being properly monitored. Read up on the discomforts and problems of typical pregnancies so you can better understand and talk about these things with the pregnant woman. You are a special mom-in-waiting. Enjoy and be part of every step along the way.

PREGNANCY FACTS

Surrogate moms and intended parents can get information and support through these sites:

- The American Surrogacy Center: www.surrogacy.com
- Organization of Parents Through Surrogacy: www.opts.com
- Surrogate Mothers Online: www.surromomsonline.com
- Surrogate Mothers, Inc.: www.surrogatemothers.com

Multiples!

Whether you're excited or distressed about having twins, triplets, or more, this is going to be a very adventurous nine months. Right from the get-go, multiples give you more of everything: The uterus grows bigger and faster, and usually you feel much more nauseous, have more indigestion, and experience more swelling of the fingers and ankles than other expectant mothers.

You'll also need more medical attention than moms expecting only one baby. More than one fetus makes yours a high-risk pregnancy. That's why you will see your doctor more often (usually every other week after the 20th week and weekly after the 30th). Complications common in multiples include hypertension, anemia, diabetes, and abruptio placenta. Multiples are also more likely to be born prematurely.

The good news about carrying and delivering multiples in this day and age is that the news rarely comes as a surprise at the moment of birth. With consistent prenatal care and the use of ultrasound technology, expectant moms know about the crowded conditions in their uterus long before delivery—with the use of ultrasound, you'll know in your fourth month. (The massive size of your belly is also a giveaway clue.)

Knowing about your twins (or triplets or more!) in advance gives you the opportunity to do things that will keep your babies safe:

- Get quality prenatal care. Don't skip a single checkup or put off following doctor's orders. A lot is on the line here.
- You will gain about 50 percent more weight throughout your pregnancy with multiples than you would if you were carrying only one baby. You don't want to gain too much more or less than this amount, so carefully monitor your weight and expect to gain about 1½ pounds a week after the 12th week.
- Low birthweight is a major problem with multiples. Make sure your diet is doubly filled with nutritious foods (especially protein).

HEY MOM!

There is a support network for high-risk expectant moms. You can contact it at Sidelines National Support Network, P.O. Box 1808, Laguna Beach, CA 92652; 1-888-447-4754; www.sidelines.org.

- Your doctor will prescribe special, fully loaded vitamin supplements. Don't forget to take them. Extra babies need extra nutrients such as iron; folic acid; zinc; copper; calcium; and vitamins B, C, and D.
- Because your body is working twice as hard to create more than one baby, you might be twice as tired. Fatigue can plague your pregnancy if you don't frequently answer the cry for rest. At every opportunity, put your feet up, take a nap, go to bed early, and cut down on your busy schedule.
- Exercise with caution. Although it's very important to stay in good physical shape during any pregnancy, carrying multiples is risky business. Talk to your doctor about any exercise program you would like to follow.

Asthma

Women with asthma sometimes need a little extra attention during pregnancy because an asthma attack can reduce the amount of oxygen the fetus receives (causing a condition called fetal hypoxia). Research indicates that women with asthma are at increased risk of hypertension in pregnancy, which might cause a slight increase in the risk of preeclampsia (a serious condition marked by high blood pressure and swelling; this condition is further explained in Chapter 21). But with close medical supervision and quick response to attacks, asthmatics can certainly expect to have a safe pregnancy and a normal delivery.

Asthma sufferers might notice a change in their asthma during pregnancy. Some have fewer attacks; others have more. Many notice an increase in attacks in the last trimester, when the enlarged uterus crowds into the lung area and sometimes makes breathing difficult even in the best of circumstances.

As soon as you know you are pregnant, talk to your doctor about your asthma medication. Some medicines are safer than others during pregnancy. After you have a pill or inhaler approved by your doctor, don't hesitate to use it when you need it. Any possible negative effect on the fetus from the medication is less than the effect of oxygen deprivation. If it ever happens that your medication can't stop an asthma attack, get yourself to an emergency room—this is an emergency. Also, let your doctor know if you feel symptoms of a cold or the flu. Immediate treatment (maybe with antibiotics) can head off an asthma attack.

DES-Exposed Moms

Between 1940 and 1971, a medication called diethylstilbesterol, or DES, was given to expectant moms to prevent miscarriage. These included women who had a history of miscarriages, those with diabetes, and those who experienced bleeding in early pregnancy—approximately two million women in all. The medication was often started in the seventh week of pregnancy—just the time when the female fetus is developing vaginal and cervical features.

PREGNANCY FACTS

There is no evidence that the granddaughters of DES moms are at risk for DES-related miscarriages.

We now know that this medication caused gynecological changes in the daughters of these women that can result in vaginal and cervical cancer and can also cause infertility, ectopic pregnancy, and miscarriage.

If you are the pregnant daughter of a woman who took this drug, you must tell your health-care provider. You are at high risk for a miscarriage in your second or third trimester. This might happen because in some DES-exposed women, the cervix isn't strong enough to hold the weight of the growing fetus. (The technical term for this is "incompetent cervix.") Also, the DES-exposed uterus might be smaller than average and *T*-shaped. This might not allow proper fetal growth and it puts pressure on the cervix to open.

Today, all is not bad news for DES-exposed pregnant moms. If the cervix begins to dilate early in the pregnancy (indicating that the body is getting ready to deliver the baby), the doctor can sew the cervix closed to prevent the miscarriage. This technique has saved many babies of DES-exposed women. Some doctors routinely sew the cervix closed in DES-exposed women after the 12th week of pregnancy. Because not all of these women will dilate early, other doctors wait to see if there is a need. Management of a DES-exposed pregnancy should be discussed with your doctor long before your due date.

Diabetes

Before the early 1900s, diabetic women were advised not to get pregnant. There were just too many risks involved in exposing a fetus to high blood sugar levels: miscarriage, stillbirth, and birth defects, to name a few. Today, there is no reason a diabetic woman can't have a perfectly normal pregnancy and healthy baby *if* she receives exceptional care and works hard to control the disease.

The excess glucose in a diabetic pregnant woman can be absorbed by her fetus. This is likely to cause the fetus to grow faster than normal and make vaginal delivery very difficult. That's why it is vital to monitor glucose levels throughout the pregnancy. If you don't already have an at-home glucometer, now is the time to buy one. This is something you should talk to your doctor about.

Your doctor will give you many directions, suggestions, and tests. Pay close attention, because all these things will determine whether you have a safe, successful pregnancy or not. You should pay particular attention to …

- **Your diet.** Together with your doctor and probably a trained nutritionist, you will need to create a diet plan that will keep your disease in check and properly feed your baby.
- **Weight gain.** Diabetes often affects overweight women. If you are overweight at the start of your pregnancy, this is not the time to worry about gaining more weight—you must not sacrifice calories now. On the other hand, this is not the time to decide you can stop worrying about your weight and eat everything in sight. Eat nutritious, well-balanced meals and keep your weight within the limits set by your doctor.

- **Exercise.** All pregnant women need exercise to stay in shape for delivery. Diabetic women also need it to regulate blood sugar. But your program of exercise must be approved by your doctor and monitored carefully. The intensity of your program depends in part on your prepregnancy physical health. If you became pregnant in tip-top shape, you'll probably be able to continue your exercise program. But if you were out of condition before pregnancy, you'll need guidance to develop a plan of exercise now.
- **Your medication.** If diet alone doesn't control your blood sugar, you might need to take insulin. If you were already on insulin before your pregnancy, the dosage will need to be adjusted. This adjustment will continue throughout the pregnancy, as the baby grows.
- **Blood sugar levels.** You will test your blood sugar (probably with a simple finger-prick method) several times a day. This will give you and your doctor clues about changes you might need to make in your diet, exercise program, and medication.

HEY MOM!

For advice and information about diabetes during pregnancy, contact the American Diabetes Association, 1701 N. Beauregard Street, Alexandria, VA 22311; 1-800-342-2383; www.diabetes.org.

Some previously healthy women develop diabetes during pregnancy—a condition called *gestational diabetes.* This is a temporary type of diabetes that develops in 3 to 5 percent of all pregnancies (most commonly in older or obese women) when their bodies don't properly regulate the amount of sugar in the blood. Severe cases often require treatment with insulin, but milder ones can be controlled with diet changes. You will be tested for this problem some time between Weeks 24 and 28. (See Chapter 3 for information about this test.) Although gestational diabetes is temporary and ends after delivery of the baby, your risk of developing diabetes later in life increases. Be sure your doctor monitors you continually.

Epilepsy

Fortunately, you are not the first or only woman with a seizure disorder to become pregnant. Your doctor is well equipped to help you experience a perfectly normal pregnancy and childbirth. This doesn't mean you won't be taking extra precautions; it just means that if you relax and follow your doctor's instructions, all should work out just fine.

Pregnancy often has an effect on the frequency of seizures. Some women suddenly have none at all; some have more; others have fewer. There's no telling how you will react. But you will need to work with your doctor to monitor your medication carefully. There is some risk that the medications prescribed for epilepsy might cause birth defects, but the risk is quite low. Your doctor might decide to lower your dosage level during this period or maybe stop it completely, but you should not make any changes without medical approval. You endanger your baby more by risking frequent seizures.

Some studies report that epileptic moms seem to experience more nausea and vomiting than other expectant moms. But on the good news side, they don't seem to have an increased number of serious problems such as miscarriages or premature birth.

To avoid seizures during pregnancy, you might make a special effort to get plenty of sleep and avoid stress. Keeping your body rested and calm seems to ward off problems. Also, if you smoke, it is absolutely vital that you stop now. In recent studies, women with epilepsy who smoked were at increased risk of preterm delivery compared with non-epileptic women who smoked.

Heart Disease

If you have heart disease and are pregnant, you have a lot to talk about with your doctor. If you have mild to moderate symptoms that do not cause exceptional fatigue, heart palpitations, breathlessness, or chest pain, and if you have no limitations on your daily activities, you should have no trouble safely carrying your baby to term, with the helping hand of your doctor. But if your symptoms of heart disease are so severe that even light activity must be limited, the stress of pregnancy might be too much for your body. If this pregnancy endangers both your life and the life of the fetus, your doctor might recommend an abortion.

If you and your doctor feel you can safely carry to term, you will probably be given very strict instructions to help you stay healthy. These might include …

- **Taking your medication regularly.** Be sure to ask your doctor to double-check your medication for its effect on your baby. Some medications are more fetus-friendly than others.
- **Staying calm.** It will be important to avoid any physical or emotional stress that would excite your heart. Some women might need to stay in bed throughout the pregnancy.
- **Watching your weight.** Of course you are expected to gain weight during the pregnancy, but you must be careful not to add any unnecessary pounds that would put additional strain on the heart.
- **Quitting smoking.** If you smoke, this is definitely the day to quit.

In the last few months and weeks of your pregnancy, your doctor will frequently monitor the health of your baby with ultrasound scans and nonstress tests (see Chapter 3). If all goes well during the pregnancy, you can expect to have a safe and normal vaginal delivery. Your doctor will probably advise using some method of local anesthesia during delivery to shorten the pushing stage and reduce the stress of labor.

High Blood Pressure

Every pregnant woman is checked for high blood pressure (also called *hypertension*) at each prenatal visit because this condition is known to have negative effects on the fetus and the mother. If you've come into this pregnancy with high blood pressure, your doctor will be very involved in helping you keep the level down over the next few months.

High blood pressure can decrease the blood flow to your baby, which reduces the amount of oxygen he or she receives. This is why women with high blood pressure who don't receive prenatal medical attention often deliver babies who are small and have a low birth weight—and therefore are at increased risk for medical complications and even death. Fortunately, modern medical advances make high-risk complications, such as high blood pressure, easily manageable. By following the instructions of your doctor, you and your baby should come through the pregnancy and delivery with flying colors.

Tips for Managing Blood Pressure

- **Learn to relax.** A calm body and mind will keep your blood pressure from skyrocketing. Take a good look at the relaxation exercises described in Chapter 18.
- **Plan a healthy diet.** By decreasing your intake of salt and increasing the intake of calcium, fruits, and vegetables, you can keep your heart pumping at a steady rate.
- **Drink!** As your fingers, feet, and ankles begin to swell, you might want to cut down on your fluid intake, but don't. Water will wash away the excess fluids that are causing this swelling.
- **Take it easy.** If you have a very stressful job, you might have to take an early leave. You need to find time to put your feet up and rest every day.
- **Double-check your medication.** There are some hypertension medications that are safe to take during pregnancy. Make sure that you're taking one of the safe ones.

- **Stick close to your doctor.** You will need very careful monitoring during your pregnancy to make sure your high blood pressure doesn't cause toxic substances, which can harm your baby, to build up in your blood (a condition called preeclampsia).

The Least You Need to Know

- High-risk pregnancies are usually cared for by an obstetrician along with a high-risk specialist called a perinatologist.
- Women who are over age 35 or under age 20 are generally placed in the high-risk category, along with women having multiples and those who achieved pregnancy through assisted reproductive techniques.
- Women with preexisting medical conditions that require close monitoring are also in the high-risk category. These conditions include women who have asthma, those whose mothers took a drug called DES during their own pregnancy, and women who have diabetes, epilepsy, heart disease, or high blood pressure.
- Most women can expect a safe and healthy pregnancy if they get early and consistent medical care and carefully follow all their doctors' instructions.

Part 2

The Countdown

A human pregnancy is nine months long, right? Well, wrong. Actually, the average pregnancy lasts 40 weeks, which is really 10 months—but it's really not. The pregnancy calendar uses what's called lunar months; they're 28 days long (just like the average menstrual cycle). But that makes counting the months a little confusing, so I've devised a simple plan to break 40 weeks into 9 months.

In the medical profession, we don't start counting the weeks of a pregnancy from the day you think you got pregnant—that's too iffy. Instead, we start with what we know for sure: the first day of your last menstrual period. Conception doesn't take place until about two weeks after this date. (See the week-by-week breakdown at the end of Chapter 5.) That's why the first month is broken into six weeks. By the time you're one month pregnant, you're six weeks into your pregnancy. The rest of the pregnancy months are four weeks long, until you get to the ninth month. Here you'll see another six-week month. To keep everybody on track, most events in a pregnancy are marked by the week in which they occur (Week 5, for example), not the month.

Chapter 5

Month Number One: Weeks 1 to 6

In This Chapter

- Finding the best health-care provider for you
- Knowing what to expect at your first medical visit
- Undergoing the first round of routine prenatal tests
- Noting the first sign of body changes: bigger breasts, frequent urination, mood swings, and fatigue
- Calculating your due date
- Taking a week-by-week peek at your baby's development

The first month of your pregnancy is often over before it sinks in that you're really pregnant. This is a time for making plans, choosing a health-care provider, and getting used to your new body.

Finding the Care That's Best for You

When you first discover you're pregnant, it's like trying to walk across a very busy intersection. The cars zip by at break-neck speeds. The huge tractor-trailers brush you back off the curb. Traffic rushes past from the right and the left, from in front and from behind. How are you supposed to get safely to the other side? What you need is a kind and understanding crossing guard who will step into the fray, blow his whistle to stop the traffic dead, and invite you to cross without risking your life.

Your health-care provider is your crossing guard. He or she will make a path through all your fears and uncertainties and guide you safely through your pregnancy, labor, and delivery. The person you choose to direct the traffic at this crossroads should be someone who is experienced and competent (after all, somebody in your support group needs to know what's going on) and with whom you feel comfortable enough to entrust with your life. This is a decision you should take some time to consider. You'll have to choose this individual from the list of practitioners participating in your insurance plan.

The Alphabet Soup of Professional Credentials

Luckily there are lots of options for health-care providers, but their credentials can be a little difficult to decipher. Most women are familiar with "OBs," but what on earth is an "FP" or a "CNM"?

The *family practitioner (FP)* is an updated version of the old family GP (general practitioner) who treated all family members for whatever ailed them. The FP has had special training in obstetrics and can be your primary care provider, your obstetrician, and eventually your baby's primary care physician. Some people like the continuity and the familiarity of this kind of practice.

The majority of women in this country choose an *obstetrician* to care for them during their pregnancies and to deliver their babies. These doctors are specially trained in the field of neonatal and maternal health care. They are usually gynecologists as well, so you might already be under the care of an obstetrician. But the person who has prescribed your birth control or cured your yeast infections might not necessarily be the person you want to see you through this pregnancy. It's okay to change to a new doctor at this point. Spending nine months with a doctor who will deliver your baby is different than the once-a-year hello-goodbye relationship you might have now with your gynecologist. Take your time and think about what kind of doctor you really want.

PREGNANCY FACTS

Until the mid-1700s in America, physicians did not attend at childbirth. Expectant women looked to female friends and family for help and comfort. They turned to midwives for skilled assistance.

In many areas of the country, the use of certified midwives has risen dramatically, and their services are usually covered by health insurance. *Certified nurse-midwives (CNMs)* are licensed health-care practitioners who have been educated in both nursing and midwifery at a medical institution accredited by the American College of Nurse-Midwives (ACNM). They are certified and active in all 50 states and the District of Columbia. The ACNM says that California has the largest number of CNMs, followed by New York, Florida, Pennsylvania, Illinois, and Massachusetts. In some states, women are being trained and licensed as midwives without first becoming nurses. In these cases, they are called *certified midwives.*

If you are looking for a health-care provider who is known for giving that extra personal touch and an emphasis on natural deliveries with minimum high-tech intervention, you might want to investigate midwifery. Most midwives today are employed by physicians, hospitals, or birth centers, but they also attend at home births. Some CNMs work independently with women who are expected to have low-risk pregnancies (see Chapter 2 for more on high-risk factors). An independent CNM should always be affiliated with a physician, whom the CNM can call on for consultation or in case there is an emergency. Nurse-midwives cannot assist in the care and childbirth of women who develop problems during the pregnancy. In this case, the woman is considered "high-risk" and is referred to a physician who will manage the rest of the pregnancy and birth.

Male or Female?

When you choose a health-care provider, you should think about whether you want a male or female practitioner. Some women have no preference in this area—they simply want the best. But for some, the gender of their health-care provider is very important. I don't believe there is any difference in expertise or ability between men and women. The decision to choose one or the other is a deeply personal one.

PREGNANCY FACTS

More than 50 percent of graduating obstetrician/gynecologists are female. This number is rising every year.

Solo or Group?

Next you should decide whether you want a practitioner who is in a solo or a group practice. As the name implies, a solo practitioner works alone. This is the only person you will see during your pregnancy. He or she will be the one to deliver your baby. Many women prefer this arrangement because they get to know and trust this person. The downside of a solo practice in obstetrics is the fact that one person can't be in two places at one time. If this one-and-only is on vacation or has the flu when you go into labor, you'll be delivering with a covering doctor you have never seen before. It's also a problem when a solo practitioner is called away from the office for a delivery at the same time you're scheduled for an office appointment. You can sit in the waiting room all day or come back another time; either way, it's an inconvenience.

A group practice has its own set of pros and cons. In this setup, there are several practitioners who work together. Although you might have one favored doctor, you can't get too attached. In most group practices, a different doctor attends each monthly checkup until you have met all members of the team. Also, each member takes a turn at being on call for deliveries in the middle of the night (is there any other time babies come knocking?). So you can't be sure who will do the delivery until you arrive in labor. On the upside, because doctors in group practices are not required to attend a birth in the middle of the night and then be at the office for early morning appointments, they are more likely to be alert and refreshed. Also, if one doctor is called out to deliver a baby, another is back in the office to handle the daily appointments. If one is busy delivering a baby when you go into labor, another one is there to give you a hand. And at least you'll have a nodding acquaintance with whoever shows up.

Due to the medical insurance crisis across the country, many doctors, even those in group practices, do not feel that it is a financially sound business practice to be available 24/7. Many have combined their group practice with other group practices to create rotating delivery schedules. In this case, the chances are high that your baby would be delivered by someone you have never met and who is not even a member of your doctor's group. This is becoming more and more common, so if you're thinking of choosing a physician who belongs to a group, be sure to ask whether that group has combined with other groups to deliver babies.

The Final Pick

After you've decided whether you want a physician or a midwife, a man or a woman, and a solo or group practice, you're ready to choose from a small group of health-care practitioners. After you have your criteria (and your insurance company's list of participating practitioners) in hand, it's time to zero in on a few and then pick the best.

Ideally, you can decide whom to interview for the position of your health-care provider based on a personal recommendation. If you have a relative or friend who has had a wonderful experience with her doctor or midwife, that's a good start. But if you're not ready yet to spread the word about your pregnancy until you get a definite medical confirmation, this might not be possible. In that case, you'll just have to pick up the phone, call from the list of selected practitioners, and ask a few pointed questions that will help you narrow your list down to one.

It is important to find a doctor who meets all your needs, from ease of scheduling appointments to philosophy about husband involvement. If you have a low-risk pregnancy, you will see this person (or a member of this team) once a month for the first six months. When your baby is about 28 weeks along, you'll visit every two weeks; then, from 36 weeks to delivery, you'll be examined by your doctor once a week. If yours is a high-risk pregnancy (see Chapter 2), you'll probably visit the doctor more often to be monitored and to have additional tests.

Questions to Ask Health-Care Providers

When you interview health-care providers, refer to a written list of the questions you want to ask, including the following:

- I just want to double-check my information: Is this a solo or group practice? (Things sometimes change between the time you get information and when you sign up.)
- Are you still participating in the health-care program _______? (Fill in the blank with the name of your insurance company.)
- What are your office hours? (If you work all day and there are no evening or Saturday office hours, you can cross this candidate off your list.)
- What hospitals are you affiliated with?
- Do these hospitals have a neonatal intensive care unit? (This is a special nursery for babies born with medical complications. It is vital for women with high-risk pregnancies.)
- Does the hospital allow the baby to room with the mother? (Some new moms think this is important; others would prefer having the time to recuperate without their babies next to them. Either way is fine; just find out what the hospital offers.)
- Can my husband be present at my monthly exams? (If this is important to you, find out now! And pay attention to the tone in the person's voice when he or she answers. If a "yes" sounds more like an "if you're going to be a pain about it and I have no other choice," that will tell you to keep looking.)
- Will my husband be welcomed in the labor and delivery room? (Some practitioners welcome new fathers; others merely tolerate them.)
- Do you encourage natural childbirth or anesthetized childbirth? (The right answer here should say something about this being your choice and preference, not the doctor's.)
- What is your position on pain relief during delivery? (Some doctors withhold pain medicine until the woman demands it; others give it freely. Ask.)
- What is your opinion about cesarean section deliveries? What is your (or your group's) cesarean rate?
- Do you encourage vaginal birth even if I've previously had a cesarean?
- What is your group's induction rate? (This is the rate at which labor is forced or "inducted.")

- What is your group's VBAC rate? ("vaginal birth after a cesarean": This is the number of people in your practice who have cesarean births and then go on to have subsequent vaginal births.)
- How do you support breast-feeding women?

What to Expect at the Medical Checkup

After you've chosen your health-care provider, you'll be given an appointment for your first medical checkup. Although every medical practice has its own way of handling this first visit, you can expect your first medical exam to go something like this:

1. You will fill out a medical record sheet that will ask for information such as your name and address, your age and marital status, and your insurance information. You'll also supply your medical history (chronic illnesses, hospitalizations, surgeries, medications, and allergies, for example). You'll give information about your family's medical history (such as heart disease, cancer, and birth defects). You'll provide facts about your gynecological and obstetric history (length of your menstrual cycle, duration and regularity of your periods, past births, abortions, and miscarriages). Your health-care provider will also want the details of your life-style and habits (exercise, smoking, drinking, diet, occupation, and such).
2. You'll be asked to give a urine sample in a small cup.
3. You will be escorted into an examination room and given one of those glamorous dressing gowns. (Those of you with an innate fashion sense always put the opening in the back.)
4. A nurse will record your weight (the lowest you'll see it for a long while), take your blood pressure, and ask you a few easy questions ("How are you feeling?").
5. The doctor will come in, talk to you for a while, and then get to work. First, he or she will check your heart, lungs, and breasts. Then you will lie back and put your feet up in the stirrups, and the doctor might insert an unappealing (but painless) metal device (called a speculum) into your vagina to widen the opening to the vagina. Here he or she can assess your reproductive system: the cervix, vagina, uterus, and fallopian tubes. To check the physical signs of pregnancy, the doctor will slip two fingers of his or her gloved hand into your vagina as far as they will go, while pressing down with the other hand into your abdomen. This allows the doctor to feel the top of the uterus. If it is

more than six weeks since the first day of your last period, he or she can also feel the already softened part of the uterus, which is now slightly enlarged, and the changing texture of the cervix (the neck of the uterus). This examination will not be painful, just a little uncomfortable. And don't worry about your baby. The fetus is well protected and cannot be dislodged from the uterus by this internal examination. In many practices, this is the last internal exam you will have until near the end of the pregnancy (unless some medical complication makes another one necessary).

6. Most likely you will be given a prescription for prenatal vitamins. These vitamins give your body the added nutrients you will need to nourish your growing baby. Ideally, you will take in most of the needed nutrients from the good foods you eat; these vitamins are just insurance.
7. Before you leave, you will be given a date for next month's checkup. Don't lose track of this date.

PREGNANCY FACTS

The pregnancy countdown: Most pregnancies last 280 days, which is 40 weeks. This is 10 lunar months or 9 calendar months.

Your monthly checkups are an absolutely vital part of ensuring a healthy pregnancy and delivery. They are not something you can skip.

Testing

If you thought you left testing back in school, you are in for a surprise. You will take a series of routine tests at every medical visit for the next nine months. Some provide a base to measure changes against during the pregnancy. Others check for health factors that should be addressed immediately if problems are detected. These routine tests include an evaluation of weight, blood pressure, urine, and blood. (See Chapter 3 for more details about these tests.)

DADDY ALERT!

Don't feel shy about going with your partner to her medical checkups. If you want to be there, just say so. Expectant dads are encouraged to participate in every aspect of the pregnancy and, if it's okay with your partner, you should feel free to go right into the examination room to watch and ask your own questions. If the health-care provider says you can't, then it's time to look for a new health-care provider.

This first weigh-in records a weight you won't see again for many months. Your total weight gain (which should be between 25 and 35 pounds) will be measured against your weight at this first visit.

Blood pressure is tested every month. At your first visit, your health-care provider will take note of your normal pressure (not influenced by the pregnancy just yet). A sudden rise in blood pressure in later months signals a problem, such as preeclampsia—a high-tech word for high blood pressure during pregnancy. (See Chapter 23 for details.)

You might be asked to bring your first morning urine to every checkup, or you might be given a little cup to urinate in at each visit. This urine is tested for a number of things: (1) infection; (2) protein, which can be a sign of high blood pressure; and (3) sugar, which can be a sign of diabetes.

Blood will be drawn either at this first visit for routine blood analysis or at a later visit for the Alpha-fetoprotein (AFP) test. (The AFP is a screening test given between Weeks 16 and 18 that identifies a potential risk of birth defects.) A nurse will take your blood by inserting a needle into a vein on the inside bend of your elbow. As explained fully in Chapter 3, this blood will tell your blood group (A, B, or O), your Rh factor, and your immunity to rubella (German measles), and will be used to test for sexually transmitted diseases, such as hepatitis B, HIV, and syphilis.

A finger-prick blood test will be taken periodically throughout your pregnancy to check for anemia. To take this blood, the health-care provider will prick the tip of your finger and then squeeze the finger to draw a drop of blood. This blood is placed on a glass slide for laboratory analysis.

Body Changes

In the first month of pregnancy, no one except you might even know you're pregnant. Obvious physical changes aren't shouting the news to the world just yet, but if you listen carefully, your body has a whole lot to say about the newcomer growing inside you.

This is the month when reproductive hormones kick in overtime and begin to send you signals about your pregnancy. It's hard to say exactly how you will feel—some women need to listen very closely to their bodies to hear any message at all, whereas others are hit hard and have no doubt that they are hosting a new living organism in their body. (See Chapter 1 for an in-depth look at all the following body changes.)

Bigger Breasts

Almost immediately, your breasts might feel swollen and sore. They will also begin to grow! This is one of the first obvious physical signs you might notice. Suddenly your bra is killing you. It's tight and uncomfortable. Your sweaters start to look like they've shrunk. Your breasts might know about your new arrival before you do!

Frequent Urination

You might find yourself getting up in the middle of the night to urinate. In fact, you might find yourself spending a good part of the day in the bathroom also!

DADDY ALERT!

Don't panic if you start to feel "pregnant." You wouldn't be the first expectant father to embrace a pregnancy with physical symptoms of your own. You might feel nauseous; you might start putting on a few pounds around your middle; and you might feel emotionally fragile. These sympathetic discomforts are nothing to worry about.

Mood Swings

Your emotional state is on shaky ground right now. One minute you're ecstatic, the next you're in tears. You're not losing your mind—you're pregnant. If you suffer the mood swings of premenstrual syndrome (PMS), you'll know the feeling, but you'll be surprised by the timing. The mood swings of pregnancy don't go away after a few days!

Fatigue

Boy, are you tired! If you're having trouble mustering the energy to put one foot in front of the other when you walk, put your feet up, rest, and remind yourself that all pregnant women feel like this.

Your Due Date

The expected date of your baby's arrival is probably the biggest piece of news you'll take away from your first checkup. It's the date you'll memorize and engrave on your heart. Unfortunately, it's probably not the date your baby will arrive. The due date is nothing more than an estimate that gives you and your doctor an idea of when to expect your bundle of joy. Because the exact date of conception is almost impossible to pinpoint, and because babies have their own time schedule for arrival, you should use this date only as an indicator of when you might be due.

Your health-care provider will determine when your baby is due by using a handy little "due-date calculator" that figures out the date by simply targeting your last menstrual period. To do this calculation yourself, try one of two formulas.

- Take the date of the first day of your last normal menstrual period and add seven to it. To that date, add nine months. That's your estimated due date.
- Note the date of the first day of your last menstrual period. Add 40 weeks to this date. This could be your due date.

If your periods are a predictable 28-day cycle, your calculated due date should be fairly accurate. But if your cycles are longer or shorter than 28 days, your actual due date might fall before or after the projected date.

As your pregnancy progresses, your health-care provider will double-check the many factors that indicate the age of a fetus. She'll note the growing size of the uterus. She'll mark the time you first feel movement and when the heartbeat is detected. If these dates don't match up with your projected due date, your doctor might suggest that you take an ultrasound test (see Chapter 3 for the details on this test). The ultrasound will show the size of the fetus and give a very good indication of its age.

Week by Week

The development of a baby in 40 weeks is an amazing thing. There's something new happening every week!

Week Number 1

You're not pregnant. This is the week of the start of your last period. As the uterus sheds its lining and causes bleeding, the hormones are preparing another egg for release.

Week Number 2

You're still not pregnant. The uterine lining is thickening and ovulation (the release of an egg) is getting ready to occur. You might feel a twinge of pain as ovulation occurs.

Week Number 3

This could be the week! When an egg is released into your fallopian tube, it meets up with your partner's sperm. (During the average ejaculation, 350 million sperm have a chance at making the trip into the fallopian tube. The ones that make it will wait there for an egg for as long as four days.) When the sperm penetrates an egg, fertilization (conception) occurs. The fertilized egg is called a *zygote*. Immediately, the egg begins dividing into identical cells as it floats down the fallopian tube to the uterus. *Now* you're pregnant.

Week Number 4

There's lots of action going on that you're completely unaware of. Your little zygote finds its nesting place in the uterus and is now called a *blastocyst.* When in the uterus, it divides in half: One half sticks to the uterine wall and becomes the placenta (the life-support system that brings nourishment into your baby and takes waste out). The other half will become the baby. Transvaginal ultrasound (which is an ultrasound in which a small probe is placed into the vagina, giving a very close look inside the uterus) shows a gestational sac (a small circle that will become the baby's home). By the end of this week, you will have missed your period, giving you the first sign that something's up. Some women see a slight spotting called implantation bleeding that happens when the blastocyst nestles into the uterine wall.

BABY TALK!

The fertilized egg is called a **zygote.** When the zygote finds its nesting place in the uterus, it is called a **blastocyst.**

Week Number 5

At this point, a pregnancy test can confirm the pregnancy. Your baby, now about the size of an apple seed, is now called an embryo and has a beating heart of its own. The placenta and the umbilical cord are in full operation. You would be shocked to see how rapidly your baby is developing:

- The head and the tail folds are distinct.
- The primary brain vesicles form.
- The nervous system begins to develop.
- Two heart tubes are fused in the midline and begin to contract.

Week Number 6

Your little embryo is dropping its calling card. This is the week the physical sensations of pregnancy usually appear: Nausea, sore breasts, fatigue, and frequent urination are all signs of this incredible growth process. The embryo looks more like a tadpole than a human, but the body is growing rapidly.

- The head, tail, and arm buds are easily recognizable.
- The optic vesicles and lenses form.
- Limb buds are present.
- The earliest form of the liver, pancreas, lungs, thyroid gland, and heart appear.
- Blood circulation is well established. The heart bulges from the body.
- The cerebral brain hemispheres are enlarging.
- In the stomach area, the primary intestinal loop is present.

PREGNANCY FACTS

Organogenesis is the period of time that the fetus's important organs are developing. This begins at 6 weeks and extends to 10 weeks. It is during this period that the fetus is most at risk from birth defects caused by external factors (such as drugs and other toxins).

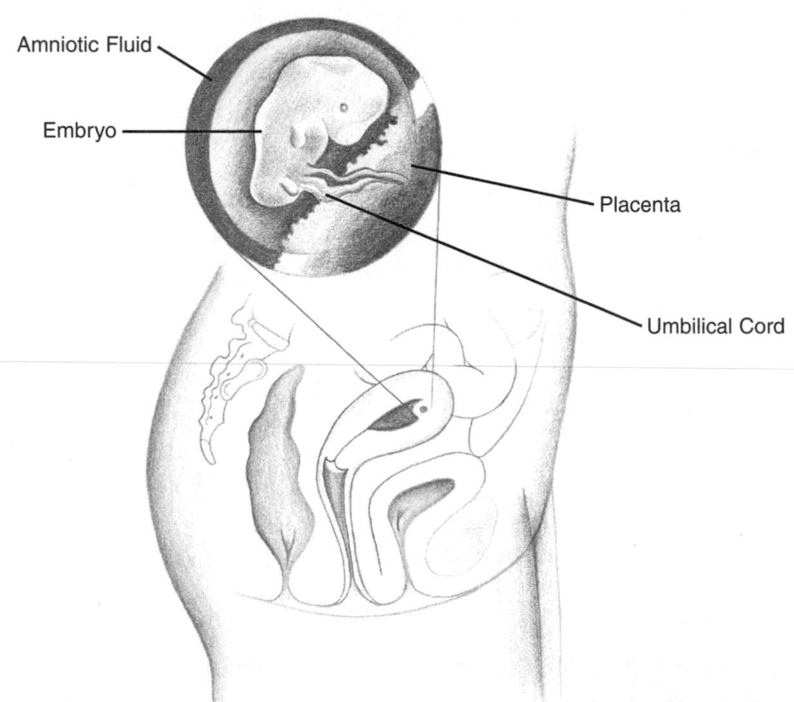

A human embryo at 6 weeks. At this time, your baby will weigh 1/1,000 of an ounce and be 1/4 inch long.

In these few weeks in the first month of pregnancy, so much is happening. Just because you don't see your belly growing yet, don't be fooled into thinking there's nothing going on that needs medical attention. Don't let this first month go by without a visit to your health-care provider.

The Least You Need to Know

- You are pregnant for 10 lunar months.
- Take time to select the health-care provider who's just right for you. Decide whether you want a physician (family practitioner or obstetrician) or a nurse-midwife. Do you want your caregiver to be a man or a woman, in a solo or group practice?
- Your first visit to your health-care provider is vital for recording baseline information.
- In the first month, you will notice body changes such as sore breasts, expanding waistline, nausea, increased need to urinate, mood swings, and fatigue.
- Your due date is only an estimate based on a simple mathematical formula.
- In the first six weeks, your baby is rapidly growing.

Month Number Two: Weeks 7 to 10

Chapter 6

In This Chapter

- The second month medical checkup includes routine tests, a look at common leg problems, and time to ask questions
- Body changes to look out for include constipation, nausea, vaginal discharge, excess saliva, and a growing waistline
- There are facts about pets and toxins you need to be aware of

The second month is a critical month in the development of a fetus. During this month, the organs (such as the heart and kidneys) are forming and any assault on the fetus (from alcohol, medications, drugs, or environmental toxins, for example) can have lasting effects. This is a time to take very good care of yourself.

What to Expect at the Medical Checkup

In the beginning of your pregnancy, you will most likely go to your health-care provider every month for a routine checkup. Although every medical practice has its own way of following a pregnancy through its 40-week course, generally at this second visit you can expect to be evaluated for the following:

- **Weight.** Since conception one month ago, you might have put on some weight due to increased breast tissue and blood volume—but not very much. If you have gained more than three pounds in the last month, you're taking in too many empty calories. See Chapters 14 and 15 for help in putting together a healthy diet.
- **Blood pressure.** This is a routine test. The doctor is still watching for any sudden changes that can indicate a problem. Remember to take a deep breath and relax as your blood pressure is being recorded.

PREGNANCY FACTS

Blood pressure is recorded in two numbers: The top number measures the peak pressure in your arteries as the heart pushes blood to your organs. The bottom number is the pressure that remains when the heart is at rest just before it contracts again and pushes more blood through the body. Ideally, you want your blood pressure reading to be 120/80.

- **Urine tests.** Every month your urine is tested for: (1) infection; (2) protein, which can be a sign of high blood pressure; and (3) sugar, which can be a sign of diabetes.
- **Leg trouble.** Your doctor might look for signs of varicose veins in your legs—this is a good time to head off trouble that might be down the road as your baby gets heavier and puts more strain on your leg veins. She will also examine your ankles and feet for signs of edema (swelling); this could be caused by blood pressure problems. (See Chapter 2 for a detailed discussion of varicose veins and edema.)
- **Questions.** Every visit should allow time for you to ask questions. This pregnancy idea is still new to you, so don't be shy about telling your doctor what you're worried about or what you don't understand. Speak up and get the most out of these visits. Anything that you wonder or worry about when you're home alone is a good subject of discussion at your monthly checkup.

Body Changes

In the second month of your pregnancy, you might still look your prepregnancy self, with little to give you away. But you'll know without a doubt that your body is changing.

Constipation

In the second month, your bowel becomes sluggish and distended. Your stools become hard, dry, and difficult to pass. You have constipation.

Constipation is a universal problem with pregnant women because of the rush of hormones in the body, but the iron in prenatal vitamins is also notorious for causing bowel and digestive problems. Just because constipation is common in pregnancy doesn't mean you have to accept it.

While you pass this second month dreaming of all that lies ahead of you, be kind to your behind by drinking lots of fluids; eating fiber-rich foods; limiting your intake of sugary, processed foods; and exercising! Revisit Chapter 2 for the details on keeping your bowel movements soft and regular.

Be sure to talk to your doctor before taking any medicated remedy for constipation. Not only can laxatives and stool softeners wash necessary nutrients out of your system, they might be harmful to your baby.

Nausea

About one half of all pregnant women get nauseous—many start to upchuck sometime during the second month. If you're going to have "morning sickness," this is the month you'll know about it. Whether you feel seasick morning, noon, and night, or feel queasy only on occasion, the cause is probably the rising level of hormones in your body at this time. (There's a theory that nausea might be the body's way of keeping you away from harmful foods, as well.) If month number two finds you in the bathroom with your head in the toilet, flip back to Chapter 1; it's chock-full of ideas (from sucking on a lemon to pressing on acupressure points) to help you control nausea.

Vaginal Discharge

You might begin to see a vaginal discharge that is thin and milky-colored and has a slight odor. Although this discharge can be quite heavy and might continue throughout the pregnancy, it is no cause for alarm—it might actually be your body's way of protecting against infection. Let your doctor know if the discharge becomes thick and yellowish, looks bloody, or is very watery. It might be a sign of trouble.

Excess Saliva

You might find your mouth filled with saliva during the first few months of pregnancy. This condition (called ptyalism) is especially common in women who have morning sickness. It's a harmless but annoying problem (especially when you find yourself spitting all over everyone you speak to). Mint is an herb that can help dry up the mouth a bit. Try using mint-flavored toothpaste, mouthwash, breath mints, and chewing gum.

Waistline

Although there's probably no sign of a pregnancy belly just yet (unless this isn't your first pregnancy or you're expecting twins), some women lose their waistline very quickly. You might have trouble closing the top button on your pants—especially if you're slim and have little room for the growing uterus to expand into. The problem might also be caused by digestive problems that swell the bowel and give you a bloated feeling.

Whatever the cause, you might want to pull out those slacks and skirts with elastic waistbands from the back of your closet. They are the best choice for this in-between time. Experienced expectant mothers learn to find creative ways to keep up a pair of pants. For example, you can take a long, thick elastic band and loop it through the buttonhole and slip the ends over the button. Hide this handiwork with a large blouse or sweater and you can use your prepregnancy wardrobe for just a bit longer.

What's on Your Mind?

You've now had several weeks to think about all the things that can go wrong during a pregnancy. This month, you might be especially concerned about being pregnant with pets in the house, the possibility of a miscarriage, and the damage the wrong foods, medications, and toxins can do to a fetus during Weeks 7 to 10.

The Down Side of Kitties, Dogs, and Turtles

Household pets, like cats and dogs, are a part of the family. They give you love and joy, and I'm sure there's no chance they'll be moving out to make room for your baby. But keep in mind that pets can bring more than fun into your home—they bring in diseases that can be dangerous to both you and the fetus.

Your cat can quite innocently cause some trouble during your pregnancy. Cat feces can contain a microscopic protozoan (a very tiny organism) called *Toxoplasma gondii.* This protozoan can be passed to a human in two ways:

- **By direct contact.** This can happen if you touch the feces while cleaning the litter box or when gardening in an area where a cat has relieved itself.
- **By simply breathing.** If the feces are disturbed (say by the way the cat scratches at its litter) and the sacs containing the *Toxoplasma gondii* become airborne, people nearby can inhale them through the mouth or nose.

Being infected by this organism causes a condition called toxoplasmosis. The symptoms of toxoplasmosis are quite mild and are often passed off as some kind of cold or flu. An infected person might get a low-grade fever, cough, headache, fatigue, and swollen glands. If you have had a cat in your home for a long time, it's very likely that you've already had toxoplasmosis—this is a good thing! After being infected, the body builds up antibodies (disease-fighting cells) to protect itself from a repeat infection.

If you already have toxoplasmosis antibodies, it is unlikely that exposure during pregnancy will cause your baby any harm. (It is estimated that about one half of the American population has been infected.) But if you have never been exposed to toxoplasmosis or if you're not sure, it is very important to protect yourself now. If toxoplasmosis crosses the placenta in the first few months of pregnancy (especially in the second month), it can severely damage the fetus. Problems can range from premature birth or low birthweight to serious central nervous system defects and even stillbirth.

Don't let this information scare you. Toxoplasmosis is rather rare. It is estimated that the chances of contracting toxoplasmosis for the first time during pregnancy are approximately 1 in 1,000. Still, be smart and follow these steps:

- If you have a cat, take it to your vet to be tested for *Toxoplasma gondii.* If your cat has an active infection, ask a friend to take care of it until you're further along in your pregnancy. After the sixth month, the chances of this organism crossing the placenta are slim.
- If your cats are not infected, keep them that way: Don't let them eat raw meat and keep them inside as much as possible (where they can't get at mice or birds that might be infected and where they aren't exposed to infected cats).
- Stay away from the litter box! It must be cleaned daily, but somebody else will have to do the job.
- Stay away from stray cats and don't hold cats you don't know.
- Avoid gardening in soil that might be contaminated with cat feces. Always wear gloves.
- Wash fruits and vegetables thoroughly. (The ground they fall on before harvest might be contaminated.)
- Cook all meat thoroughly. Inadequately cooked or cured meat is a main risk factor for infection with toxoplasma.

DADDY ALERT!

This is your chance to be the hero. Don't let your wife clean the cat's litter box—that's now your job. Change it daily because the sacs containing *Toxoplasma gondii* are not infectious for the first 24 hours (although they have the ability to survive in soil and water for as long as 18 months). Wear gloves and wash your hands thoroughly afterward.

You can ask your doctor to test you for toxoplasmosis, but right now the results won't tell you much. If they show that you have been infected, there's no telling if you were exposed before or during your pregnancy. Later, around Weeks 20 to 22, tests of fetal blood or amniotic fluid can determine whether the baby has been infected. If so, an immediate and aggressive course of antibiotics might limit the damage.

Even if you don't have a cat, you can still be exposed to toxoplasmosis by handling or eating raw meat. The organism is found especially on pork, beef, and mutton. It's a good idea to wear gloves when handling raw meat, cook meat thoroughly, wash your hands with soap before eating, and clean all kitchen counters and utensils exposed to the meat.

If your dog has been to the vet this year and is up to date on its rabies shot, you shouldn't worry about caring for it during your pregnancy. As an extra precaution, you might have it examined for parasites at regular intervals (especially if it is allowed to run loose). Animal parasites have been known to infect humans. Although the effect of a parasitic infection on a fetus is unknown, the illness experienced by the mother cannot be good for the baby.

Pet turtles are on the list of animals to be careful around when you're pregnant. That's because they are known to transmit salmonella bacterial infections to humans. (This is the same bacterium you can get from raw chicken that causes food poisoning.) If you have a turtle, try to avoid touching the animal and the water it swims in. Be sure to wear gloves when you clean the tank or change the water.

Fetal Assault

Wow! Your baby is growing by leaps and bounds this month as many vital parts and pieces fall into place. But watch out: This astonishing growth can go awry if the embryo is assaulted by anything that interferes with healthy growth. To keep your baby safe during this crucial month, you must be very careful about what goes into your body.

For starters, stay away from alcohol! In addition to the many problems fetal alcohol syndrome hands to a newborn (see Chapter 17), alcohol can affect the way the baby's face is formed in the second month of pregnancy. Babies born with fetal alcohol syndrome have very distinct facial features that include a small head circumference, underdevelopment of the jawbone, low-set ears, abnormalities of the eyelids, and underdevelopment of the bridge of the nose. These deformities occur in the second month of pregnancy, when the facial structure is forming.

In Chapters 16 and 17, you'll find discussions about the dangers of certain medications, drugs, and environmental toxins. Each in its own way can interfere with the normal development of a fetus throughout a pregnancy. But it is in the second month, when so many vital organs are forming, that these "poisons" are most dangerous. If you are in your second month, jump over to these chapters and read them carefully.

Week by Week

The second month is a busy one for your little embryo; there's so much to do and so little time to do it.

Week Number 7

- The heart is completely formed.
- The limb buds are present.
- On the face, the nostrils have overhanging borders.
- The eyes appear as dark spots.
- The tongue is beginning to form.
- Permanent kidneys begin to form.
- The head is relatively larger.
- The trunk of the main body is elongating and straightening.
- The eyelid folds are forming.
- In the middle area, the appendix and pancreas are present, and the mid-gut (or primitive intestine) herniates into the umbilical cord.
- The pituitary gland is forming in the middle of the brain.
- Spleen and liver ducts are forming.
- The intestines elongate.
- The cerebral cortex (the part of the brain that directs motor activity and intellect) can be seen.
- The stomach and esophagus begin to form.

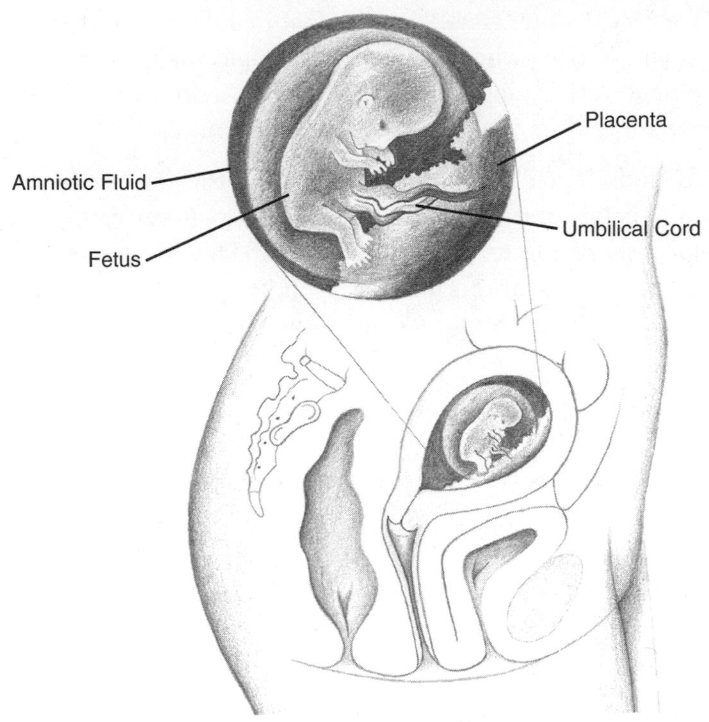

A human fetus at 10 weeks. At this time, your baby will weigh 1/3 of an ounce and be 1 1/4 inches long.

Week Number 8

- The embryo is half an inch long.
- The leg buds have divided into thigh, leg, and foot units.
- The arm buds have divided into hand, arm, and shoulder units.
- The gonads, testes or ovaries, are forming.
- Cartilage and bone are forming.
- The hands are flexed over the wrists and meet over the heart bulge.
- The feet are approaching the midline and might meet.
- The eyelids have almost covered the eyes.
- The external ear is well advanced in form.
- The head is in a more erect position and the neck is more developed.

- The limbs are longer.
- Cartilage appears where bones will later develop.
- The head is bent forward onto the chest.
- The eyes develop pigment.
- Nerve fibers connect the olfactory lobe of the brain, laying the groundwork for the sense of smell.
- The brain stem is now recognizable.

Week Number 9

- The abdomen and chest cavities become separated.
- The eye muscles and upper lip develop.
- Using ultrasound, the first fetal movements can be detected.
- The nerve cells of the eyes' retinas form.
- The semicircular canals of the ears form.
- The nasal passages open to the outside.
- The nerve connections from the retina to the brain are established.
- A distinct neck connects the head to the body.
- All fingers and toes are present.
- The urinary and rectal passages are completely separate.

Week Number 10

- The embryo now weighs $\frac{1}{3}$ ounce and is $1\frac{1}{4}$ inches from the top of the head to the rump.
- The eyes have moved from the sides of the head closer to the front of the face.
- Bones begin to replace the cartilage.
- The palate and roof of the mouth form.
- The stomach moves into its final position.

- Taste buds begin to form.
- Neck muscles are forming.
- The clitoris appears in females and the testes begin to descend in males.
- The two lobes of the lungs extend into many tiny tubes (bronchioles).
- The diaphragm begins to separate the heart and lungs from the stomach.

In month number two, your baby is rapidly growing and your hopes are high. Now is the time to balance the discomforts of the hormonal surge with the knowledge that it will all be worth it in the end when you hold your newborn in your arms.

The Least You Need to Know

- You can't skip your medical checkup this month; month number two is a crucial time for fetal development.
- As the level of hormones skyrocket this month, you might experience constipation, nausea, vaginal discharge, excessive saliva, and an expanding waistline.
- This is not the time to bring a cat into your house. Cats can transmit toxoplasmosis, which is harmful to the fetus.
- Cut out alcohol and other toxins; they can cause deformities as organs and facial features develop this month.
- During Weeks 7 to 10, there is incredible development of internal organs and sensory organs.

Month Number Three: Weeks 11 to 14

Chapter **7**

In This Chapter

- What to expect during the medical checkup: routine tests and a milestone event
- How to accommodate your expanding waist, breasts, and buttocks
- Why the room keeps spinning
- What the facts are on birth defects and genetic counselors
- How your baby grows week by week

Month number three brings you to the end of the first trimester. (Remember, the nine months of pregnancy are broken into three trimesters of three months each.) Now your baby graduates from being an embryo to being a full-fledged fetus! By the end of this month, the fetus is completely formed—all organs are in place and the fingers and toes are accounted for. When you reach the end of the third month, you can exhale—the high-risk period for a miscarriage is over.

What to Expect at the Medical Checkup

The medical checkup in the third month of pregnancy offers the same routine tests and questions as last month, but it also holds the possibility of a wonderful surprise!

- **Weight.** By end of this month, you will probably have gained four to five pounds. Unfortunately, some women gain 10 to 13 pounds in the first trimester because they let go of the fear of weight gain. When you know you're going to be as big as a house in a few months, what's an extra piece of cake? The big deal is that those extra pounds make fat, not a baby, and they will be hard to get rid of after the baby's birth. They also affect your health.

Excess weight places extra stress on the blood vessels and organs (such as the heart and kidneys) from the extra fluid volume; it also increases the risk of developing gestational diabetes. If you're gaining more than you should, see Chapters 14 and 15 for help in putting together a healthy diet.

- **Blood pressure.** Your blood pressure is recorded at every checkup. The doctor is still watching for any sudden changes that can indicate a problem.
- **Urine tests.** Every month your urine is tested for: (1) infection; (2) protein, which can be a sign of high blood pressure; and (3) sugar, which can be a sign of diabetes.
- **Size check.** Your health-care provider can measure the size of the growing uterus by pushing down on your abdomen and feeling the upper edge. The location of the top of the uterus will tell the doctor whether the size of the fetus matches the expected date of delivery.
- **Doppler.** Here is the most exciting part of the three-month visit: You might be able to hear your baby's heartbeat! With a hand-held *Doppler* (which is a small device that is simply placed against the woman's abdomen and magnifies the sounds within), your practitioner should be able to pick up the wonderful heartbeat "thud-lump" of life. A stethoscope can't yet pick up the sound, but a Doppler can. Your doctor will probably use the Doppler to listen to the heartbeat at every visit after 10 weeks.
- **Questions.** Don't leave your checkup until you've asked all the questions you've thought of since your last visit. Books and magazine articles give you lots of facts, but they don't know you and your pregnancy—your doctor does.

Body Changes

In the third month, you're in an in-between stage. You don't quite fit into your prepregnancy clothes, but you're not big enough for maternity clothes, either. This is a month for wearing loose dresses and large sweaters and jackets that cover your midsection.

Breasts and Buttocks

Your breasts are still very full and tender. You might notice a darkening in the skin color of the areola (the darker area of skin surrounding the nipple). As the blood supply increases throughout your body, you might also see bluish veins under your skin.

Make sure you're wearing a bra that gives your breasts plenty of support. Maternity bras are a good choice because they are made differently than fashion bras. They have broader straps; they are wide in the back to ease muscle strain, and they don't press into breast tissue (which can clog milk ducts). Get a bra that fits correctly on the tightest row of hooks. This will give you some room to expand.

While you're in the lingerie department, you should pick up some new underwear also. Because your hips and buttocks expand during pregnancy (I guess you've noticed that by now), you're going to need a larger size. Maternity underwear (which has a special stretchy panel across the front) is probably too big for you right now, and buying regular underwear in larger sizes might fit at the waist but bag out at the legs. Try this: Buy bikini-style underwear a size larger than usual. This will accommodate wider hips but stay out of the way of an expanding belly.

HEY MOM!

Maternity bras are different from nursing bras. Nursing bras will be very useful after the baby is born if you plan to breast-feed. They have little panels in the front that open and close for easy access to your nipples. This is not the kind of bra you need right now.

Dizziness

Have you noticed that when you stand up quickly, the room begins to spin? This is nothing to worry about. It happens because a sudden change of position makes it hard for the circulatory system to keep up a steady supply of blood to the brain. This is common in early pregnancy because there is an increased demand for blood throughout the body, but there isn't quite enough to handle a sudden call for more, if you go from lying down to a sitting or standing position.

If you get dizzy even when you're not changing positions, ask yourself when was the time you last ate. If you wait too long between meals, your blood-sugar levels can drop and set the room a-swaying. You might need to eat small meals more often.

Don't worry about feeling dizzy. Nothing is happening that can hurt your baby. But you should worry about hurting yourself if you should fall down.

You can avoid dizzy spells in several ways:

- Rise from a sitting or lying position slowly; jumping up to answer the doorbell can start the room spinning.

- Don't let your blood sugar drop. Eat several small meals a day and snack on raisins or fruit.
- Stay out of hot, stuffy rooms. If you feel yourself getting overheated, go outside and get some fresh air.
- Avoid standing still for long periods of time. Walk around and move your feet so that your blood doesn't pool in your legs.

If you feel like you're going to faint, don't ignore the feeling. Sit or lie down. If the feeling continues, prop your feet up so they are elevated higher than your head or sit with your head between your knees. If there's no place at hand to sit or lie, kneel down on one knee and bend forward. This should stop the feeling of faintness.

If you faint, call your doctor as soon as you recover.

Nausea

There's good news on the nausea front: Most pregnant women leave morning sickness behind by the 13th week. There are the unlucky few who feel nauseous for the full nine months, but generally, nausea should end by now.

What's on Your Mind?

The third month is a critical month in the development of your baby. During this month, you might be concerned about birth defects, the effects of stress, enrollment in childbirth classes, and chicken pox.

Birth Defects

All pregnant women worry about bearing a child with a birth defect, but some women have more reason to worry than others. If you are over age 35, have a history of bearing a child or children with a birth defect, or have a family medical history that puts your child at risk for inheriting a genetic disorder, your doctor will suggest that you consider genetic counseling and prenatal testing this month to determine the health of your baby.

Genetic counseling is a wonderful support program for couples who fall into a high-risk category for birth defects. A genetic counselor has advanced training in genetics, which is the study of how traits are passed on from parent to child. With this training, the counselor can explain the likelihood of a baby having a problem and the various prenatal tests available.

Before you meet with a counselor, make some phone calls to your parents or other relatives (and get your partner to do the same with his family!). Gather as much information as you can about family medical history. How did your grandparents die? Why did your cousin go to a special school? Has anyone in the family had a child with a birth defect or mental retardation? Ask specifically about inherited disorders. These include Tay-Sachs disease (which affects French Canadians and Middle European Ashkenazi Jews), sickle-cell anemia (which affects African Americans and some Mediterranean Caucasians), thalassemia (which affects primarily Southeast Asians), and cystic fibrosis.

The genetic counselor will tell you all about amniocentesis and chorionic villus sampling, which can detect defects in the womb. (See Chapter 3 for more details on these tests.) He or she will also explain the outlook for a child born with birth defects as well as the treatments that might be necessary, both immediately after birth and throughout the child's life.

A genetic counselor will not tell you what to do. He or she will tell you your options, give you the facts, and answer your questions. But the final decision is up to you. If you should choose prenatal testing and find out that your child has a birth defect, you will have all the information you need to help you decide what to do next. Either you will need to prepare for a child with disabilities or make arrangements to end the pregnancy.

If you meet with a genetic counselor, bring your partner with you. You both need to hear information that can be easily mixed up in the retelling, and you both need each other for support.

Stress

Don't let worrying about stress add more stress to your day. Stress is a part of life—it has weaseled its way into your schedule before your pregnancy, and it will continue to accompany you throughout your pregnancy. Even when you're pregnant, there will still be traffic jams that make you late, inconsiderate and pushy people who drive you nuts, deadlines to meet, and arguments with friends and co-workers. In these kinds of situations, stress will not harm your baby.

On the other hand, stress that is intense or chronic can be a problem for you and your baby. If this is an unplanned pregnancy, for example, or if you have separated from your partner, are grieving the death of a close friend or family member, or have a job that's making you want to jump off a cliff, your body's physical reaction to this kind of stress can be harmful to both you and your baby in many ways:

- **Extreme stress changes your breathing pattern.** When you're upset, you take shorter, shallower breaths that bring in less oxygen. (That's why people who are distraught are always told to take a deep breath.) Your body needs a plentiful supply of oxygen right now, so make a conscious effort to maintain a normal, deep breathing pattern.
- **Stress can affect your diet.** If you lose your appetite, your baby won't get the daily nutrients necessary for healthy growth. If you find yourself bingeing on sweets when you're upset, you'll add fat to your weight gain, raise your blood-sugar levels, and give your baby empty calories that can't be used for healthy development.
- **Stress can affect how well you sleep.** Sleep is a restorative time that allows your body to rid itself of toxins, such as free radicals and excess brain chemicals that are released during the day and can zap good health if allowed to build up in your system. Sleep also allows the body to discharge the effects of everyday stress that can build up and cause anxiety. Your body craves sleep (especially in the first trimester) for a good reason.
- **Stress can weaken the immune system.** When your body diverts much of its energy and internal resources to battling the fatiguing effects of intense or chronic stress, your immune system has little left to fight off invading germs. You are much more likely to catch a cold, the flu, or anything else in the air when you're stressed.
- **Stress can cause physical pain.** Tension headaches and backaches, unexplained muscle aches, and even chest pain are all signs of extreme stress.

If you read through these stress-related symptoms and say, "Hey, that's me!" it's time to talk to your health-care provider about finding ways to ease stress. Maybe it's time for an early maternity leave from your job, for example. In the meantime, make the relaxation exercises in Chapter 18 a part of your daily routine.

Childbirth Classes

I know the birth of your baby seems like a long time away, but it's not too early to start thinking about childbirth classes—they fill up quickly, and you'll want to get yourself enrolled in a class that runs during your seventh or eighth month.

DADDY ALERT!

Childbirth classes are for you, too. They give you an opportunity to ask questions, find out what to expect, and most importantly, support your partner. She didn't get into this situation alone, so don't ask her to go through it by herself.

If going to a childbirth class isn't already on your list of things to do during this pregnancy, think again. Yes, it's true that women have been having babies without going to school to learn how to do it since the beginning of time, but things are different today. Now the birth of your baby is something you have the right to participate in. Unless you're admitted for an emergency cesarean birth, you're going to be awake during your delivery. Don't you want to know what's going on? Don't you want to be able to help? Childbirth classes prepare you in advance for one of the most monumental events in your life. Regardless of the kind of delivery you choose—in-hospital, at-home, medicated, or natural—childbirth classes help to ease your fears. They tell you what's going to happen from start to finish. Ignorance is a scary thing—these classes give you the facts and some courage. See Chapter 23 to help you choose the kind of class you'd like to enroll in.

Chicken Pox

Chicken pox is a childhood disease that covers the body with itchy scabs. It is the kind of infection you get only once. If you had chicken pox as a kid, you are now immune to it and don't have to worry about getting it during your pregnancy. But if you haven't had chicken pox, you have to be very careful that you don't get it now. Women who contract chicken pox between the second and fourth months of pregnancy have a slightly higher rate of miscarriage and are at a slightly increased risk for delivering babies with birth defects.

If you haven't had chicken pox, you'd be smart to avoid young children who have not had chicken pox—at least until you're out of your fourth month. This viral infection is contagious one day *before* the telltale rash appears. So you might be at a family birthday party with all your nieces and nephews, who look perfectly healthy, and then get a call the next day telling you little Johnny has come down with chicken pox.

This would mean that you were exposed and are in danger of contracting the infection yourself. (Exposure to chicken pox is not dangerous to your baby, however, unless you actually come down with the disease.)

HEY MOM!

Of course, you can't stay away from your own young children who have never had chicken pox. The key is to keep them away from situations where they might be exposed to the disease and bring it home.

If you have never had chicken pox and are exposed to the disease, call your doctor immediately. You should have your blood tested to see whether you are already immune or whether you should be given a drug called varicella-zoster immunoglobulin. If it is given within 96 hours of exposure, this drug can prevent a severe form of the disease. It will not stop chicken pox from developing or prevent it from being passed to the fetus, but it will reduce the risk of complications if you suffer from a severe case.

Week by Week

As the third month ends, your baby is officially a completely formed fetus!

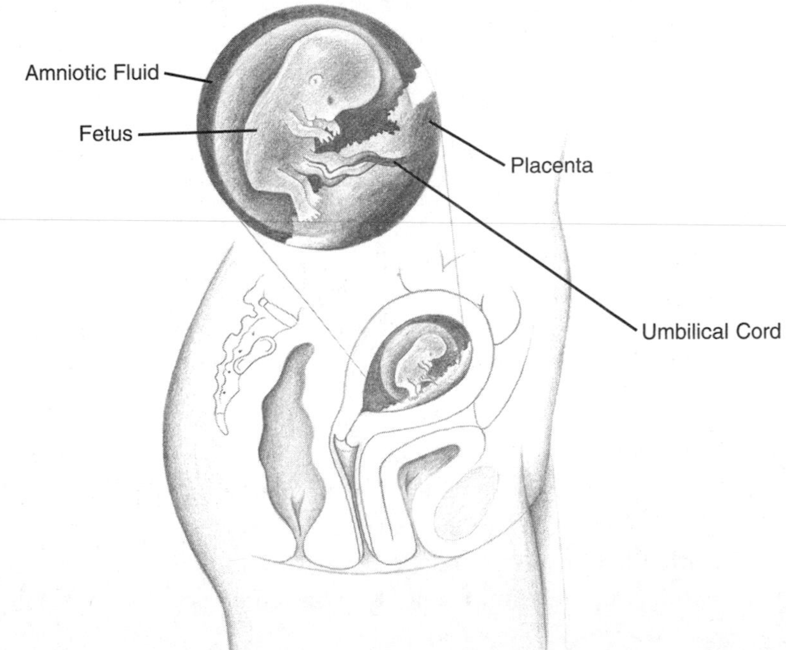

A human fetus at 14 weeks. At this time, your baby will weigh 1 ounce and be 3 inches long.

Week Number 11

- The head is almost half the size of the fetus.
- The eyelids have fused and will stay that way until Week 24.
- The external sex organs are developing.
- The hair follicles of the skin are forming.
- The ears are still abnormally low on the sides of the head.
- Teeth are beginning to form.

Week Number 12

- A skeleton of cartilage is forming.
- The gallbladder secretes bile from the fetus.
- The lungs are completely formed.
- The thyroid gland and pancreas are now complete.
- If the forehead is touched, the fetus will turn its head away.
- The liver is functioning to make blood cells. This organ accounts for about 10 percent of the entire weight of the fetus.

Week Number 13

- The fetus is about three inches long (double its length at Week 7).
- The fingernails appear.
- The beginnings of finger- and footprints begin to form.
- Tooth buds appear for all 20 baby teeth.
- The vocal cords begin to form.
- The trachea, lungs, stomach, liver, pancreas, and intestines develop into their final functioning form.

Week Number 14

- The ears have moved from the neck onto the head.
- The sex organs have fully differentiated into male or female.
- The digestive glands are complete.
- The taste buds are numerous and the salivary glands form.
- The vocal cords are complete.

At the end of the third month, take some time to celebrate. Your baby is fully formed and secure in your womb, and you're starting to feel more like your old self, with less fatigue and nausea. As the first trimester ends, you can look back, breathe a sigh of relief, and pat yourself on the back for getting through a tough period with flying colors. Now you can look forward to the days ahead when your baby (and you!) will grow in size.

The Least You Need to Know

- In addition to all the routine tests at your monthly checkup, you might be able to hear your baby's heartbeat this month.
- Get yourself to the store and stock up on new bras and underwear; your swollen breasts need more support, and your expanding waistline makes it tough to squeeze into your prepregnancy underwear.
- If you are over age 35 and have either a history of bearing a child with a birth defect or a family medical history that puts your child at risk for inheriting a genetic disorder, your doctor will suggest that you consider genetic counseling and a prenatal test to determine the health of your baby this month.
- Extreme and/or chronic stress can affect your health, and therefore the health of your baby.
- It's time to enroll in a childbirth class (even though you won't attend until your seventh or eighth month).
- Women who contract chicken pox between the second and fourth months of pregnancy have a slightly higher rate of miscarriage and are at a slightly increased risk for delivering babies with birth defects. If you've never had chicken pox, talk to your doctor about this and stay away from young children who are infected with this disease.

Month Number Four: Weeks 15 to 18

Chapter 8

In This Chapter

- The medical checkup: routine tests
- A discussion of Alpha-fetoprotein and amniocentesis, two prenatal tests that are often given in the fourth month
- A look at abdominal pains, nosebleeds, and breast, hair, and skin changes
- Concerns about staying healthy, carrying more than one fetus, and working

Month number four begins the second trimester. You might find these three middle months to be the best of the pregnancy. You've probably gotten past the fatigue and nausea of the first trimester and you're not yet into the discomforts of being so large in the third trimester. You finally look pregnant, you get lots of attention, and you should feel great!

What to Expect at the Medical Checkup

Your medical checkup in the fourth month offers routine tests and examinations, but it is also a month for prenatal testing and major decision making.

- **Weight.** By the end of this month, your weight is probably up about nine pounds. Keep in mind that most of this weight is *not* your baby. At the beginning of the second trimester, the fetus weighs only about *one ounce.* Continue to nourish your baby with healthy foods and stay away from the empty calories of sugary, processed foods that add weight in fat.
- **Blood pressure.** Your blood pressure is recorded at every checkup. The doctor is still watching for any sudden changes that can indicate a problem.

- **Urine tests.** Every month your urine is tested for: (1) infection; (2) protein, which can be a sign of high blood pressure; and (3) sugar, which can be a sign of diabetes.
- **Size check.** Your health-care provider can measure the size of your growing uterus by pushing down on your abdomen and feeling the upper edge. The location of the top of the uterus will tell him or her whether the size of the fetus matches the expected date of delivery. If it does not match by the fourth month, he or she might order a sonogram (see Chapter 3), which will give a more accurate account of the baby's age.
- **Doppler.** Again, you will have the chance to hear the baby's heartbeat with the hand-held Doppler. Last month the sound might have been difficult to detect, but this month it should be loud and clear. If your partner wasn't able to be with you last month, ask him to come this month. Because the heartbeat is an unmistakable sign of human life, it can help your partner begin to feel close to the baby.
- **Questions.** This month, your doctor will discuss the prenatal tests available in the fourth month to screen and detect birth defects. (See Chapter 3 for more specific details about these tests.) Listen closely and ask questions.

Sometime between Weeks 16 and 18, your doctor will take a blood sample from you to check the level of the Alpha-fetoprotein (AFP) and to run the triple and quad screens (see Chapter 3) which can give an indication of the risk of certain birth defects. High levels of AFP indicate the possibility of a neural tube defect, such as spina bifida (a deformity of the spinal column) or anencephaly (the absence of all or part of the brain). Positive tests flag the baby to be at risk for a birth defect called Down's syndrome. Most likely, your doctor will strongly recommend this test, but it's up to you if you want it or not.

DADDY ALERT!

That little fetus growing inside your loved one has your genes, too. If possible, ask your own parents for details about your family's medical history. This information can determine whether your partner should consider amniocentesis.

These tests are just like any other blood test, and are not painful or risky. But remember that they are only screening tests—the results are not absolute, so they can cause much worry for nothing. If your tests are positive, for example, there is a small chance that your baby has Down's syndrome. To find out for sure, you will need to have further diagnostic testing, such as amniocentesis (see the following paragraph).

For certain at-risk women, a test called *amniocentesis* (amnio for short) is performed between 15 and 18 weeks to detect birth defects (results are then available within two weeks).

At-risk women include the following: (1) women over age 35, (2) women who have received a positive result on their AFP test or triple and quad screens, and (3) women who have a family history of certain birth defects (or women whose partners do).

Amniocentesis is a procedure that involves inserting a needle into the womb in order to obtain a small amount of amniotic fluid (the water in the sac surrounding the fetus) for analysis. Analyzing fetal cells found in this fluid can help diagnose a number of birth defects with approximately 99 percent accuracy. In fact, amniocentesis can detect hundreds of disorders in addition to chromosomal abnormalities such as Down's syndrome. You will be tested for other genetic conditions only if the physician knows you might be at risk for them. These conditions include cystic fibrosis, Fragile-X syndrome, Gaucher's disease, muscular dystrophy, sickle-cell anemia, Tay-Sachs disease, and Huntington's disease. If you have a family history of a specific disease, check with a genetic counselor to see whether it's detectable through amnio.

Before having an amnio, many couples talk with a genetic counselor (a person trained to explain the risks of birth defects, as described in detail in Chapter 7). There is a lot to think about: Roughly 1 in every 200 to 300 women who takes the test miscarries as a result of the amniocentesis. This might happen if the placenta or the amniotic membrane is disrupted or an infection is introduced during the procedure. If the amnio is given earlier in the pregnancy, there is increased risk of a miscarriage due to performing this test in a very small sac.

Many women, however, feel that the benefits of this test outweigh the risks. If the results of an amnio show the baby has a birth defect, the expectant parents have time to decide to either terminate the pregnancy or plan the safest timing, location, and method of delivery (with the appropriate specialists available immediately after birth).

If you have an amniocentesis this month, you'll have one more decision to make: Do you want to know the gender of the baby? The amnio can tell with great accuracy whether you're carrying a boy or a girl—but that doesn't mean you have to know. If you prefer to discover the gender of the child at birth, be sure to let your doctor know and ask him or her to record your wish on your chart so there's no chance that a nurse or technician down the line will let the secret out of the bag.

Body Changes

As you begin your second trimester, get ready for some surprises. Your ligaments, breasts, sinuses, hair, and skin are all going through some changes.

Sharp Abdominal Pains

This month, your uterus is starting to enlarge, which can cause a sudden sharp pain across the abdomen and into the groin. This pain is caused by the stretching of round ligaments, the structures that support the uterus. These ligaments attach from the top of the uterus down to your groin. The pain happens most often when you move quickly or during sleep.

When you get one of these sharp twinges, don't feel alarmed—your baby is fine. It's just your body adjusting to the changes of a growing uterus. You can ease the pain by applying heat, rising and sitting slowly, and avoiding sudden movements.

Leaking Breasts

This month, a yellowish or whitish fluid called colostrum might ooze or leak from your nipples. Don't worry—this is normal. Colostrum is a kind of "premilk" that is richer in protein and lower in fat and milk sugar than the breast milk that comes a few days after delivery. It also contains antibodies that might help protect your baby from disease. If colostrum spots your clothing, you can put a panty liner or a gauze pad in your bra. If the colostrum forms a crust on the nipple, wash it off gently with warm water during a bath or shower. The area around the nipples (the areola) now becomes larger and darker also, and small raised spots might appear in this area; these are normal skin glands.

Nosebleeds

Some pregnant women who have never had a nosebleed in their lives suddenly find themselves groping for a tissue to stop the flow. This is more likely to happen in the wintertime, when dry air from indoor heating dries up mucous membranes in the sinuses. These membranes are soft and swollen already because of the increased flow of blood in your body brought on by pregnancy hormones. When you blow your nose, you might rupture the membranes and end up with a nosebleed.

To treat a nosebleed, don't throw your head back. Instead, lean slightly forward and pinch your nostrils closed. Stay like that for about five minutes. If the bleeding hasn't stopped at the end of that time, do it again. If you find that your nose bleeds often or very heavily, tell your doctor.

If nosebleeds are a problem, you can plan ahead to prevent them. Ask your doctor if you can try an extra 250 milligrams of vitamin C to strengthen the capillaries. And use a humidifier in your home or office to keep the air moist. To keep nose membranes from drying out, try a daily dose of saline nose drops. After that, don't worry. Nosebleeds are just one more little reminder of the bundle of joy you're carrying.

Hair Changes

Even your hair won't escape the effects of the reproductive hormones that increase blood circulation and metabolism. By the fourth month, you'll probably notice that your hair is growing faster and looks thicker and healthier than before. Or you might be one of the few whose hair becomes thinner, oilier, or drier. Either way, there will be noticeable changes in your hair.

Some women see drastic changes when their light hair turns darker, curly hair falls flat, or pencil straight hair turns curly. Most often the change is temporary, occurring during the pregnancy only. But many women claim their hair texture or color changes forever. (See Chapter 17 for information about hair dyes and permanents.)

PREGNANCY FACTS

Hair goes through two stages: growth and rest. During pregnancy, the majority of your hair is in the growth stage, giving you a fuller head of hair. Two to four months after delivery, your hair moves into a resting stage that causes a noticeable increase in hair loss.

The hair on your head is not the only hair on your body that grows longer and gets thicker during pregnancy. Increased amounts of facial hair (particularly on the lips, chin, and cheeks) are the most obvious. But you might also see thicker hair on your arms, legs, back, and belly. Even the area covered by your pubic hair might expand. Much of this growth disappears within six months after the baby is born.

DADDY ALERT!

This is not a good time to test your partner's sense of humor. A woman who has always been quick to laugh at herself will surprise you with a wailing retreat from the room if you dare mention the fact that she seems to be growing a mustache.

If your body hair is dark, you might find this unexpected feature of your pregnancy a bit embarrassing. Plucking and shaving are options, but avoid depilatories or bleaching cream. It's possible that they might be absorbed into the bloodstream and circulate into your womb.

Skin Changes

Because skin is the body's largest organ, it's probably no surprise that your pregnancy can drastically affect it.

DADDY ALERT!

Your partner's face isn't the only thing that will be changing color. The lips of her vagina (the labia) change color, too. They get darker and more engorged with blood. If you notice this change, don't get alarmed. It doesn't cause pain or soreness and will be gone after the baby is born.

You might be one of the women who wear the "mask of pregnancy." This is a scary-sounding name for a change in the pigmentation of the skin on the face, particularly the forehead, nose, upper lip, and cheeks. As a result of the high levels of hormones in your body, patches of darkened skin sometimes appear on the face (light patches might appear on dark-skinned women). Don't get upset—this is most likely a temporary condition that will disappear when the baby is born.

You might also notice that your moles or beauty marks are getting darker and bigger during pregnancy. As if that's not enough, 60 percent of women will get "vascular spiders," which are red blotches on the face, upper chest, and arms. Fortunately, these skin changes disappear when pregnancy ends.

You can try to lighten skin discoloration with cosmetic creams used to lighten birthmarks, but you'll have better luck using makeup to blend the skin colors. You can also keep skin discoloration, such as the mask of pregnancy, from darkening or getting worse, by staying out of the sun and wearing a sunscreen. Whether it's spring, summer, fall, or winter, use a sunscreen with a sun protection factor (SPF) of at least 15 every morning.

What's on Your Mind?

This month, you have lots to think about. You might find it a bit harder to stay physically healthy. This is the month you might find out you're carrying more than one baby. It is also the right time to start making a few career decisions.

Staying Healthy

If it seems like you're getting sick more often than usual, you could be right. During pregnancy, the immune system slows down to prevent the body from rejecting the fetus. In fact, the Centers for Disease Control now recommend that women who will be in the second or third trimester of pregnancy during the flu season receive a flu shot. If you feel a cold or flu coming on, get extra rest and drink plenty of fluids. Always call your doctor before taking any over-the-counter medications.

More Than One

Feeling exceptionally big? Worrying that there might be more than one boarder in your womb? This is often the month when you find out for sure. You and your doctor will begin to suspect twins (or triplets?) when you …

- Have watched your diet, but still put on more weight than expected.
- Have had the symptoms of pregnancy (such as nausea, edema, indigestion, and fatigue) in double doses.
- Have a large-for-date uterus. Each month, the doctor checks the position of the growing uterus; if it is larger than it should be for your due date, this is an important clue.
- Have a predisposition to multiples. This means you have a family history of nonidentical twins on your mother's side, and/or you are over 35 (women over 35 often release more than one egg), and/or have used fertility drugs or in-vitro fertilization to conceive.
- Have more than one heartbeat showing up on the Doppler. (This isn't as telling as you might think; the heartbeat of a single fetus might be heard at several locations because you can hear the blood flow in both the placenta and the umbilical cord.)

HEY MOM!

You can connect with other mothers of twins through the National Organization of Mothers of Twins Clubs; visit their website at www.nomotc.org.

Read more about mothers of triplets and more at the website of MOST: Mothers of Supertwins: www.mostonline.org.

If you experience one or more of these signs, your doctor can order an ultrasound exam. This test (see Chapter 3 for the details) can "see" inside the womb and, in almost all cases, accurately tell whether you are carrying more than one fetus.

If you find out you are carrying multiples, don't feel guilty if you're not immediately overjoyed. The news can be tough to take at first. Your dreams of rocking a sleeping infant while singing a lilting lullaby are suddenly replaced by the prospect of having two or three screaming babies demanding your attention round the clock. This requires a major mental adjustment. Give yourself time to adjust and seek out support. Other mothers of twins, especially, will have lots of support and helpful advice to offer.

If you're expecting multiples, you've just landed in the high-risk category. This is because your pregnancy will need special attention and your babies might be born prematurely. Your pregnancy is different from others' because the demands on your body are doubled. For starters, you'll need …

- **Extra rest.** All expectant moms feel tired by the end of the day, but you might find that you can't keep your eyes open by noon. This is your body's way of telling you that it's working overtime. Don't fight this craving for sleep. Nap whenever you can, get to bed early at night, and make time to put your feet up and rest during the day. When the babies arrive, you'll still be tired, but you won't have much opportunity for resting, so take advantage of any chance you have now to give your body a break.
- **Extra nutrients.** It takes more calories, vitamins, and minerals to nourish two or more babies. Ironically, as the babies grow, your stomach gets squished and can't hold as much food. The digestive problems of pregnancy often make eating a chore. That's why it's vital to fill yourself with quality foods that will supply the nutrients you need. Try not to waste your precious digestive energy on empty calories. (See Chapters 14 and 15 for information about nutritious meal planning.) Your doctor might also prescribe a stronger dose of vitamins and mineral supplements.
- **Extra weight.** Not only will you now carry the weight of another baby, you also have to factor in the weight of the extra placenta and amniotic fluid. Your pregnancy weight gain should jump into the range of 35 to 45 pounds. (That sounds like a lot, but it's only half a pound a week over the recommended weight gain for carrying a single baby.) If you're very careful about eating the right foods and putting on weight that goes to the baby (instead of going to your own fat cells), you can be proud of yourself for doing

something positive to avoid the most common problem of multiple pregnancies: low birth weight. Unfortunately, many twins are born weighing less than five pounds, but those nurtured with a healthy, closely monitored diet often grow in the womb to a robust seven pounds or more. That is your goal—give your babies supernutrients.

- **Extra medical attention.** Home birth with a midwife is rarely attempted with multiples. You will need medical monitoring by an obstetrician, who will be watching you very closely for signs of complications. (High blood pressure, edema, anemia, preterm labor, and problems with the placenta are more common in multiple pregnancies.) To keep a close watch, he or she will want to see you more frequently—perhaps every other week after Week 20 and then weekly after the 30th week.

HEY MOM!

Don't play around with over-the-counter vitamin and mineral supplements. Your babies need a regulated amount of nutrients, such as iron, folic acid, zinc, copper, calcium, B_6, vitamin C, and vitamin D. Let your doctor choose the supplement that's best.

If you find out you are carrying twins (or more!), keep reading. All the information in this book is still meant for you. The only difference is that the recommended weight gains will be higher for you; your checkups will happen more often after the 20th week, and your birth plan might be different. (See Chapter 12 for more information about birth plans.) Otherwise, you're in the same boat with every other expectant mom.

Work Concerns

This is the end of the line for hiding your pregnancy. Very soon (if it hasn't happened already), your belly will stick out just a bit too far to pass it off as "a little extra weight gain." Most likely, you've told your family and friends about your pregnancy, but many women wait until the beginning of the second trimester to spring the news at work.

There's no doubt that pregnancy complicates the career of any working woman, but it should never be a reason to lose your job if you choose to stay. If your pregnancy is uncomplicated (meaning you don't fall into any of the high-risk categories discussed in Chapter 2), and if your job doesn't expose you to an environment that is harmful to the growing fetus, there is no reason not to work right up to the moment labor begins. Chapter 19 will give you the facts regarding the law and pregnancy, and it will offer some advice on how to work safely and comfortably throughout your pregnancy.

DADDY ALERT!

Worried about paying the bills when your partner stops working? Join the crowd! There's no doubt about it: Going from two incomes to one is difficult. But if your partner is healthy and is not in a high-risk pregnancy, there's no reason for her to stop working before the baby is due (assuming she doesn't work in a dangerous or toxic environment). This will give you both a little extra time to store up some savings. Talk to her this month about how long she plans to keep working so you both have the same expectations.

Week by Week

In the fourth month, your baby's face looks more human. Her eyes, which started out on the sides of her head, have moved closer together. Her very thin skin is covered with hair (which usually disappears before she's born).

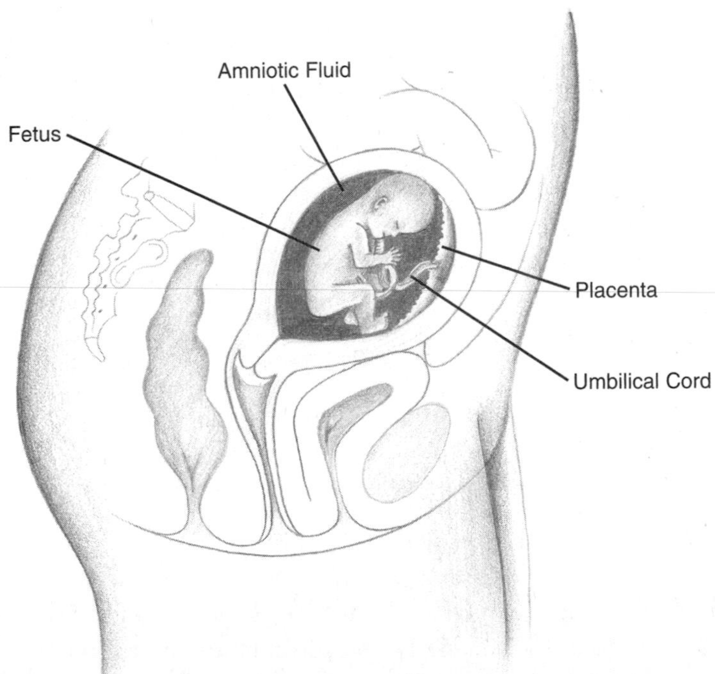

A human fetus at 18 weeks. At this time, your baby will have grown to about 5 inches long and weigh 6 ounces.

Week Number 15

- Blood vessels can easily be seen through the skin, which is very thin and translucent.
- The legs are longer than the arms.

Week Number 16

- The fetus can make a fist, open its mouth, move its lips, and swallow.
- The fetus might suck its thumb.
- Fine hairs can be seen on the head.
- The nails are well formed.
- The heart is beating 117 to 157 times per minute.
- The stomach is producing digestive juices.
- The kidneys are producing urine.

Week Number 17

- Brown fat begins to form.
- The rapid growth rate begins to slow down.
- White fatty material begins to enclose the nerve fibers of the spinal cord.
- Between the 17th and 20th weeks, hearing develops; the fetus can hear internal-organ and outside-world sounds.

Week Number 18

- The skeleton can be clearly outlined on x-rays of the fetus.
- Ears stand out from the head.
- Lanugo hair covers the entire body.

The Least You Need to Know

- At the beginning of the second trimester, the fetus weighs about one ounce and is three inches long, but you will probably have gained about nine pounds.
- In the fourth month, you and your physician will discuss two tests that check for birth defects: Alpha-fetoprotein and amniocentesis.
- This is a time of changes. Your breasts might start producing colostrum and you might experience nosebleeds. Changes in your skin (complexion, color, and texture) and in your hair (it might get thicker and grow faster) are all normal signs of pregnancy.
- If you're carrying twins (or more), this is the month you'll probably find out.
- Now is the time to think about how pregnancy and childbirth will fit in with your career.

Chapter 9

Month Number Five: Weeks 19 to 22

In This Chapter

- The monthly checkup: routine tests, another chance to hear the baby's heartbeat, and an opportunity to discuss the symptoms of anemia
- Body changes: vaginal discharge, acne, dry skin, and a distended navel
- Concerns, including fetal movements, cord blood banking, heavy lifting, an overload of advice, and overwhelming fears and anxieties
- Week-by-week development

This is the month the action begins—you can now feel your baby kick, turn, roll, and wiggle. Hallelujah—you've got interactive company! And the whole world knows it, because this month, as your belly grows, you begin to look pregnant.

What to Expect at the Medical Checkup

Your medical checkup in the fifth month offers the same routine tests and questions you've become accustomed to by now.

- **Weight.** There's just no way you can skip this part of your checkup, so off with your shoes and onto the scale. By the end of the fifth month, you should be weighing in somewhere around 10 to 13 pounds over your prepregnancy weight. If you're gaining more than you should, see Chapters 14 and 15 for help in putting together a healthy diet.
- **Blood pressure.** Your blood pressure is recorded at every checkup. The doctor is still watching for any sudden changes that can indicate a problem.

- **Urine tests.** By now your aim should be getting better as you urinate into that little cup. Again this month your urine will be tested for: (1) infection; (2) protein, which can be a sign of high blood pressure; and (3) sugar, which can be a sign of diabetes.
- **Size check.** Your doctor can measure the size of the growing uterus by pushing down on your abdomen and feeling the upper edge. At five months, your uterus reaches your bellybutton!
- **Doppler.** Again you'll have a chance to hear the baby's heartbeat—louder than ever this month. If you'd like to hear that wonderful sound over and over again (or share it with family and friends at home), bring a small tape recorder and tape it!
- **Questions.** Keep those questions coming. Let your doctor know if you are concerned about anything at all. At the five-month checkup, you might want to ask about *anemia*, a blood condition in which there is an abnormally low number of red blood cells.

HEY MOM!

If you eat iron-rich foods along with a cup of coffee, the caffeine can wash the iron right out of your system.

On the first prenatal visit, your blood was drawn and tested for a number of things, including anemia. You might have cleared that test, but now around the 20th week (when expanding maternal blood volume and your growing fetus require more iron), you might end up with iron-deficiency anemia.

You should ask your doctor about having another test for anemia if you are experiencing extreme tiredness, weakness, breathlessness, a pounding heart, pale skin, or fainting spells. You might be especially susceptible to anemia if (1) you have had several babies within a short period of time, (2) you are carrying multiples, (3) you have had severe morning sickness, or (4) your diet is very poor.

The treatment for anemia is simple. Your doctor will prescribe a new daily vitamin/mineral supplement with an increased amount of iron. You can also improve iron intake by using iron cookware and by eating more iron-rich foods such as whole grains, dried beans, dark green leafy vegetables, blackstrap molasses, tofu, spinach, beet greens, bulgur, prune juice, and dried fruits.

Body Changes

In the fifth month, the most noticeable body change is the fact that you've suddenly expanded! You now look slightly pregnant and will need to make some adjustments in your wardrobe. You might also notice changes in vaginal discharge, your complexion, your skin texture, and the appearance of your navel.

Vaginal Discharge

Just as you're rejoicing over the fact that you don't have to deal with monthly bleeding during pregnancy, you might begin having a vaginal discharge that is thin and milky-colored and has a slight odor. Although this discharge can be quite heavy and might continue throughout the pregnancy, it is no cause for alarm. It is thought that it might actually be your body's way of protecting against infection by cleansing out the vagina.

To protect your clothing, wear a panty liner or sanitary pad and change it frequently. Be sure to keep your vaginal area very clean, wear cotton underwear, and avoid tight pants and exercise suits. Don't douche, use a tampon, or wash with heavily perfumed products. Let your doctor know if the discharge becomes thick and yellowish, very watery, or bloody. These could be signs of trouble.

Acne

If you thought you left pimples behind in high school, you might not be so happy to hear that the hormonal changes of pregnancy can cause an increase in oil secretion. More oil can mean more pimples. This is especially likely if you had a tendency to break out before your monthly period.

To reduce flare-ups, follow the same kind of eating, drinking, and washing routine advised for all teens (whose increased hormone levels give them the same problem): Eat a nutritious diet, drink lots of water, and wash your face frequently.

Dry Skin

Many women find they have dry, itchy skin during pregnancy. This becomes especially apparent on your abdomen as the baby grows and the skin stretches across it. If the itching is bothering you, try these simple remedies.

- Don't scratch. This makes you itch more!
- Avoid soap. This removes natural oils and causes itchy skin. Use soapless cleansers.
- Keep your baths and showers short and don't use hot water. Hot water dries out skin. Stick to warm water.
- Smooth on a moisturizing cream immediately after your bath or shower; applying it right onto damp skin is best.
- Use a humidifier if the air in your home is particularly dry.

PREGNANCY FACTS

If you use a humidifier to keep the air in your home from getting dry, be sure to clean it with bleach daily. You'll have a whole new set of problems if the vapor contains bacteria.

The Bellybutton Pop

As your belly grows larger, you might wake up one morning and find that your bellybutton now sticks out (kids call this an "outie"). Don't panic. It's perfectly natural, and your bellybutton will revert to an "innie" after delivery. If it bothers you when your navel pokes at your blouse, hide it by simply putting a Band-Aid across it.

What's on Your Mind?

This month, you might find yourself thinking about fetal movements ("Is the baby moving around enough?"); heavy lifting ("Just how much is safe to lift?"); wardrobe dilemmas ("What do I have that fits?"); an overload of advice ("Whom should I listen to?"); and overwhelming fears and anxieties ("Is my baby developing normally?").

Kick Boxing

Let the games begin. Sometime in the fifth month, your baby will give you a hello kick. (It's been moving since the ninth week, but you haven't been able to feel it.) This is an absolutely thrilling moment, which you can easily miss if you aren't paying attention. Women describe these first movements as a feeling of butterfly wings flapping inside them; others feel a faint twitch or a punch. You might even think you are feeling hunger pains or gas.

After a while, you might be able to tune in to your baby's sleep/wake schedule. Often she'll wake and move around as soon as you lie down to rest. Although your baby's activity at this time might seem like an intentional plan to get you used to staying up all night, it probably means that you're simply more focused and aware of her movements than you are when you're active yourself. Also, babies like motion; it lulls them to sleep.

If you don't feel any kicking this month, tell your doctor—but don't panic. If the heartbeat is strong and all other vital signs are stable, there's no reason to worry. It might simply be that you're due later than you thought (making your baby a few weeks younger).

Heavy Lifting

It is not true that you can harm your fetus by lifting something heavy. You cannot dislodge it or tear the placenta from the wall of the uterus. But it's still not a good idea to heave two-ton grocery bags into your car. Your back won't like it. During pregnancy, the usually stable joints of the pelvis begin to loosen up to prepare for childbirth. This, combined with your growing abdomen, will throw your weight off balance and cause you to counterbalance by walking with a curved lower back. This puts strain on the lower-back muscles that will be aggravated by heavy lifting.

HEY MOM!

When you have to lift something heavy, do it correctly. Stand with your feet about a foot apart. Bend at the knees (not at the waist) and lift with your arms and legs rather than with your back.

Give your back a break. If you have a young child at home, now is a good time to get some use out of the stroller and let her practice walking more often. Put your groceries in several lightweight bags. Ask someone else to carry heavy suitcases or packages. Your back muscles will be strained even more in the pregnancy later on; try to ease their burden now.

Umbilical Cord Blood Banking

Umbilical cord blood banking is something you might want to talk to your doctor about before your baby is born. Cord blood is the blood in your baby's umbilical cord following birth that is usually discarded. However, some parents are now saving and storing cord blood because it has been found to be rich in stem cells.

Stem cells are the building blocks of the blood and immune systems. They can divide to become other types of cells. The stem cells found in umbilical cord blood and bone marrow can divide and become all three types of blood cells: red blood cells, white blood cells, and platelets. Stem cells are able to restore function to the blood-making system and immune system. This is especially valuable when the systems have been damaged by radiation or chemotherapy. In a stem cell transplant, patients with a marrow or blood disease (such as leukemia) first undergo chemotherapy and/or radiation therapy to wipe out their diseased blood or marrow cells. Then blood stem cells from a healthy donor are transplanted into the patient, where they grow and develop into healthy marrow and blood cells.

BABY TALK!

Umbilical cord blood banking is the process of saving and storing cord blood at the time of birth for its therapeutic stem cells.

Stem cells are currently used in the treatment of nearly 40 life-threatening diseases, including certain cancers (such as leukemia) and immune and genetic disorders. And researchers are now looking for ways to use cord blood to address medical problems such as stroke, heart disease, diabetes, and muscular dystrophy.

How Umbilical Cord Blood Banking Works

The blood collection process is easy and painless, and it does not interfere with the delivery or care of your newborn. (The collection process is essentially the same with a cesarean birth as it is for a natural birth.) After your baby is born, but before the placenta is delivered, your obstetrician or midwife cleans a four- to eight-inch area of umbilical cord with an antiseptic solution and then inserts the blood bag needle into the umbilical vein. When the blood has been collected, the blood bag is clamped, sealed, and labeled. The collection typically takes two to four minutes. Two tubes of maternal blood are also drawn at this time. The procedure is painless and noninvasive. There is no risk to you or your child.

The cells in your blood cord sample must then be processed and frozen within 48 hours by a laboratory specially equipped to handle umbilical cord blood banking.

Why Do It?

Some parents choose to save and store umbilical cord blood so they will have a supply available in case it is ever needed by their child or a family member. Cord blood stem cells are a perfect match for the donor baby; they have 25 percent probability of being an exact match for a sibling, and can be potentially used for parents and grandparents. Others choose to save cord blood because of the possibilities that science might provide in the future. The blood can be collected only at birth, so many don't want to miss the opportunity. And some collect the cord blood and donate it to a public blood bank.

Umbilical cord blood donation is a new idea that is picking up after a slow start. Currently, there are just 11 public cord blood banks in the National Marrow Donor Program (NMDP) registry that accept donated cord blood. The NMDP website (www.nmdp.org) lists 10 non-NMDP centers around the country that also accept cord blood donations (but often only for related transplant recipients). The American Red Cross currently has seven active cord blood collection sites around the country, and the National Institutes of Health has committed $30 million to establish three national public donation banks.

Women who donate their cord blood can, theoretically, retrieve their own donation should they need it before the units have already been used by another individual who needs a stem cell transplant. Because donation is free, it is liable to be a more accessible option for many families. (But be aware that if your doctor charges a fee for drawing the blood, that will not be covered by the blood bank.) However, because cord blood donation is a newer stem cell option, donating is not available in all communities. If there is not a participating hospital in your community, you might want to try contacting a major university hospital or medical center in your local area to explore other options. Be sure first to check the NMDP's website (www.nmdp.org) for registered blood banks and more information about cord blood donations or call the NMDP at 1-800-MARROW2.

Words of Caution About Cord Blood Banking

As the concept of umbilical cord blood banking becomes more popular and common, the methods of obtaining the blood will become more standardized and routine. But right now, here are some factors you should carefully consider.

The hospital where you deliver is unlikely to offer umbilical cord blood banking. You must make all arrangements yourself and supply your doctor with the collection kit. If you talk to your doctor well in advance of your baby's delivery about your interest in cord blood banking, he or she might be able to refer you to a reputable cord blood bank in your area who will give you all the information and collection equipment you need.

Not all umbilical cord blood banks are equal. The federal government is in the process of developing industry standards for the collection, processing, and storage of cord blood, but at this time, uniform regulations do not exist. You should, at the very least, make sure that the laboratory you choose is accredited by the American Association of Blood Banks.

There is no way of knowing at this time how long stored cord blood will last. One study out of Amsterdam produced viable cord blood stem cells from blood frozen for 15 years. But estimates of the "shelf life" of cord blood are still tentative.

In most cases, medical insurance companies do not pay for umbilical cord blood banking. This is an out-of-pocket expense that can be very costly. You will also pay an annual storage fee to the blood bank for storing the blood. If you choose to move the cord blood to a different blood bank, you'll have to pay preparation and shipment charges.

If you give birth to multiples and want to draw umbilical cord blood, each child needs his or her own collection—the only direct match is from the direct donor. This, of course, raises the cost. However, some cord blood banks offer discounts for multiples and for additional children the parents might have at a later time.

Find out who has access to the cord blood's hidden information—the diseases and genetic traits shared by both infant and parents. Ask questions about the bank's policy regarding screening cord blood and ask whether all identifiers are stripped from the blood samples in order to protect the donor's privacy. Many physicians will advise their patients against donating cord blood to a blood bank that retains patient identifiers.

An Overload of Advice

After you put on maternity clothes, pregnancy experts will start coming out of the woodwork. Everywhere you go, people will have advice about what you should and shouldn't do.

Perhaps much of the advice will come from your mother or mother-in-law. This is a playing field where you need to know the rules if you ever hope to come out the winner. These women's genes are floating around in your womb, so they might feel divinely entitled to tell you how to nourish and protect their progeny. (*Warning:* This belief grows even stronger after the birth of the baby.) On the one hand, they have a point. Their lineage is invested in the outcome of your pregnancy and they speak from experience. They've been through this themselves and have done a pretty good job, judging by you and your partner. They have experiences to share and helpful tidbits to pass on that might actually make this pregnancy easier for you. So take advantage whenever you can.

DADDY ALERT!

You might have to choose sides if your mother and your partner get into ongoing debates over the best way to get through a pregnancy. Although your mom means well, somebody (like you) might have to run interference if her advice is persistently upsetting your partner.

If your mom insists that you rest on the weekend and let her come over and do your laundry—don't fight it. Sure, you're not sick and there's no reason you can't do your own laundry, but if it makes your mom feel involved and needed when she helps you, why not? When she gives advice, don't get yourself stressed out by arguing or contradicting. Just say, "Thanks." Many things have changed since she gave birth, and her intentions are good. You can let it go in one ear and out the other with no stops along the way if you like, but a simple smile and a nod of appreciation will save your family many unnecessary battles. And don't forget that there is always the possibility that in this case, your mother and your mother-in-law really do know more than you.

More advice might come from your friends. Co-workers, neighbors, lifelong friends, and even vague acquaintances will all have words of wisdom to share. Some might hover over you as if you've just turned into a delicate piece of glassware that will break at the slightest jostle or bump. Others will scold you about not exercising enough and will nag you to join classes, programs, gyms, and spas. Some will push all sorts of exotic diets, herbs, and supplements your way. And a surprising number will insist on recounting all the horrors of their own experiences with childbirth (in gory detail).

This is a good time to learn how to sort out the gems from the fakes. If you have women friends whom you've known a long time, whom you trust, and who have gone through their own pregnancies, look to them for support. Ask their opinions and share your experiences. A woman you feel close to and who has been through the same experience in recent years makes a great sounding board. But to handle all your other "friends," you'll need to develop a deaf ear. If you find yourself listening to tales that scare or upset you, don't hesitate to interrupt. Simply say, "Please don't tell me that story. I'd really rather not hear it." If you have concerns and questions, find out the facts from reputable sources. Do your own research by reading books and magazines, and save important questions to ask your doctor.

Another batch of advice will come from complete strangers. Being noticeably pregnant makes you fair game for every person on the face of the earth who has something to say. You'll be asked questions in the supermarket and on street corners that will make you wonder about the sanity of the human race: "Did you plan to have this baby or was it a surprise?" "How much weight have you gained?" "Will you have natural childbirth?" These questions will be followed by far-fetched stories of pregnancy and childbirth—along with unwanted advice. When this happens, try not to take offense. Even when strangers suddenly reach out and rub your tummy, try to keep cool. If the questions and advice of strangers bother you, the easiest way to escape is to look at your watch, exclaim that you're late, and hurry away. If someone corners you (say on a bus or in the checkout line), quickly turn the attention away from yourself and ask the stranger questions such as, "Do you have children? How many do you have? What are their ages?" and so on, until you can make a getaway.

You are now a walking magnet that attracts know-it-all people. Out of nowhere, they'll swarm to tell you what you should and shouldn't be doing. Don't let this onslaught of advice overwhelm you. Choose a few trusted people to be your confidants and turn a deaf ear to the rest.

Worry and Anxiety

Making a baby really is a miraculous, complex, intricate process—it's no wonder you worry that something might go wrong along the way. All this talk about birth defects, prenatal testing, and miscarriage is enough to drive any expectant mother to fits of anxiety. These fears are natural—but not necessary in most cases.

If you're losing sleep because you're worrying so much about the health of your baby, you've got to get a grip. Extreme stress can be harmful to both you and your baby.

Try this mental trick every time your mind starts to go down a scary path: Stop and redirect. Make yourself stop the worrisome thoughts immediately—just don't let your mind dwell on anxious thoughts for another second. Then redirect your mind to something happy and pleasant. The thought could be of a day at the beach or a time in the future when you are holding your perfectly healthy newborn in your arms. Use any image that brings you mental peace. Remember: Stop and redirect.

DADDY ALERT!

Be careful what you say—your baby is listening! Don't be shy about talking to him or her. Read bedtime stories, sing, and talk about the weather if you like. If your baby becomes accustomed to your voice now, you'll be pleasantly surprised, a few months from now, to find that your newborn recognizes your voice and is attracted to it.

If you find you can't let go of fear, talk to your doctor about it. Maybe you have reason to worry (a history of drug or alcohol abuse, a poor diet). He or she will be able to give you the facts and offer a plan for keeping you and your baby healthy through the pregnancy. If you can't shake your fears, maybe the doctor will schedule a sonogram (see Chapter 3) so you can both see how the baby is developing.

All expectant moms worry about their baby's health at some time in the pregnancy, but if your fears are overwhelming and are keeping you from eating, sleeping, or relaxing, you might need professional help to deal with these worries. Ask your doctor for advice and a referral to a mental health professional if he or she thinks it's appropriate.

Week by Week

In the fifth month, your baby's skeleton is mostly rubbery cartilage that will harden later. The baby might spend some time sucking his or her thumb.

Week Number 19

- Parts of the legs have now grown in proportion to the rest of the body.
- You can feel the fetus kick, move its arms, and wiggle its fingers and toes.

Week Number 20

- A skin covering called vernix caseosa forms to protect the baby's skin from the amniotic fluid.
- Delicate eyebrows are forming.

Week Number 21

- Body parts, tissues, and organs continue to mature.

Week Number 22

- The eyelids are very well developed.
- Fingernails are completely developed.

The fifth month is a very busy one. Your body is changing in ways that can no longer be hidden and you're carrying around a baby who's ready to rock and roll. Fears and anxieties might keep you awake at night. But there's good news, too: You're more than halfway there!

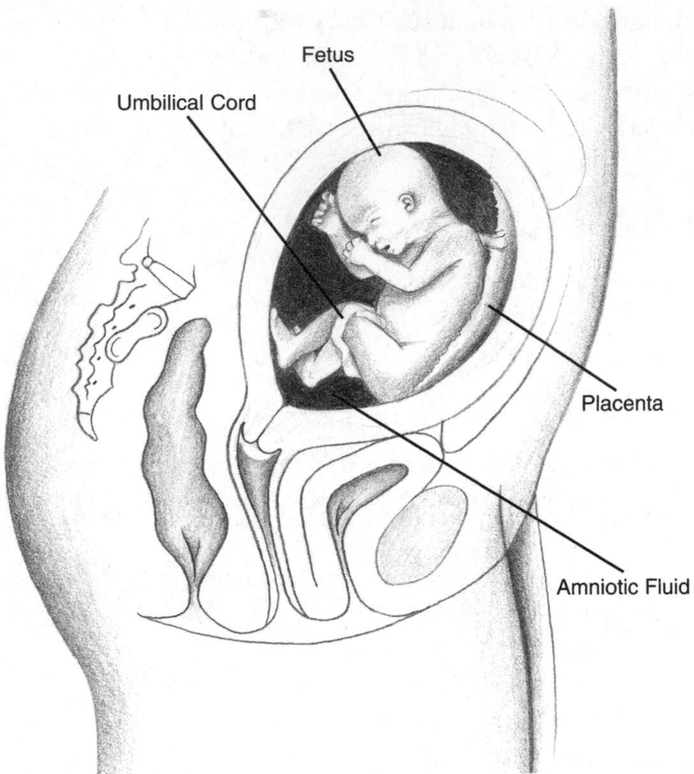

A human fetus at 22 weeks. At this time, your baby will measure about $6^1/_2$ inches long and weigh 9 ounces.

The Least You Need to Know

- Your doctor might test your blood for anemia if you show symptoms of this blood disease. Anemia can be caused by your body's increased demands for iron.
- This month you will see changes in your body that might include vaginal discharge, acne, dry skin, and a distended navel.
- This is the month you'll feel your baby roll, kick, and punch!
- In the fifth month, your concerns might focus on the monthly checkup, umbilical cord blood banking, body changes, and understandable fears and anxieties.

Month Number Six: Weeks 23 to 26

Chapter 10

In This Chapter

- The medical checkup: evaluation of weight, blood pressure, uterine growth, fetal heartbeat, and scheduling of a glucose-screening test
- Body changes: increased fetal movement, rising body temperature, and dizziness
- Concerns of the sixth month
- Week-by-week development

This is the last month of your second trimester. Although your baby's lungs are still filled with amniotic fluid, he or she has started to practice breathing movements—a sure sign that the end is almost here. This month is special because the "pregnancy belly" you now have is like a walking billboard that yells out to everyone you meet: I'm going to have a baby!

What to Expect at the Medical Checkup

Your medical checkup in the sixth month will include routine tests as well as a discussion about the glucose-screening test.

- **Weight.** You've probably added a hefty 17 to 19 pounds to your weight by now! Your whole body is ballooning—your face, upper arms, thighs, and buttocks are all daily reminders that you are pregnant. Still, most of this weight is not the baby (he or she weighs only about 1½ pounds). Continue to nourish your baby with healthy foods and stay away from empty calories in sugary, processed foods that add hard-to-shed pounds.

- **Blood pressure.** As always, your blood pressure will be taken at your monthly checkup. Your doctor is always on the lookout for any sudden changes that can indicate a problem.
- **Urine tests.** Ready, aim, fire. Once again you'll hand over your little cup of urine, which will be tested for: (1) infection; (2) protein, which can be a sign of high blood pressure; and (3) sugar, which can be a sign of diabetes.
- **Size check.** By the sixth month, your uterus should be two fingers above the navel.
- **Doppler.** This is the best part of every visit: listening to the sound of the baby's heartbeat. With the little, but mighty, hand-held Doppler, you can hear the presence of life inside of you.
- **Questions.** Before the visit is over, take out your little notepad, where you've been recording your questions, and fire away. Talk to your doctor about what's on your mind. Ask the questions you've been wondering about since your last visit. And then pay close attention as the doctor explains the screening test he or she will schedule for you this month.

Most expectant moms are given a glucose-screening test between the 24th and 28th weeks of pregnancy to check for gestational diabetes. (See Chapter 4 for information about the effects of diabetes on a fetus and Chapter 3 for more details about this test.) Although all pregnant women are given this test, you are at risk for developing gestational diabetes if you fit into any of the following categories:

- You have had gestational diabetes during an earlier pregnancy.
- You have previously delivered a very large baby.
- You are greatly overweight.
- You are over 35.
- You have high blood pressure.
- You have a parent or sibling who is a diabetic.
- You have previously given birth to a stillborn or malformed baby.

The test for gestational diabetes is a two-parter. The first part is a screening test in which you drink a sugar solution; then, an hour later, a blood sample is taken to test your blood-sugar level. If the level is abnormal (which happens about 20 percent of the time), you'll be scheduled for another test (called a three-hour glucose tolerance) to verify the results.

HEY MOM!

Keep in mind that the first glucose test is a screening test only. If you get a high sugar reading on this test, don't get too worried. Approximately 85 percent of those with a positive result on this screening test show normal blood-sugar levels in the glucose tolerance test.

Body Changes

This is the month everyone knows you're pregnant because you can't hide your pregnancy any longer. You will also get a reminder of your condition every time your baby kicks and rolls in your womb. Don't worry if you start to feel warm and sweaty occasionally or feel some dizziness—both are perfectly normal.

HEY MOM!

It's natural for you to be caught up in all the physical and emotional changes that occur during pregnancy, but take some time to consider what this might mean to your partner. Ask him if he has any worries or concerns he'd like to talk about today. Sometimes all it takes is an invitation to encourage a man to open up.

Body Bouncing

Those gentle flutterings of life you were so thrilled to feel last month will probably turn into kicking, punching, and body blows this month. Although you might notice only a bit of body slamming during the day, the real action begins when you lay your tired body down at night. Your little gymnast will begin to turn and twist and kick, with no regard for the fact that you're trying to sleep. This seeming lack of consideration for your need to sleep is something you should probably get used to—it will continue long after your baby is born.

Body Heat

If you find yourself sweating more than usual, you can add one more item to your list of things caused by pregnancy hormones. During pregnancy, your basal metabolic rate (the rate at which your body expends energy at total rest) rises about 20 percent. This is going to make you feel very warm. Even women who always bundle up against the cold and sleep with two blankets in the winter now find themselves throwing back the covers and wearing T-shirts when it's cold.

Keep this fact in mind when you shop for maternity clothes. It's best to dress in layers that can be shed when your body begins to overheat. Buy clothes that are not too tight around the neck or arms and that give you room to breathe (and sweat). Also, stick to fabrics that breathe and absorb sweat (such as cotton) and stay away from those that hold in the heat (such as polyester and wool).

If you find yourself sweating up a storm, take some time to make yourself feel fresh and comfortable. Take daily showers or baths, use a good antiperspirant, and sprinkle on a little talcum powder after you wash. Be sure to drink lots of water to replace what you're sweating out.

The Spinning Room

For a variety of reasons, your blood pressure will fluctuate during pregnancy, which can cause dizziness (especially if you stand up too quickly). If this happens to you, don't get upset. Fainting because of pregnancy is quite rare. (See Chapter 7 for more details on that dizzy feeling.)

What's on Your Mind?

During the sixth month, lots of things are bound to be on your mind. You might be concerned about premature birth, disturbing dreams, sex, or forgetfulness, but, at the same time, you might be preoccupied with the ongoing search to find clothes that fit comfortably and keep you cool.

Premature Birth

Twenty years ago, a baby born in the sixth month of pregnancy was called a miscarriage. There was no hope of survival. But thanks to new procedures, medical equipment, medications, and reams of research, today's *micropreemies* (babies born before the 26th week of pregnancy) often have a 50 percent chance of survival (especially those born closer to the 26th week). Although this is good news, premature labor and/or delivery in the sixth month is still very dangerous.

Some women know in advance that they are at risk for a premature birth (see Chapter 21 for details). Their high-risk pregnancies are closely watched for any signs of premature labor, and they know what to look for and what to do. But 60 percent of the women who deliver prematurely have no risk factors that could have forewarned them—it's a complete surprise. That's why you should know the signs of premature labor and contact your doctor immediately if you think your baby has plans for an early entrance. Drugs called tocolytic agents can be given to relax the muscles of the uterus and often delay childbirth.

Symptoms of Preterm Labor

- Menstrual-like cramps that might be constant or occur intermittently.
- A feeling of heaviness or pressure on the rectum.
- Lower-back pain.
- Cramps (which might be accompanied by diarrhea).
- Change in vaginal discharge. It might be heavier, watery, or blood-tinged.
- Contractions.

Dreams

If you're suddenly having tons of dreams that you remember vividly, you're in good company. Many expectant moms find that their dream life explodes during pregnancy. There are two common reasons for this:

- Your daytime thoughts are so intently focused on the pregnancy that they push all other concerns and subjects into your subconscious.
- The discomforts of pregnancy disrupt your sleep, causing you to wake more often throughout the night. When you wake during the night, you can catch your dream just as the dream cycle is ending—that's when you're most likely to remember what you dreamed.

The dreams of pregnant women are as indecipherable as any other sort of dreams. You can take dreams as omens or dismiss them as mere fantasies of the mind. In almost all cases, they are normal, healthy occurrences that help you sort out worries and fears.

If you find that your dreams during pregnancy are more vivid and frequent than usual, don't worry. It's perfectly normal and nothing to worry about. Even nightmares have something to tell you about your feelings and emotions during this very unique time. Listen carefully, but don't add to the daily load of stress by worrying that your dreams are sending messages you can't understand.

Forgetfulness

Are you finding yourself standing around lately wondering what you're supposed to be doing? Do you forget important appointments? Does your mind feel too full to take in any more data? Yep—you're pregnant. This mental fog is a natural result of the body's intense focus on baby making. Powerful hormonal changes are going on that affect your ability to concentrate and remember. Don't fight it—you'll only get more flustered. Work with it.

If you can't count on your memory anymore, try these memory aids:

- **Become a list maker.** Write down exactly what you're supposed to do each day. Write down what you want to buy at the store. Write down everything, and you won't forget anything.
- **Ask for help.** Tell your partner and your co-workers to remind you of important dates and appointments. Two minds are always better than one—during pregnancy, they can be a necessity.
- **Lighten your load.** Pregnant or not, doing too much at one time can muddle the thinking process. Being pregnant makes an overload all the more difficult to manage. Make an effort to drop projects that aren't absolutely necessary. Learn to delegate to others. Practice saying "no."
- **Get more sleep.** If you're burning the midnight oil, you have no hope of being clearheaded the next day. Your mind needs the restorative power of sleep to be sharp, clear, and efficient.

These things will help reduce that scatterbrained feeling—but they won't get rid of it. You can expect to be just a little less efficient for the remainder of your pregnancy. Then the sleeplessness caused by caring for a newborn will give you a brand-new set of excuses for having a brain that feels like it's turned into mashed bananas.

PREGNANCY FACTS

Although pregnancy can temporarily muddle your thinking powers, it might also cause permanent changes in your brain that will improve your thinking powers in the future. New studies suggest that the hormones released during pregnancy and nursing dramatically enrich the parts of the brain involved in learning and memory. Scientists have found that these are significant permanent changes that make learning a much more efficient process. (This explains why mothers always seem to know everything!)

Wardrobe

Well, it's official: You've got a pregnancy belly and the whole world knows it. You can't hide behind your baggy sweaters any longer—you need maternity clothes. To begin building your new wardrobe, you'll probably find yourself in a maternity shop. Here the sales ladies are attentive and sympathetic. They know what you're going through, they don't mind lending an understanding ear, and they'll let you gab on and on about your pregnancy as long as they can keep showing you outfits (most, remember, are on commission). This setup is good for both of you: They can sell you something you need, and you get the attention you crave. But be careful. It's easy to get caught up in the new wardrobe idea and forget that the clothes are going to be in your closet for only three to four months. Your best bet is to buy a few very basic pieces of clothing that you can mix and match and layer—especially if the remainder of your pregnancy will bring you into a different season of the year.

Maternity shops are the best place to buy things such as maternity bathing suits, stockings, underwear, and bras. Outerwear is available less expensively from other stores, including ...

- **Department stores.** The selection is not so great here, but you can get many of the basics you need and save a lot of money. If you have the time to weed through the cutesy styles with bows and ribbons, you'll often come up with things just right for you.

- **Friends.** This is a time when relatives and friends who have young children are a valuable resource. Don't be shy; ask if you can borrow any maternity outfits they're not using right now. If five friends each loan you one outfit, you've just saved a couple hundred dollars and have an instant core of clothes to work with.
- **Consignment shops.** Here you'll find gently used maternity clothes for a bargain. Remember that you're not building a wardrobe to last a lifetime—you're just looking for things you can cover yourself with until the baby arrives.
- **Online shopping sites.** Like everything else, maternity clothes are sold online for those of you who like to cyber-shop. Even eBay has a maternity site for gently worn clothing. Check it out at www.maternitycloset.com.

Shopping for maternity clothes is fun, but it's easy to waste your money on an impulsive buy (that will never fit just right). See Chapter 20 for more tips about choosing just the right clothes.

HEY MOM!

There's a marketing concept sweeping the country: maternity clothes for rent! Why not? We rent wedding gowns, tuxedos, and party dresses for special occasions; why not rent for this special occasion? In shops like Maternity Rental Successwear in Nashville, Tennessee, you can rent a maternity business suit for $20 a month—which is far better than buying it for $400. A Google search for "maternity clothes rentals" brings up over 300,000 hits. There's lots of places where you can rent a temporary wardrobe!

Sex with Three in Bed

Now that your baby has made his or her presence known in both size and movement, you might begin to feel a little awkward about lovemaking. Don't worry about hurting the baby. Unless you're in a high-risk pregnancy, intercourse doesn't bother the baby, who is resting securely in the womb. Pushing on your pregnancy belly during lovemaking won't hurt the baby, either—but it might be uncomfortable for you. This is a good month to start experimenting with new intercourse positions. Many couples find it more comfortable for the woman to assume the position above (on top of) the man. Side or rear entry positions can also ease the pressure on your big belly and add some novelty to your sex life. For more information about sex during pregnancy, take a look at Chapter 20.

Week by Week

In the sixth month, your baby's brain is growing rapidly and hearing is well developed. (In fact, studies have found that unborn babies can communicate a preference for classical music over rock.)

Week Number 23

- Eyebrows and eyelashes are forming.
- Lips are becoming more distinct.
- Eyes are becoming more developed, but they still lack color.
- The first signs of teeth appear beneath the gum line.

Week Number 24

- Blood vessels in the lungs are developing.
- The head is still large compared to the body.
- The baby can swallow.

Week Number 25

- The body is beginning to become plump.
- The skin becomes wrinkled.
- If the baby were born now, he or she would attempt to breathe.
- Taste buds are forming.

Week Number 26

- The face and the body generally assume the appearance of an infant at birth.
- The baby begins to make breathing movements, although there is no air in the lungs.
- The baby will respond to touch.

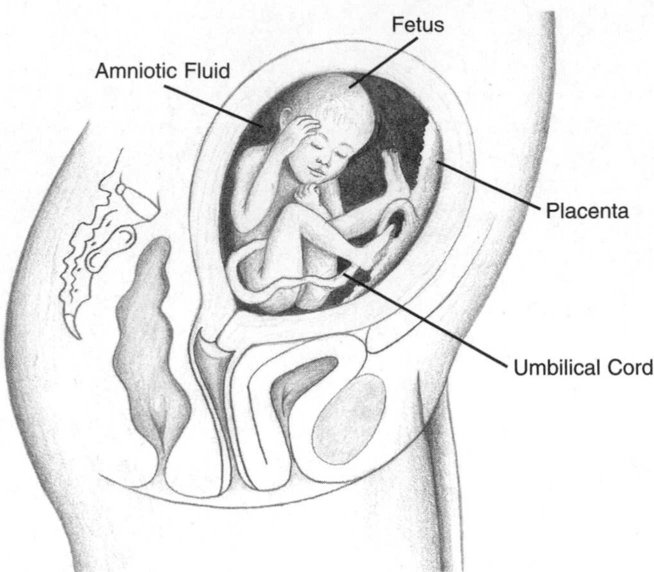

A human fetus at 26 weeks. At this time, your baby will weigh about $1\frac{1}{2}$ pounds and be 9 inches long.

As your second trimester ends, take some time to sit back and enjoy it. Very soon your pregnancy will be over and all the days you dedicated to creating a new human being will be only a vague memory. Cherish them now.

The Least You Need to Know

- In addition to performing the routine tests of your monthly checkup, your doctor will discuss the glucose-screening test that's usually given between the 24th and 28th weeks of pregnancy.
- Those gentle fetal movements you strained to feel last month now become all-out body slams that you can't mistake for anything but your baby's kicking, turning, and punching.
- Babies born in the sixth month have a chance of survival (especially those born closer to the 26th week).
- The dreams of a pregnant woman can be wild and exciting, but they're rarely omens of what's to come.
- It's time to break out the maternity clothes. Your pregnancy is obvious to the world now!
- As your belly grows, you might need to experiment and use a bit of creativity to find a comfortable position during sex.

Month Number Seven: Weeks 27 to 30

Chapter 11

In This Chapter

- The medical checkup: the routine exam and a look at Rh factor compatibility
- Stretch marks, edema, indigestion, and heartburn
- Warm up for the real thing: Braxton Hicks contractions and fetal position
- Childbirth classes, fetal health, personal safety, and choosing a name for baby
- Week-by-week development

Welcome to the last trimester of your pregnancy! In these last three months, you'll see your fetus grow to full size and prepare for birth. This is a time for both daydreaming and anxiety. One minute you'll probably say you can't wait for the baby to come; the next you'll be dreading the moment. Either way, this seventh month puts you on the fast track to mommyhood.

What to Expect at the Medical Checkup

Your schedule for medical checkups has just jumped into high gear. After the 28th week, you will probably see your health-care provider once every two weeks. At each visit, you'll go through the same routine tests and procedures. You should be a pro by now!

- **Weight.** By the end of the seventh month, you should be weighing in somewhere around 17 to 20 pounds over your prepregnancy weight. If you've been watching your weight and diet for the last few months, don't fall apart now that you're so close to the end. If you ever say to yourself, "What difference does it make now? How much could I gain when I only have three months to go?" stop and remind yourself how little of your pregnancy weight is actually your baby. (He or she will probably weigh a hefty three pounds by the end of the month.) Much of your pregnancy weight in the third trimester comes from the amniotic fluid, the placenta, the uterine muscles, your increased blood and body fluid levels, your breasts, and the fat around the internal organs. These gains are natural and necessary, but you should be careful about adding extra pounds of excess fat. See Chapters 14 and 15 for help putting together a healthful diet.

- **Blood pressure.** Your blood pressure is again recorded. The doctor is still watching for any sudden changes that can indicate a problem.
- **Urine tests.** This should be old hat to you by now, but your doctor is still on the lookout for: (1) infection; (2) protein, which can be a sign of high blood pressure; and (3) sugar, which can be a sign of diabetes.
- **Size check.** By pushing down on your abdomen and feeling the upper edge, your doctor will check the size of your uterus. At seven months, your uterus should come up to your rib cage.
- **Doppler.** Is it ever possible to get tired of this sound? The Doppler will let you hear the baby's heartbeat again—louder than ever.
- **Questions.** After the relative calm of the second trimester, you might be distressed to find that your level of discomfort shoots back up again in the third trimester. You might feel tired all the time, digestive problems might reappear, and sleep is disturbed. Keep your questions coming. Let your doctor know if any of these discomforts are upsetting you.

This is the month when your doctor will check the Rh factor results of your early blood tests. If your blood is Rh-negative and your partner's is Rh-positive, you will be tested in the 28th week for Rh antibodies. If you have not developed these antibodies (which is likely in your first pregnancy), you will be given a vaccine dose of Rh-immune globulin. Another dose will be given within 72 hours of your baby's delivery. If you have developed antibodies at this point in your pregnancy, an amniocentesis might be scheduled to check the health of the fetus. See Chapter 25 for more information about Rh incompatibility.

Body Changes

The calm of the second trimester is over. Body changes in the third trimester can cause you renewed discomfort. Be on the lookout for stretch marks, practice contractions, swelling, the "black line," and indigestion and heartburn.

PREGNANCY FACTS

A dermatologist can treat any stretch marks that remain after a birth. Some doctors use topical prescription treatments that contain formulations such as glycolic acid. A recent study found that retonoic acid reduced the length of stretch marks by 14 percent and the width by 8 percent. Laser treatments are also now being used to minimize the appearance of stretch marks.

Stretch Marks

How do you think you'll look with stretch marks? Well, you might want to convince yourself that you'll look great, because about 50 percent of pregnant women get stretch marks. As the name implies, these pale to dark red or purple streaks occur when the skin stretches to accommodate the growth of your belly. They can occur just about anywhere, but breasts, hips, abdomen, and thighs are the most common spots. If you're dark-skinned and/or have a mother or sister who had stretch marks, it's very likely you will join the club.

Don't get too upset about these badges of motherhood; there's nothing much you can do about them and you probably won't be wearing a bikini anytime soon anyway. Some women rub on special creams made to minimize these marks. The rubbing might make them feel better, but no cream currently on the market has been medically proven to effectively reduce stretch marks. Most stretch marks on light-skinned women fade on their own to a silvery white color.

Rib Kicks

The acrobatics of your young athlete continue. During particularly strong kicks, you might actually be able to grab hold of a little foot as it pushes against your insides. Sometime this month, you might begin to feel a frequent twitch in your rib cage just below one of your breasts. This is a good sign that the baby is in birthing position, with the baby's head down and the feet poking into your upper ribs.

Practice Contractions

Isn't the body amazing? Well before your due date, the muscles in your uterus begin practicing for the delivery! These muscles have a lot to do on the big day. When it's time to deliver your baby, they will contract and relax, contract and relax, to push the baby down the birth canal. This takes a lot of muscle power. And just like any major physical event that requires muscle power, the uterus needs to be prepared in advance. Your body automatically exercises the muscles of the uterus during the last trimester with *Braxton Hicks contractions.* These practice contractions feel like a sudden hardening or tightening and then a gradual relaxing of the uterus. Some women say the contractions feel as if an elastic band around the belly is being drawn tight and then relaxed. Braxton Hicks contractions aren't painful, they're just a little uncomfortable. As you get closer to your due date, these contractions might become more frequent and intense. They are usually felt earlier and more intensely by women who have had a previous pregnancy.

Swelling

Just when you thought you couldn't get any bigger, you might notice that your feet, hands, face, and ankles have become quite swollen. This is caused by water retention (a condition called edema, which is explained in detail in Chapter 2). You might notice this especially late in the day and during warm weather. Ironically, the best way to keep water from building up is to drink lots of water. This helps flush out the system. If any swelling appears overnight, call your doctor; it can be a sign of high blood pressure.

The Black Line

Around the seventh month, you might notice a dark vertical line going down the middle of your stomach. This is particularly obvious if you're dark-haired. The technical name for this line is *linea nigra,* and it will disappear after the baby's birth.

Indigestion and Heartburn

If you've suffered indigestion and heartburn in your prepregnancy days, you know that eating spicy foods and too much food at one time leaves you feeling miserable. Well, nothing's changed. You still need to watch what you eat to avoid these digestive problems. But now you have other reasons for indigestion and heartburn that you can blame on your growing baby. In the last three months of your pregnancy, your baby might push into your stomach, making it difficult to eat and digest properly. Indigestion and heartburn become part of life.

To ease the bother of indigestion and heartburn, try these strategies:

- Eat five small meals rather than three large meals each day.
- Stay away from spicy foods, fried foods, and carbonated sodas.
- Keep your clothing loose (underwear and stockings, too).

- If heartburn bothers you at night while you're sleeping, prop up your upper body to keep the stomach acids from going back up the esophagus.
- Talk to your doctor before using an antacid or any medication for indigestion. Some are perfectly safe during pregnancy; others are not.

Because so many pregnant women suffer from indigestion and heartburn, many myths have sprung up over the years. For example, one of these myths asserts that a pregnant woman who has heartburn will have a baby with a full head of hair. Don't listen to these stories; the only thing we know for sure about heartburn and indigestion during pregnancy is that they are annoying.

What's on Your Mind?

As you enter the last trimester, you'll have so much on your mind, it'll be hard to sort it all out and keep track of what you want to do and the decisions you need to make. This is a great time to start a diary, if you haven't done so already.

Childbirth Classes

The months of fantasy and mystery are over. When you begin childbirth classes, you'll know that this is really going to happen—pregnancy does lead to childbirth and you're about to find out exactly how that happens. Although there are many different kinds of classes (some are explained in Chapter 23), all of them have the same basic goal: to prepare you for a safe and satisfying birth. Of course, every birth is unique, but these classes let first-time parents in on the "secrets" of delivery that are common to all births.

- You'll learn what labor is like, how to recognize it, and what to do.
- You'll get the chance to talk to other expectant parents and share your concerns and questions.
- You'll be taught techniques for coping with the anxiety and pain of labor and birth.
- You'll get an introduction to your partner's role in the birth process.
- You'll learn (usually through lectures and movies) exactly how that baby gets out of your body.
- You'll learn the practical aspects of delivery, including hospital procedures, anesthesia options, the reasons for cesarean births, and the after-birth care of your newborn.

Don't skip this opportunity. Childbirth classes often run for about eight weekly sessions and are offered to both the expectant mom and dad. The reassurance and confidence you'll gain from these classes make every minute you spend in them worthwhile.

Fetal Health

In the seventh month, when your baby seems so alive and active, you might worry if there's a sudden stillness in your womb. If you're concerned that the baby is moving less than he or she should, try this simple test:

1. Drink some orange juice or have a small snack.
2. Count the number of movements you feel in the next two-hour period.

If you count at least 10 movements in this period, your baby is doing just fine. Maybe he or she has just cut back some aerobic activities in favor of rest for a while. But if you don't feel at least 10 movements, contact your doctor.

If your doctor has any concerns about your baby's level of activity, he or she might perform a *nonstress test.* This test is given at any time during the last trimester when the health-care provider wants to evaluate the fetal heart rate (which usually ranges between 120 and 160 beats per minute). It might even be performed every day in the last month of particularly complicated and risky pregnancies.

To record fetal heart rate, an ultrasonic detector (called a Doppler transducer) is strapped to your abdomen over the area where the fetal heartbeat is most easily heard. The heartbeat is recorded on a strip of graph paper, which runs through a monitoring machine. A second detector (called a tocodynamometer) is strapped to the upper abdomen at a point over the top of the uterus. This detector records the frequency and strength of the uterine contractions. Also, the mother records her contractions on a monitor by clicking a device whenever she feels the baby move. It is expected that the fetal heart rate will increase in response to fetal movement. That's why this test generally lasts 20 to 40 minutes—waiting for a number of fetal movements. If the fetus happens to be sleeping, this test can take even longer.

Safety

In the last trimester, you're just not as secure on your feet as you used to be. Your center of gravity has shifted forward, your joints are less stable, and you can barely see your feet. All of these things make it more likely that you're going to fall down if you're not careful.

Although the heroines of many soap operas still lose their babies when they fall tragically (or get pushed) down the stairs, a fall during pregnancy is not as dangerous to the baby as was once believed. Your baby is cradled in an incredibly shock-resistant womb. He or she is protected by amniotic fluid; tough membranes; the flexible, muscular uterus; and the abdominal cavity, which is made up of muscles, bone, and fat. It would take quite an accident to penetrate that fortress.

If an accident were severe enough to cause a problem, however, the damage would most likely be to the placenta. (Remember, this is the organ that attaches to the uterine wall and supplies the fetus with nutrients and carries away wastes.) Trauma to the abdomen can cause the placenta to pull away from the uterine wall. This occurrence needs immediate attention. If you notice vaginal bleeding, leaking amniotic fluid, abdominal pain, or uterine contractions after an accident, call your doctor immediately. He or she will probably want to meet you in the emergency room.

As you begin to feel yourself getting wobbly on your feet, pay attention to things in your environment that could be hazardous, including the following:

- **Avoid slipping while bathing.** Make sure the tub has a nonslip surface or a slip-resistant mat.
- **Don't climb on anything to reach high shelves.** Call your partner or a friend.
- **Watch your feet.** It's time to give up high-heeled shoes completely.
- **Trip-proof your house.** Look around for potential hazards.
- **Work with the weather.** Don't risk a fall on wet, icy, or snowy days!

You can also avoid trouble by getting more sleep. In the third trimester, you're bound to feel more fatigued and clumsier than usual and this can put you at risk for accidents.

Premature Birth

If your baby is born during the seventh month of pregnancy, he or she will have a very good chance of survival. The head of a baby born at seven months gestation is disproportionately large in comparison to the body. The skin is wrinkled and has a red-purplish tinge. It also has a clear transparency that makes the surface arteries and veins visible. Without the layers of fat that full-term babies are born with, these preemies appear skinny and bony. The eyeballs bulge out against eyelids that often don't have eyelashes. The baby's ears lie close against the head and have little or no cartilage. The baby has just the beginning buds of soft finger- and toenails and has no creases on the soles of the feet. A child born in the seventh month has almost no muscle tone. The baby does not lie in the expected fetal position, but rather with the arms and legs flat out at the sides. If you were to lift an arm or leg off the bed and then let it go, it would flop back down to the mattress.

GREEN FROM THE START

The delivery of a baby uses lots of natural resources and therefore carbon emissions caused by the energy used to run the delivery room and its equipment. You can offset the carbon footprint of your delivery day by contributing to projects that promote clean, renewable energy. Go to www.carbonfund.org and you'll find a menu of certified carbon offset projects that play an important role in the fight against climate change and include renewable energy and methane projects, energy efficiency and carbon credits, reforestation projects, and projects to prevent deforestation.

Week by Week

In the seventh month, almost all the parts are in place. Your baby is very busy making faces, hiccupping, crying, kicking, and elbowing you.

Week Number 27

- The network of nerves to the ear is completed.
- The fetus takes some breaths. Although your baby is breathing in water, not air (in utero, babies breathe in amniotic fluid through the nose and it passes through the lungs and exits back into the amniotic sac), it is good practice for his or her lungs.
- Because the retinas of the eyes are not finished forming yet, an eye problem called retinopathy of prematurity can occur in babies born at this time.

Week Number 28

- Brain tissue continues to develop.
- The baby begins to dream.
- The eyes open and close.

- The baby sleeps and wakes at regular intervals.
- Although the lungs are still immature, they are capable of sustaining life in the event of a premature birth (often with the help of a respirator).

Week Number 29

- Your baby can turn his or her head to find the source of a bright light.
- The fat layers continue to form.
- Fingernails are budding.

Week Number 30

- In male babies, the testicles move from near the kidneys through the groin en route to the scrotum.
- In female babies, the clitoris appears large and exposed because it's not yet covered by the folds of skin called the labia.
- The baby's head is getting bigger.

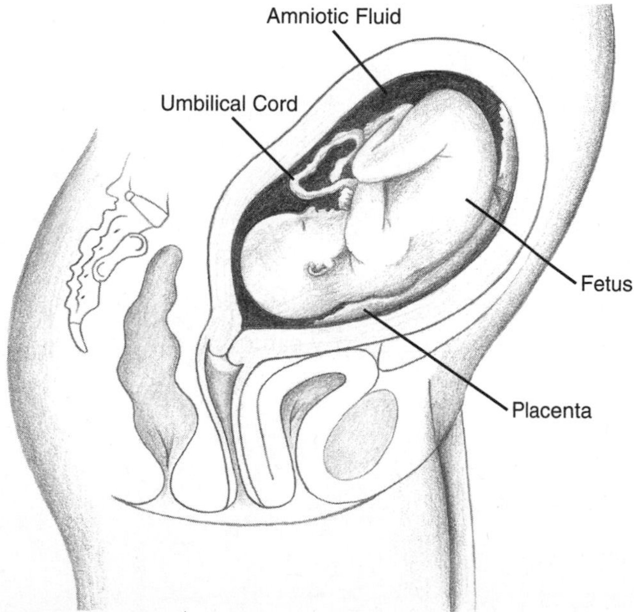

A human fetus at 30 weeks. At this time, your baby weighs about 3 pounds and is about 15 inches long.

The seventh month is both busy and long. There's so much to do, but there's still so long to wait. Your baby seems anxious to join the world, too, as his or her kicking and punching become stronger and more frequent.

The Least You Need to Know

- The seventh month begins the third trimester.
- After the 28th week, you will probably see your health-care provider once every two weeks.
- If you are Rh-negative, you will be tested for Rh antibodies during the 28th week.
- Stretch marks, rehearsal contractions, edema, indigestion, and heartburn are all part of the fun in the third trimester.
- Childbirth classes are a great way to prepare for the real deal.
- Fetal health can be checked with a nonstress test.

Month Number Eight: Weeks 31 to 34

Chapter **12**

In This Chapter

- The medical checkup: evaluation of weight, blood pressure, uterine growth, fetal heartbeat, and a discussion about Braxton Hicks contractions
- Coping with body changes: backaches and shortness of breath
- Boredom, lovemaking, choosing a doula (labor coach), making a birth plan, and finding a pediatrician
- Week-by-week development

Month number eight puts you on the home stretch. You can see the finish line, but it's still out of your reach—there's so much to do before you cross it.

What to Expect at the Medical Checkup

Seeing your doctor every other week now gives you an opportunity to keep close watch on your baby's progress (and your own).

- **Weight.** There's no hiding the fact that you're big! But your weight gain should stabilize at about a pound per week—making you 24 to 30 pounds over your prepregnancy weight by the end of this month. Keep in mind that excess weight increases your discomfort and general immobility. It aggravates problems such as varicose veins, backache, leg pain, and sleeping discomforts. Although women who gain 40 or 50 pounds sometimes give birth to large babies, usually they have the same six- or seven-pounder that women who gain only 25 pounds have.

- **Blood pressure.** As usual, your blood pressure will be taken at your monthly checkup. Your doctor is always on the lookout for any sudden changes that can indicate a problem.
- **Urine tests.** Your urine will be tested for: (1) infection; (2) protein, which can be a sign of high blood pressure; and (3) sugar, which can be a sign of diabetes.
- **Size check.** By the end of the eighth month, the uterus should be located about five fingers below the point where the ribs meet in the middle (by the heart). Your doctor will feel very carefully for the position of the baby. By this time, he should be positioning himself for a head-first birth.
- **Doppler.** Once again, you'll hear the heartbeat of life within you. The location of the heart can give you a pretty good idea of your baby's position. Ask your doctor to help you figure out where your baby is nestled in.
- **Questions.** During the eighth-month checkup, you might want to talk to your doctor about Braxton Hicks contractions (see Chapter 11 for the details). As your due date nears, these contractions can become more intense and you might worry that you're going into labor. Call your doctor immediately if they occur more than four times in an hour and/or are accompanied by pain in the abdomen or back or by any kind of unusual vaginal discharge.

Body Changes

The discomforts of pregnancy might begin to multiply this month. Digestive problems might worsen, your varicose veins might throb more, and headaches and lightheadedness might occur more frequently. This all happens because the baby's demands on your body increase as his or her size and weight increase. The only good news is that such discomfort won't last much longer. In the eighth month, you might have a few new problems, especially backaches and breathlessness.

Backache

As your belly has grown, you have probably changed your posture to carry the extra weight in front. This strains the back muscles and causes backache. In your eighth month, when you're near the end of pregnancy, the ache can get really bad—not only is the weight getting heavier, the baby's head might be in a position that pushes against the lower spine.

To prevent backache and reduce back pain, stand and sit tall. Don't let your shoulders slouch when you sit or let your back sway forward when you stand. Forget high heels. They just can't give your legs the support you need to carry around the extra weight. Avoid standing still for too long. If you must stand still, keep one foot elevated on a step stool, which you should keep nearby. Raising one leg in this way will relieve some of the pressure on the spine. Sleep on a firm mattress. If yours is too soft, put a board underneath it to give your back more support. Exercise your back muscles. See Chapter 18 for some exercises that will keep the lower-back muscles strong.

PREGNANCY FACTS

Not only is a hot bath relaxing, it is good medicine for a backache. Heat increases blood flow and brings more oxygen and nutrients to the painful area. It also speeds the flow of the body's natural painkillers (called endorphins) to the site. In addition, heat eases the muscle tension that is so often responsible for lower-back pain. Hot towels, heating pads, hot water bottles, or hot baths can help soothe the backaches of pregnancy. (Don't let the water get too hot—say over 102°F—and don't stay in more than 10 minutes at a time. It can harm your baby.)

During pregnancy, most back pain is caused by poor posture or pressure on the spine. As the uterus gets bigger, it might push against a nerve in the spine (the sciatic nerve), causing pain (sometimes really bad pain) that runs from the lower back, down the buttocks, and down one leg. If you're lucky, the pain will pass when the baby changes position, but sometimes it lasts until the end of the pregnancy. Talk to your doctor before taking any pain reliever. In the meantime, rest and a heating pad might give you some relief.

Sometimes back pain in pregnancy is a sign that something else is happening (perhaps a slipped disk, a kidney stone, or preterm labor). As your body gets ready for childbirth, you might feel a persistent dull backache (along with cramps sometimes). If this happens, call your doctor, even if you don't think you're ready to deliver.

Breathlessness

Your uterus has grown so large that it presses up against your diaphragm (the large flat muscle that helps you breathe). This can make you feel like you can't get enough air. Although it is an uncomfortable feeling, don't worry that it will deprive your baby of oxygen. During pregnancy, changes in your respiratory system ensure that you and your baby get even more oxygen than usual.

To ease the discomfort of breathlessness, watch your posture. Take the pressure off your diaphragm by standing tall and sitting up straight. If you can't breathe easily when you lie down to sleep, try using extra pillows to prop up your shoulders and head.

Feelings of breathlessness will probably end two to three weeks before delivery, when the baby moves down into the pelvic area (and away from the diaphragm) to prepare for birth.

HEY MOM!

Although shortness of breath is normal in the last trimester, call your doctor if the feeling becomes severe or causes rapid breathing, blueness of lips and fingertips, chest pain, and/or rapid pulse.

What's on Your Mind?

There's so much to think about this month—so much to do! Take a deep breath and get ready to deal with the boredom of being pregnant, spending time and energy finding a comfortable sleeping position, working out a satisfying way to make love, choosing a labor coach (called a doula), making a birth plan, and finding a health-care provider for your baby. Whew!

Boredom

Had enough? Ready to get this pregnancy phase over and move on to motherhood? This is probably the longest nine months you'll live through, and by this point in the pregnancy it's not at all unusual to be bored to tears by the whole thing. You're big and uncomfortable. Your day is consumed by the discomforts of constipation, heartburn and indigestion, leg cramps and backaches, swollen ankles and feet, Braxton Hicks contractions, and fatigue—just to name a few. This isn't fun.

Don't feel guilty if you're not having a great time this month. Wishing the pregnancy was over isn't a covert sign that you don't have the patience to be a good mother. It simply means you're human, tired, and ready to move on to the next stage of your life.

Making Love

If you can't sleep, maybe there's something else you can do in bed. If you're still in the mood (and not all pregnant women are in their eighth month), talk to your doctor about the pros and cons of sexual intercourse and orgasm at this late date. In most cases, it's perfectly safe right up to the moment you go into labor.

DADDY ALERT!

Sex during pregnancy is a whole new game. Some men love it; others just can't do it. The physical discomforts of the last two months make even the thought of intercourse revolting to some women. Don't take it personally if your partner turns you down—many women feel this way at this time. On the other hand, if you have lost your desire, don't be hard on yourself. This, too, is perfectly natural. Talk to your partner about it. If the fact that you're worried about hurting her or the baby during intercourse makes it impossible to feel romantic, say so. But don't give up on all expressions of love—hold her hand, rub her back, kiss her. All of these things will reassure her of your love.

In some cases, however, it's best to avoid intercourse in the last month or so. This is especially true if the following conditions apply:

- You are at risk for a premature delivery (because you're carrying multiples, your cervix has started dilating, or you have a history of premature labor).
- You have placenta previa or abruptio (problems with the placenta).
- You are experiencing unexplained bleeding.
- Your membranes have ruptured.

HEY MOM!

To help prevent infection and to avoid exposing the woman's cervix to irritants in the man's semen, some physicians recommend the use of a condom during sexual intercourse in the last eight weeks of pregnancy. Talk to your doctor about this.

If you can't have intercourse in your eighth and ninth months, it doesn't mean you can't make love. A full body massage for you and a penis massage for your partner are always perfectly safe and satisfying. (See Chapter 20 for more information on sex during pregnancy.)

Choosing a Doula

If you're getting very nervous about delivering your baby, you should think about hiring a *doula* (a private labor coach) to help you. Many women have their husbands or a trusted friend on hand for support during labor, but these "labor coaches" are rather inexperienced and might not be all that much help. If you are delivering in a hospital, labor and delivery nurses will be assigned to help you, but they are also assigned to other women at the same time; when their shift is over, they're replaced by new faces. If your labor is long and drawn out, your support team might tire and feel stressed, too. Given this reality, many women give themselves a great deal of reassurance by finding a doula to assist with the delivery.

Most doulas are certified childbirth assistants and have had experience with hundreds of women and babies. Their fees usually include being present during the labor and delivery, as well as several prelabor and postpartum visits. You can get a referral to a doula in your area free by calling Doulas of North America (DONA) at 1-888-788-DONA. You can also reach the organization online at www.DONA.com.

Talk to Your Baby

A developing fetus begins to hear at about 30 weeks. As this ability develops, researchers have found that the baby can distinguish his or her mother's voice from that of a stranger.

In a recent study, 60 women were divided into two groups and fetal heart rates were measured before, during, and after a recorded two-minute poem was played through a speaker held above the mother's abdomen. The heart rate increased about five beats a minute in 21 of the 30 fetuses who heard recordings of their mother's voice. Heart rates slowed about four beats a minute in 21 of the 30 fetuses who heard a recording of a stranger's voice. This was an exciting discovery for the researchers, who feel it provides evidence of attention, memory, and learning by the fetus. Research studies are now being performed to see if this voice recognition ability plays a role in mother-infant attachment.

So don't be shy about talking to your baby. Read to him, sing to him, and talk to him. It won't matter what you talk about—he can't understand words yet anyway. It's the sound of your voice that excites him.

A Birth Plan

A birth plan is a written list of your needs and preferences during your labor, delivery, and hospital stay. Birth plans are very popular right now and most pregnancy books include information about them. A birth plan will help you think about what you would like during labor and delivery, but it isn't a binding contract or a set of rigid instructions for your health-care providers. After all, these are the people you have chosen to care for you, and you trust them to make sound medical decisions. The point of a birth plan isn't to "tell" your health-care providers how to deliver a baby, although some books say that your birth plan should instruct your physician if you want an IV during labor or if you want internal or external fetal monitoring. But how can you possibly know what will be medically necessary at your delivery? More often than not, these kinds of decisions are based on your needs at the time. Perhaps the best policy is to trust your caregiver to do what's needed, just as you have throughout your pregnancy.

DADDY ALERT!

Make sure you know what's in your partner's birth plan. When she goes into labor, it will be up to you to make sure her wishes are honored whenever possible. You might also want to make sure your own desires are included in the plan. If you want to be in the labor and delivery room at all times, and if you want to "catch" your baby as he or she comes out of the birth canal, say so!

Still, a good birth plan will help you think through the things you do have control over. It's always a good idea to familiarize yourself with options before they're needed. So if you'd like a birth plan, take the time to learn about the procedures involved in labor and delivery. Before you put your plan together, however, be sure to read through Part 5 of this book; it gives you all the information you need to consider.

The following checklist will help you get organized. Read each question and decide what you want to put in your birth plan. When you know what you want, bring the plan to your doctor so the two of you can look it over. He or she will be able to tell you whether the things you ask for are possible. It's better to discuss these things now rather than when you're in labor.

When you put the answers to these questions down on paper, you will have a birth plan to discuss with your doctor. Bring it with you wherever you go to deliver; it will help your physician and other health-care providers to better understand your needs.

Birth Plan Checklist

Labor

- Do you want to be able to walk around during labor?
- Is there a place for your partner to rest or nap during the initial stages of labor?
- Does hospital procedure require an enema or pubic shaving?
- Do you want to be offered painkilling drugs during labor? Do you want an epidural?
- Do you want your labor to be induced if it becomes very drawn out?

Delivery

- Whom do you want to be present with you for support in the delivery room?
- Do you want a natural childbirth?
- If you want medication to dull the pain during delivery, what kind of anesthesia do you want?
- Do you want to film or photograph the delivery?

After the birth

- Do you want to hold the baby immediately after the birth or wait until he or she is weighed and cleaned?
- Do you want to breast-feed your baby immediately after birth?
- Do you want a private or semiprivate room?
- Do you have any special dietary requests?
- Do you want the baby to sleep in your room during your stay?

GREEN FROM THE START

As you create your birth plan, ask your health-care provider what green options are possible for you and your newborn. If it's important to you, ask whether the birthing facility offers the option of organic cotton bed linens and gowns in the delivery room. If not, ask whether you can provide your own. Ask whether you can bring pure soap, shampoo, and lotions for your baby. You might also want to provide your own organic cotton cloth diapers or perhaps disposable brands known to have a lower impact on the environment.

The Pediatrician Search

When you go into labor to deliver your baby, your health-care provider arrives to care for you. The care of the baby falls to a *pediatrician* or to a *family practitioner*. Now is a good time to start looking for one you can trust with your very special bundle of joy.

The process of choosing a doctor for your child is similar to the one you used to find a practitioner to care for you during pregnancy:

HEY MOM!

If you don't choose a doctor before your delivery, the hospital will assign one to care for your child during his or her hospital stay. Later you can pick your own doctor. But it is far better to make this choice now, before the demands of a new baby fog your thinking and push you into a hasty decision.

- **Decide whether you want a family practitioner or a pediatrician.** The services provided by a family practitioner are a little bit like one-stop shopping, where all the members of your family are cared for by the same person who gets to know all of you. A pediatrician, on the other hand, has more specialized training in the care of young children.
- **If you have health insurance, identify the local doctors covered under your plan.** You might have a book that lists all participating doctors in your area, or you can call member services and ask for help. Try to stick close to home. Children are known to need quick emergency treatment for high fevers, deep cuts, and the like. A trip to the "big city" with a sick or injured child will soon wear you down.
- **Decide whether you want to use a doctor in a group or a solo practice.** Remember that in a solo practice the doctor works alone and in a group practice the doctor works with several other doctors. Both options have their good and bad points. See Chapter 5 for a look at the pros and cons of each.
- **Ask for recommendations.** Your own doctor is a good source of information. (Ask who he or she uses for her own kids!) Also, talk to friends and family members who have already chosen a doctor for their children.

After you have collected the names of a few possible health-care providers, it's time to interview them. (Many pediatric practices offer half-hour consultations for a nominal charge.) Call each doctor and ask for an interview. It's best not to settle for a phone interview. Although this is good for gathering information, it won't give you a good picture of the doctor's warmth and sensitivity (which are always vital in a person working with babies and children). The kind of response you get to your request for an interview will perhaps tell you all you need to know about a physician who is too busy, too important, or too disinterested to meet with an expectant mother.

Be prepared to go to your interview with a list of questions about the practical aspects of the doctor's practice as well as his or her beliefs and philosophy. For example, you might ask …

- What are the office hours? Are you available on weekends?
- If this is a group practice, will my child see the same doctor at each checkup?
- How do you handle nighttime calls and emergencies on holidays?
- At what hospitals do you have full staff privileges?
- How do you handle appointments with sick children? Are these children in the same waiting room with healthy kids waiting for a checkup?
- Who is your covering doctor when you're not available?
- What is your payment and billing policy?
- What is your advice about how to handle a crying baby?
- If I have trouble breast-feeding, will I be able to call you for help?

You don't need to take up too much of a doctor's time debating child-care procedures. This kind of interview should give you factual information about the practice and an opportunity to meet the doctors and decide whether you like them. The person you choose will care for your child into the teen years, so be sure it is someone you like and trust. When you have chosen the person you want to be your child's doctor, notify his or her office. Be ready with details such as your due date, your health-care provider's name, and the location of the delivery. Remember to tell your own doctor, too, so that he or she knows who will be in charge of your baby after birth. When you check into the hospital for your delivery, someone in receiving or admissions will also ask for the name of the baby's doctor.

Week by Week

This month you feel (and probably look) huge! Your baby is putting on more fat layers and weight every day—about half a pound a week! In fact, she'll gain more than half her birth weight in the seven weeks before delivery.

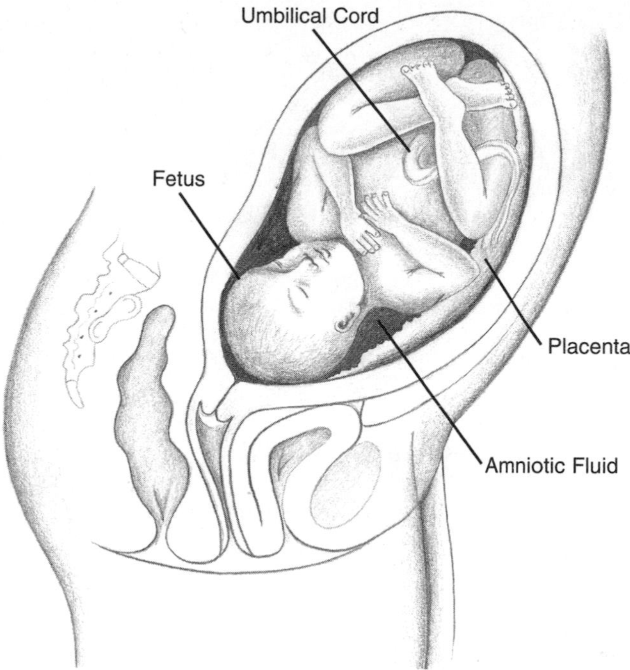

A human fetus at 34 weeks. At this time, your baby will weigh approximately 5 pounds and be about 16 inches long from head to toe.

Week Number 31

- Lungs and the digestive track are nearly mature.
- The baby can see in the womb. (If you shine a bright light on your belly, he might move his head to follow the light or reach out to touch it.)
- Eyebrows and eyelashes are complete.

Week Number 32

- Layers of fat are being deposited beneath the skin.
- Arms and legs are fully proportioned in relation to the size of the head.
- The baby is passing water from his bladder.
- The baby's movements might be less frequent and less forceful because he is running out of room to move around.

Week Number 33

- The baby is practicing breathing by inhaling amniotic fluid to exercise his lungs.
- Some babies have a full head of hair by now; others have only a bit of fuzz.
- Boys' testicles are descending into the scrotum.

Week Number 34

- The skeleton hardens, although the head remains pliable to maneuver through the birth canal.
- The skin becomes less red and wrinkled.
- The toenails are present and the fingernails have reached the tips of the fingers.

In the eighth month, you might feel this pregnancy idea is getting old. It's time to move on to motherhood! Be patient and give your baby just a little more time to plump up before he makes his grand entrance.

The Least You Need to Know

- You will see your doctor twice this month for an evaluation of weight, blood pressure, uterine growth, fetal heartbeat, and a discussion about Braxton Hicks contractions.
- You might feel quite uncomfortable as the size of the baby puts more demands on your body. In particular, you might be plagued by backaches and shortness of breath.
- This is the month you might be bored with being pregnant, and worry about your love life.
- This is the time to think about hiring a doula (a labor and delivery coach).
- Create a birth plan that will help you think through different aspects of your labor and delivery, and then discuss the plan with your health-care provider.
- It's time to find a pediatrician who will care for your baby after his birth.

Month Number Nine: Weeks 35 to 40

Chapter **13**

In This Chapter

- The medical checkup: routine examinations on a weekly schedule
- Body changes: lightening, frequent urination, pressure in the pelvic area, hemorrhoids, and easier breathing and eating
- The difference between prelabor, false labor, and real labor; plus what to buy for the baby and what to pack for your trip to the hospital or birthing center
- Week-by-week development

Ta-dah! This is it! You've made it to the end. This is a month of exhilarating highs, as you get ready to hold your baby in your arms, and deep lows, as you wonder, with each abdominal twitch, whether labor is starting. There's also a lot to do. So roll up your sleeves and get ready for the final stretch.

What to Expect at the Medical Checkup

From Week 36 until delivery, you will have a weekly checkup. Your doctor might now occasionally give you an internal exam to see whether your *cervix* is *effacing* or *dilating* in preparation for birth. At each visit, you will go through the usual routine tests.

BABY TALK!

The **cervix** is the entrance to the uterus or the gatekeeper of your womb. It must **efface** (thin out) and **dilate** (open) to let the baby pass through the birth canal.

- **Weight.** If you've been very, very careful, you'll find yourself 25 to 35 pounds over your prepregnancy weight. If you've overdone it, it's not too late to make some amends. Cut back on sweet treats and add more fruits and vegetables to your diet today. This month, you should gain very little (or nothing at all).

- **Blood pressure.** Your blood pressure will still be recorded at every checkup. It's important to watch for any sudden changes that can indicate a problem.
- **Urine tests.** This is the last month you'll be sharing this part of yourself with other people. In the ninth month, the urine is still being tested for: (1) infection; (2) protein, which can be a sign of high blood pressure; and, (3) sugar, which can be a sign of diabetes.
- **Size check.** The female body is truly amazing. Your uterus has grown 1,000 times its original volume and is now located right under your ribs.
- **Doppler.** The baby's heartbeat is checked at each visit. The strength, rate, and location of the heartbeat tell your doctor a lot about the baby's health.
- **Questions.** Because you might be a little distracted at this stage of your pregnancy, write down the information you want to remember or you'll get home and pace the floor trying to remember what the doctor said about false labor signs.

If he doesn't bring up the subject, ask your doctor about the test for *Group B streptococcus* (GBS). GBS is an infection carried in the vagina or rectum of 10 to 35 percent of all adults. It is harmless and goes unnoticed, unless it is passed from mother to baby. Then it can cause meningitis (an inflammation of the brain or spinal cord), bacterial bloodstream infections, infant pneumonia, and even stillbirth.

The risk of giving this infection to a baby is greatest if the child is born prematurely, if the mother's water breaks early (which is a sign of labor; see Chapter 21), or if there is a long delay between the time the water breaks and the baby's birth. The American College of Obstetricians and Gynecologists and the Centers for Disease Control and Prevention now recommend that every pregnant woman be screened for GBS. You'll find that the GBS test is quite simple. Sometime between Weeks 35 and 37, the doctor will rub a cotton-tipped swab over your vaginal and rectal areas. Then the cells gathered on the swab are sent to a lab for processing. If the results are positive, there's nothing to worry about. You will receive antibiotics during labor and delivery to prevent infecting the baby. That's it—it's simple but very important.

Body Changes

The most noticeable change this month is the size of your belly. It's huge—after all, you have a full-grown baby moving around inside you! You might also deal with "lightening," a pressing need to urinate, hemorrhoids, and, finally, false and real labor.

The Big Drop

Lightening and *engagement* are terms used to describe the process in which the baby drops into the pelvic cavity. (This is the bony structure at the entrance to the birth canal.) In first pregnancies, lightening might begin two to four weeks before the onset of labor. In later pregnancies, it usually happens just before labor begins. But every woman is different. You might be able to tell that your baby has dropped if your pregnancy belly is lower than before and tilts forward.

When lightening happens you'll feel changes in your body. On the good-news side, the pressure on your lungs and stomach is relieved when the baby drops. You can breathe and eat easily again! On the bad-news side, walking might become downright uncomfortable (the expected consequence of moving around while your baby's head is practically between your legs). You might also start to notice a tingling sensation or numbness in your pelvic region. This feeling, which might last until the baby is born, is caused by the pressure of the baby on the nerves in your legs and pelvis.

Frequent Urination

Remember in the beginning of your pregnancy when you spent so much time in the bathroom because you always felt like you had to pee? Well, this month that feeling is back! When the baby "drops" down into the pelvis, this month, he or she might push against the bladder, causing you to spend more time than usual in the bathroom.

HEY MOM!

Don't try to reduce the number of daily bathroom trips by cutting down on fluids. Your body needs plenty of fluids to do all the amazing work of creating a child. The only thing you can do that might help a bit is to lean forward when you urinate; this will empty the bladder fully.

Hemorrhoids

As the baby moves down into the pelvic area, he or she might push out your hemorrhoids. This pain is the last thing you need while you're waiting to deliver your baby! As painful as hemorrhoids can be, take comfort in knowing that this happens to many women in the ninth month.

To relieve the pain, use any of the over-the-counter remedies you would use if you weren't pregnant. Hemorrhoidal creams and ointments might help. Try using a compress soaked in witch hazel or even ice packs if you can stand the cold. It's safe to take a pain reliever, such as acetaminophen (Tylenol).

Be sure to tell your doctor about this problem. If it's severe enough, she might refer you to a colorectal surgeon, in which case she might try a treatment called "rubber band therapy." Tying off the piles can relieve some pain and bleeding, but it might not prevent new piles from forming (especially toward the end of your pregnancy or during delivery). Knowing you're in pain from hemorrhoids, your doctor might also choose to use more anesthetic during delivery so you won't have to deal with both the pain of hemorrhoids and labor.

What's on Your Mind?

During the last month there's so much to think about. Inevitably, labor is on the top of this list. There are three kinds: prelabor, false labor, and real labor. You'll also spend much of this month buying, buying, and buying for the tiny newcomer.

Getting Ready

Every day this month, your body is preparing for labor so that when the moment actually arrives, your body is ready. *Prelabor* signals that you're in the getting-ready-for-labor stage include:

- Lightening—The baby's head drops down into the pelvis.
- An increase in vaginal discharge and/or brownish or blood-tinged mucus discharge.
- An increase in the number and intensity of Braxton Hicks contractions (see Chapter 11 for a description of these practice contractions).
- A nesting instinct that makes you start cleaning closets and organizing your kitchen. If you find yourself filled with energy and driven to clean, primal instincts are pushing you to get your home ready for the new family member.

Practice Run

On the TV sitcoms, the pregnant woman always grabs her big belly with a look of wide-eyed surprise and announces, "It's time." Unfortunately, labor doesn't usually come on like that. You might spend a lot of time this month timing *contractions*, grabbing your suitcase, and then stopping short, realizing the contractions have stopped—*false labor!*

BABY TALK!

Birth contractions are muscle spasms of the uterus that will eventually help push the baby through the birth canal.

False labor is contractions that make you think you are in real labor when you're not. They are a false alarm.

False labor feels just like the real thing. That's why thousands of pregnant women who rush to the hospital are sent home again to wait just a little longer. This is embarrassing (especially if you've woken your spouse, your parents, and your physician to announce the news). When contractions start, you can tell, usually, that real labor has not begun if you answer "yes" to these four questions:

- Do the contractions stay the same in intensity (not getting worse)?
- Do the contractions come in uneven intervals (two minutes apart, then seven minutes apart, then four minutes apart, for example)?
- Is the pain in your lower abdomen rather than in your lower back?
- Do the contractions stop when you move around or change position?

If you're saying "yes," you're not in real labor yet. When real labor contractions begin, you will find that you cannot walk or talk through them. That's a good time to start packing.

The Real Thing

It would be so nice if there were definite symptoms of labor so every expectant mother would know exactly when labor begins. But *labor* is different for every woman—and for some women, it is a different experience for each of the children they have. The best you can do is know the signs that mean things are moving along and delivery day (D-day) is near.

BABY TALK!

Labor is the process by which the body prepares for childbirth.

If you answer "yes" to any of these three questions, you might be in labor:

- Do contractions occur at regular intervals that are coming closer and closer together and getting more intense?
- Do you have lower-back pain (which might be accompanied by a crampy, menstrual feeling)?

- Has your water broken? The expression "water broken" refers to a rupture of the membranes of the amniotic sac. When this happens, amniotic fluid will leak from your vagina and make it look like you have wet your pants (always a fun thing when you're in public). If this happens and you haven't begun labor contractions yet, this is a sign that you should begin labor within 24 to 48 hours. It is very important to keep the vaginal area very clean at this point, because the baby is now unprotected from germs. Do not take a bath, have sexual intercourse, or use a tampon to stop the flow of amniotic fluid.

Talk to your doctor about when you should call her about your labor. She'll tell you to time your contractions. Also let her know when they reach a certain frequency and intensity. She'll also tell you not to worry too much about having your baby on the living room floor by accident. All over the world, most new mothers arrive at their birthing centers not too soon and not too late. If you pay close attention, you will hear the body signals that say, "It's time to go!"

DADDY ALERT!

This is a good time to rehearse the route to the hospital. Make sure you know exactly how to get there safely.

Reaching into Deep Pockets

Are you the kind of expectant mom who buys nothing for her baby until the child has arrived safely and the gender is known? Or are you the kind who has already bought everything the child will need for the next five years? In either case, the baby eventually will need certain things. When you shop, keep the tips in this section in mind.

Car Seats

By law, all children under age nine must be strapped into a car seat when riding in a car. This is so important that most hospitals will not release a baby until they are assured he or she will sit in a car seat on the ride home. This is one time that you have to start thinking like a responsible parent even before the baby is born.

GREEN FROM THE START

Push your family and friends to give you a "green" baby shower. All the necessities—from baby bottles to bassinets, teethers to PJs, diaper bags to baby food, cribs and sheets to booties and hats—are now made from non-toxic, earth-friendly materials that protect a newborn from harsh chemicals and respect the planet the child will inherit.

You should buy the car seat this month before you deliver the baby. It's an important purchase that will require some comparison shopping. You'll also need time to practice getting it in and out of the car. Always put the car seat in the back seat—that way it's not directly in the path of an exploding airbag.

HEY MOM!

Some hospitals and the Red Cross offer free or low-cost car seats. If all the new baby paraphernalia are hurting your pocketbook, this is one expense a community agency might be able to cover. Call your local hospital and ask.

Car seats are made in two basic styles:

- **Infant seat.** This is designed for children under 20 pounds and it faces the back of the car.
- **Infant-toddler seat.** This can be used by both infants and older children up to 40 pounds. It faces the back for infant use and is turned around to face the front when the baby reaches 20 pounds.

Cribs

The American Academy of Pediatrics recommends that cribs meet the following standards:

- Slats should be less than 2⅜ inches apart or no wider than the length of your little finger. If the crib was made before 1985, it might not meet this requirement.
- Avoid cribs with cut-out designs on the head- or footboard. They can trap a child's head.
- Unscrew or cut off corner posts—your baby's clothing can get hooked on one and cause her to choke.
- The mattress should fit snugly. If you can put more than two fingers between the mattress and the crib, replace the mattress.

If you are using a rocking cradle, make sure it has stops so the baby won't be thrown out. And keep in mind that you can use it for no more than three months. By that time, the baby will be too big to be left alone in a cradle or bassinet.

Infant Seats

These reclining chairs for babies are very handy. They let the baby sit up and watch you while you work around the house and they hold the baby in a good position for feeding. (They are *not* to be used as car seats!) Unfortunately, these seats cause injuries when they fall, especially off high tables. Look for an infant seat with a nonskid, wide bottom that will discourage tipping. Never leave your baby alone in an infant seat, and place the seat only on the floor—never on top of furniture.

Strollers

When shopping for a stroller, look for one that won't tip over. As your baby grows and begins to wiggle and turn, the stroller should hold its ground. Also look for a sunshade and front wheels that pivot. It's also nice to have a model that reclines for comfortable napping.

DADDY ALERT!

Don't pretend you're not interested in shopping for the baby. Jump in there and help your partner pick out important baby items. All these things will be a big part of your life very soon, so you might as well grab the chance to have a say in what you purchase.

Baby Clothes

Who can resist buying a carload of those adorable baby outfits? But as tempting as this is, the fancy little dresses and three-piece suits are rarely used and quickly outgrown. You're better off focusing on a practical day-to-day wardrobe that includes the following:

- At least six stretchy, snap-up-the-front, one-piece pajamas. These are the most useful fashion wear for newborns. They live in them!
- At least a half dozen front-snapping T-shirts.
- Another half dozen pairs of socks or booties. (Booties that tie around the ankle will stay on longer than socks.)
- Diapers. You wouldn't be the first parent to bring home a new baby and realize an hour later that babies need diapers. Get them now. If you are using disposable diapers, look for the newborn size with a hole cut out around the navel. These are good for about three weeks while the baby's cord stump is drying out. If you're using cloth diapers, you'll need six diaper wraps or plastic pants and diaper pins, and several dozen diapers.

- A hat. Whether the weather calls for a wool hat or a sun hat, you'll want to keep your baby's head covered.
- A snowsuit if you live in a cold region.

HEY MOM!

Bundling the new baby up in a blanket for a trip home in cold weather sounds like a good idea, but if you're using a car seat on the drive home, the legs need to be free to straddle the seat belt. Instead of using bunting or blankets with a sacklike bottom, use a cozy warm fleece suit with legs so that baby can be easily clicked into the car seat.

These are the basics for now. After the baby is home, you'll find there are several hundred other items you'll need to purchase. But this list of essential items will make you feel well equipped, at least when the baby first arrives.

GREEN FROM THE START

You have two wonderful ways to go green when diapering your baby. At www.greenplanetbaby.com, you can buy cloth diapers that are made of unbleached, organic cotton grown and milled in the United States. If you prefer disposable diapers, you can avoid the traditional kind (each day approximately 10,000 tons of them end up in the landfills, where they sit for about 500 years before decomposing) by choosing chlorine-free, biodegradable disposables from companies such as Seventh Generation and Tushies.

Packing for a Delivery

Packing for your trip to the hospital or birthing center isn't like packing for a vacation. Most maternity stays are quite short and spent in bed, but unlike other short vacations you've spent in bed, your partner isn't going to be with you under the covers. And yes, you'll need to pack for the little person you haven't met yet, too. For his or her return trip home, you'll need to bring …

- A going-home suit; a one-piece stretchy PJ is best.
- A cap and coat if the weather is cold.

For you, one medium-size suitcase should be plenty to hold …

- Clothes for the return trip home. A word of warning here: Your prepregnancy jeans will not fit. Bring your maternity clothes, or a no-waist dress or an elastic-waist skirt or pants. It'll take a while for your body to return to your normal shape, so don't get upset if you still need maternity clothes for the first month after the baby's birth. Bring a pair of flat shoes you can slip on. Heels and tie shoes are both unwise choices.
- A nursing bra if you're going to breast-feed. These bras have front panels that drop down easily to expose your nipples without having to take off the whole bra each time you breast-feed the baby.
- Old maternity underwear. Your stomach will still be swollen, and you'll be bleeding heavily after delivery. There's no need to buy new underwear that won't fit yet and will probably get stained.
- Two nightgowns if you don't want to wear a hospital gown. (Again, don't worry about bringing anything new or pretty—it will get bloodstained before you leave.)
- Robe and slippers. These are handy when you want to take a stroll down the hall or walk to the bathroom. (Leave the fancy slippers with heels at home; you might be a little wobbly on your feet and need flat slippers for support.)
- Toiletries. Bring your toothbrush, toothpaste, shampoo, lotion, hairbrush, deodorant, and any makeup you might want to wear for the trip home.
- A magazine or two. If your labor drags on, these can distract you.
- Your address book. You will certainly have a lot of phone calls to make after the birth of your baby.

Do not bring anything of value, such as jewelry, cash, or credit cards. And do yourself a favor: Leave your work at home. Some brand-new moms have their laptops up and running a few hours after birth. This is a special time; slow down and enjoy it.

Week by Week

The last weeks of your pregnancy give your baby time to grow in length and weight.

Week Number 35

- Babies born at Week 35 have a 99 percent chance of survival. The lungs are fully developed and the respiratory problems that used to kill these preemies are now easily treated.

Weeks Number 36 and 37

- More fat layers are added to help control body temperature after birth.

Week Number 38

- Your baby is now "full term." If he's born today, he'll be considered a full-grown baby. Babies born before 38 weeks are called premature babies.

Week Number 39

- The baby sheds her fuzzy layer of lanugo hair and the vernix caseosa, which is the skin coating that covers a fetus to protect the skin. The baby swallows this waste and will discharge it as her first bowel movement in a blackish mixture called meconium.
- All organs are ready to function outside your womb.
- The lungs are the last organs to mature. They should be fully developed by this time.

Week Number 40

- Bingo! This is the due-date week when your baby just might make her entrance. But then again, maybe she did that last week or will wait until next week. Remember that due dates are rarely exact. (Only 5 percent of babies are born on their due dates.) Even carrying a baby to Week 42 is considered normal. After that, the baby is *post-term.*

BABY TALK!

A baby delivered after Week 42 is called **post-term.**

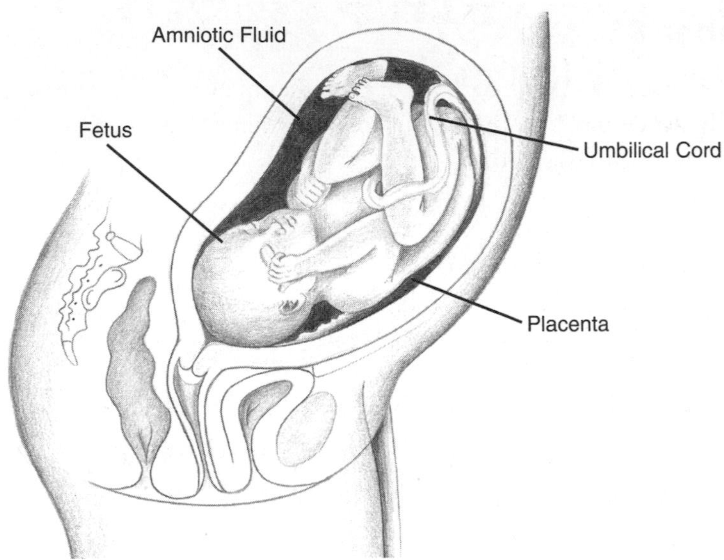

A human fetus at 40 weeks. At this time, your baby will weigh between 6 and 8 pounds and will measure about 18 to 22 inches in length.

What a month! The anticipation can drive even the calmest expectant mom crazy. But you can take your mind off this seemingly never-ending pregnancy by shopping for all those cute baby things that your new baby will be using very soon.

The Least You Need to Know

- The medical checkups in the ninth month are now weekly and might include an internal exam and a test for Group B streptococcus (GBS).
- In the ninth month, the baby might drop down into the pelvic region. This drop, also known as lightening, will make it easier for you to breathe and eat, but it can also make it uncomfortable to walk. In addition, lightening can cause pressure in the pelvic area, hemorrhoids, and the need to urinate frequently.
- This month you might experience three kinds of labor: prelabor, false labor, and real labor. You should know the signs of each.
- Reach deep into your pocket to buy all kinds of baby necessities, among them a car seat, a crib, an infant seat, a stroller, baby clothes, and diapers.
- Get your bags packed so you'll be all set when the baby says, "Here I come!"

Food and Drugs: The Good and the Bad

Part 3

It's no secret that the health of your baby depends on what you put into your body. It's a good idea to take a close look at your diet and map out a new plan that guarantees your little one all the vitamins and nutrients he or she needs to grow strong and healthy. The new MyPyramid in this part will be your guide to healthful eating. You'll also learn why fats, fried foods, sweets, and empty calories are bad for you, especially during your pregnancy. This is also a time to be very cautious about supplements and medications. This part will give you an overview of what's okay and what's not and will explain why it's so important to talk to your health-care provider before taking any supplement or medication.

During pregnancy, you'll find out suddenly that there's more to keeping your baby healthy than watching what you eat—even the air you breathe has to be considered in the total health picture. Pesticides, cleaning agents, smoke, smog, and even microwaves all flash the caution sign. Read on for the facts!

Chapter

14

Good Nutrition

In This Chapter

- MyPyramid: eating the right food for you and your baby
- Prenatal supplements
- The magic of water
- Vegetarian diets during pregnancy

It's a very simple fact: The health of your baby depends on what you put into your mouth. Diet is one area of your pregnancy where you can make a huge difference in the physical and mental health of your baby. That's a big responsibility. You need to start thinking about food as something that builds bones, nerves, and organs rather than something that simply satisfies hunger and personal cravings. Are you ready to give a good prenatal diet a try? This chapter will help you look inside the foods you eat for all the good things you and your baby need.

Follow the Stripes

The U.S. Department of Agriculture (USDA) has built a new food pyramid, called MyPyramid, that can help you choose healthy foods. The pyramid is an excellent guide to the foods that are both good and not-so-good for you.

HEY MOM!

During pregnancy, the exact number of recommended daily servings of each category on the MyPyramid depends on your height, weight, age, and level of activity. To get a personalized diet plan based on the MyPyramid, go to www.mypyramid.gov/mypyramidmoms and enter your information for a quick estimate of what and how much you need to eat.

MyPyramid illustrates each food group with a stripe—the wider the stripe, the more foods from that group you should eat each day. The staircase on the pyramid reminds you that exercise is equally important to a healthy body.

Start with Whole Grains

The wide stripe on the far left of MyPyramid represents the grains group. Grains are the foundation of a healthy diet and include breads, cereals, rice, and pasta. (Note that donuts, cookies, and pastries are not included in the healthy grain category.) The grains in these foods (such as whole wheat, oats, barley, corn, and rice, to name just a few) are a principal source of fiber—absolutely vital in the war against constipation that plagues most pregnant women! Grains are also important sources of many nutrients, including several B vitamins (thiamin, riboflavin, niacin, and folate) and minerals (iron, magnesium, and selenium).

The MyPyramid calls for a daily minimum amount of 3 ounces of grains (at least half of these ounces should be whole grains). A 1 ounce equivalent from the grains group would be any of these:

- A slice of bread
- 1 cup of ready-to-eat cereal
- ½ cup of cooked rice, cooked pasta, or cooked cereal

Whole-grain snack suggestions from the USDA include:

- Snack on ready-to-eat, whole-grain cereals such as toasted oat cereal.
- Add whole-grain flour or oatmeal when making baked treats.
- Try a whole-grain snack chip, such as baked tortilla chips.
- Popcorn, a whole grain, can be a healthy snack with limited salt and butter.

Be sure to look for "whole grains." Refined-grain products such as white rice and bleached breads (often labeled "refined" or "enriched") are not as good for you or your baby. Whole-grain products have more protein and fiber and less fat than processed grains.

DADDY ALERT!

If your partner is making an effort to eat nourishing foods for the sake of your baby, make the effort with her. When she grabs an apple while you're both watching TV, don't sit next to her and eat a bag of potato chips. Be a good sport and have a piece of fruit, too. Not only will you give moral support to your partner, your own health will improve and give you the stamina you'll need when the baby arrives.

Pile on the Vegetables

Your mother was right: You have to eat all your vegetables if you want to grow big and strong. Now that you want this for your own child, you need to stock up on a variety of different types of nature's best (not just French fries). You gain essential vitamins, minerals, fiber, complex carbohydrates, enzymes, and antioxidants from fresh vegetables.

On the MyPyramid model, any vegetable or 100 percent vegetable juice counts as a member of the vegetable group. The new MyPyramid suggests at least 2½ cups of vegetables per day. One cup would be, for example, any one of the following:

- 1 cup of raw or cooked vegetables or vegetable juice
- 2 cups of raw leafy greens
- 2 medium carrots
- About 8 ounces of tofu
- 1 medium boiled or baked potato
- 2 cups raw iceberg lettuce

Veggie snack suggestions from the USDA include:

- Try a low-fat salad dressing with raw broccoli, red and green peppers, celery sticks, or cauliflower. Many vegetables taste great with a dip or dressing.
- Add color to salads by adding baby carrots, shredded red cabbage, or spinach leaves. Include in-season vegetables for variety through the year.

- Include cooked dry beans or peas in flavorful mixed dishes, such as chili or minestrone soup.
- Decorate plates or serving dishes with vegetable slices.
- Keep a bowl of cut-up vegetables in a see-through container in the refrigerator. Carrot and celery sticks are traditional, but consider broccoli florettes, cucumber slices, or red or green pepper strips.

Vegetables may be raw or cooked; fresh, frozen, canned, or dried/dehydrated; and whole, cut-up, or mashed. However, the less you cook your vegetables, the more nutrients you'll get out of them. Raw veggies are the best, followed by lightly steamed ones. If you boil your vegetables, many valuable vitamins and minerals go down the drain with the boiled water.

Don't Forget Fruits

Fruits are full of the nutrients your baby needs, especially vitamin A, vitamin C, fiber, and carbohydrates.

The MyPyramid recommends at least 1½ cups of fruit each day. The following specific amounts count as one cup of fruit toward your daily recommended intake:

- One small apple (2.5 inches in diameter)
- One large banana (8 to 9 inches long)
- Three medium or two large plums
- About eight large strawberries
- ½ cup of dried fruits
- One cup of 100 percent fruit juice

Fruit snack suggestions from the USDA include:

- Cut-up fruit makes a great snack. Either cut them yourself or buy precut packages of fruit pieces such as pineapples or melons. Or, try whole fresh berries or grapes.
- Dried fruits also make a great snack. They are easy to carry and store well. Because they are dried, ¼ cup is equivalent to ½ cup of other fruits.

- Keep a package of dried fruit in your desk or bag. Some fruits that are available dried include apricots, apples, pineapple, bananas, cherries, figs, dates, cranberries, blueberries, prunes (dried plums), and raisins (dried grapes).
- For a snack, spread peanut butter on apple slices or top off frozen yogurt with berries or slices of kiwi fruit.
- Frozen juice bars (100 percent juice) make healthy alternatives to high-fat snacks.

Any fruit or 100 percent fruit juice counts as part of the fruit group. Fruits may be fresh, canned, frozen, or dried, and may be whole, cut up, or puréed.

A Sliver of Oil

Squeezed in tightly on the MyPyramid between Fruits and Milk is the slim stripe of the Oils group. Oils come in all shapes and forms and fall into both good and bad categories. We're all familiar with vegetable oils (such as corn, olive, and canola). Then there are solid fats such as butter, stick margarine, and shortening, as well as beef fat (tallow, suet), pork fat (lard), and chicken fat. In addition, foods that are mainly oil or that are naturally high in oil also fall into this group; these include nuts, olives, avocados, mayonnaise, certain salad dressings, and soft margarine.

Separating the good from the bad can be a bit complicated and confusing. All fats and oils are a mixture of saturated fatty acids and unsaturated fatty acids. But the solid fats contain more saturated fats and/or trans fats than oils. Saturated fats, trans fats, and cholesterol tend to raise "bad" (LDL) cholesterol levels in the blood, which in turn increases the risk for heart disease.

Other oils contain more monounsaturated (MUFA) and polyunsaturated (PUFA) fats. Most of the fats you eat should be MUFA or PUFA fats. The MUFAs and PUFAs found in fish, nuts, and vegetable oils do not raise LDL ("bad") cholesterol levels in the blood. They also contain nutrients vital to good health, such as essential fatty acids and vitamin E. Oil also helps your baby form healthy, supple skin and aids vision development. But as you can see from the size of the stripe on the pyramid, your daily intake of oils should be limited.

The daily allowance of oil for women in the childbearing age group is 6 teaspoons. Here's how that breaks down in common foods:

- Mayonnaise: 1 tablespoon = 2½ teaspoons of oil allowance
- Italian salad dressing: 2 tablespoons = 2 teaspoons of oil allowance

- Olives (ripe or canned): 4 large = ½ teaspoon of oil allowance
- Peanut butter: 2 tablespoons = 4 teaspoons of oil allowance
- Nuts (peanuts, mixed nuts, cashews, almonds): 1 ounce = 3 teaspoons of oil allowance

The high calorie content of items in the Oils group is another reason to limit your intake of these foods. Oils and solid fats contain about 120 calories per tablespoon.

Enjoy Lots of Milk

Next to the sliver of the Oils group stripe, you'll see the wider stripe for the Milk group. All fluid milk products and many foods made from milk are considered part of this food group. Foods made from milk that retain their calcium content are part of the group, while foods made from milk that have little or no calcium, such as cream and butter, are not. Most milk group choices should be fat-free or low-fat.

These milk products provide your growing baby with important nutrients such as calcium, vitamin D, and phosphorus—which are all vital for your baby's developing bones and teeth, muscles, heart, and nerves.

Calcium is especially good for pregnant women. Research shows that during pregnancy, 13 milligrams of calcium an hour—or 250 to 300 milligrams a day—pass through the placenta to the baby. That means that at birth, the baby will have accumulated about 25,000 milligrams of calcium in his body. The need for calcium is so strong that the baby will "rob" it from your bones if he or she doesn't get enough from the foods you are eating. This can have a negative effect on your health later on.

Therefore, pregnant women need about 1,000 milligrams of calcium daily. You can get that easily if you have one cup of low-fat yogurt, eight ounces of calcium-fortified orange juice, and one eight-ounce glass of skim milk during the day.

The recommended daily intake of the milk group on MyPyramid is three cups per day. In general, one cup equivalent in the milk group is found in:

- Milk or yogurt: 1 cup
- Natural cheese: 1½ ounces
- Processed cheese: 2 ounces

The USDA offers the following suggestions for getting your milk allowance:

- Use fat-free or low-fat milk when making condensed cream soups (such as cream of tomato).
- Have fat-free or low-fat yogurt as a snack.
- Make a dip for fruits or vegetables from yogurt.
- Make fruit-yogurt smoothies in the blender.
- For dessert, make chocolate pudding with fat-free or low-fat milk.
- Top cut-up fruit with flavored yogurt for a quick dessert.
- Top casseroles, soups, stews, or vegetables with shredded, low-fat cheese.
- Top a baked potato with fat-free or low-fat yogurt.

HEY MOM!

Whole milk, skim milk, ½ percent milk, 1 percent milk, and 2 percent milk all contain about the same amount of calcium and protein. They differ in the amount of saturated fat they contain, but not in nutrient content.

Go Light on the Meat and Beans Group

To the far right of the MyPyramid lies the relatively narrow stripe representing the Meat and Beans group. All foods made from meat, poultry, fish, dry beans or peas, eggs, nuts, and seeds are considered part of this group. (Dry beans and peas are part of this group as well as the Vegetable group.)

These foods give you vital nutrients necessary to a healthy pregnancy. These include protein, B vitamins (niacin, thiamin, riboflavin, and B_6), vitamin E, iron, zinc, and magnesium. However, you have to be careful which members of this group you include in your diet—healthwise, not all members of the group are created equal.

Some food choices in this group are high in saturated fat and cholesterol and therefore should be limited or even eliminated from your diet. These include fatty cuts of beef, pork, and lamb; regular ground beef; and regular sausages, hot dogs, and bacon. Also included in the saturated-fats-to-avoid group are some luncheon meats, such as regular bologna and salami, as well as some poultry, such as duck. And other foods from this group that should be avoided are egg yolks (egg whites are cholesterol-free) and organ meats, such as liver and giblets.

Most meat and poultry choices should be lean or low fat. Fish, nuts, and seeds contain healthy oils, so choose these foods frequently instead of meat or poultry.

The MyPyramid food model recommends 5 ounce equivalents from the Meat and Bean group each day. A 1 ounce equivalent looks like this:

- ¼ cup cooked dry beans.
- 1 egg.
- ¼ cup peanut butter.
- ½ ounce nuts or seeds.
- 1 ounce meat, poultry, or fish. (This is a surprisingly small portion. A small steak measuring about 2 by 4 by ½ inch, which is small by restaurant standards, is 2 to 3 ounces. That's over half your daily suggested intake in this category.)

PREGNANCY FACTS

Protein and calcium are both important nutrients, but sometimes they can work against each other. Research shows that too much protein can deplete the store of calcium in the body. This happens because sulfur-rich proteins make extra acid in the body. As acids wash through the bones, they dissolve calcium. The calcium is then eliminated through the urine. No matter how much calcium you take in, you can't keep enough in the bones if you take in too much protein. Stick to the recommended 5 ounces of meat, fish, poultry, eggs, legumes, or nuts per day. That's plenty!

You probably eat enough food from this group to meet the daily recommendation. But you should make an effort to make leaner and more varied selections of these foods. To vary your sources of protein, the USDA suggests limiting your meat intake and balancing it with dishes such as these:

- Turkey chili with kidney or pinto beans
- Stir-fried tofu
- Split pea, lentil, minestrone, or white bean soups
- Baked beans
- Black bean enchiladas
- Garbanzo or kidney beans on a chef's salad
- Rice and beans

- Veggie burgers or garden burgers
- Hummus (chickpeas) spread on pita bread

Treat Yourself

As we've run out of stripes on the MyPyramid, you might be wondering, "So where do sugary foods like cookies, cakes, and pies fit in? Surely, there must be room for an occasional treat?" Well, yes and no. The MyPyramid model itself has absolutely no room for sugary treats, but the USDA has built in what it calls "discretionary calories." These calories are the "extras" that can be used to enjoy luxuries such as solid fats and added sugars or to indulge in more food from any food group.

To better explain, the USDA gives this example: Assume your calorie budget is 2,000 calories per day. Of these calories, you need to spend at least 1,735 calories for essential nutrients, if you choose foods without added fat and sugar. Then you have 265 discretionary calories left. You may use these on "luxury" versions of the foods in each group, such as higher-fat meat or sweetened cereal. Or, you can spend them on sweets, sauces, or beverages.

Most women on a daily diet of 2,000 to 2,200 calories will end up with 265 to 290 discretionary calories if they are eating a high-nutrient diet—and that's not much to play with. One cup of vanilla ice cream is 274 calories—that's it for the day!

Although cakes and pies aren't on the MyPyramid, the sugar your body needs is found in plentiful supply in fruits and complex carbohydrates (potatoes and whole-grain breads, for example). Your body (and your baby) has no use for the kind of sugar found in candy, cakes, pies, sodas, and so on. Of course, treating yourself to an occasional sweet dessert won't hurt your baby, but don't overdo it.

Putting Together a Menu

When you're planning out your pregnancy diet, use the MyPyramid to help you select nutritious foods and to avoid empty-calorie junk foods. The suggestions are based on dietary guidelines that describe a healthy diet as one that includes foods from all food groups and subgroups, but emphasizes fruits, vegetables, whole grains, and fat-free or low-fat milk and milk products. It also includes lean meats, poultry, fish, beans, eggs, and nuts. And finally, this food model is low in saturated fats, trans fats, cholesterol, salt, and added sugars.

The suggested daily allowances listed in the previous sections for each category on the MyPyramid guide come together to offer you a varied and nutritious menu each day. Here is a sample menu containing all the recommended equivalents.

Breakfast:

1 whole-wheat English muffin with 2 teaspoons soft margarine and 1 tablespoon jam or preserves.

1 medium grapefruit

1 hard-cooked egg

1 unsweetened beverage

Lunch:

White bean–vegetable soup: 1¼ cups chunky vegetable soup and ½ cup white beans.

2 ounces breadstick

8 baby carrots

1 cup fat-free milk

Dinner:

Rigatoni with meat sauce: 1 cup rigatoni pasta (2 ounces dry), ½ cup tomato sauce tomato bits, 2 ounces extra-lean cooked ground beef (sautéed in 2 teaspoons of vegetable oil), and 3 tablespoons grated Parmesan cheese.

Spinach salad: 1 cup baby spinach leaves, ½ cup tangerine slices, ½ ounce chopped walnuts, and 3 teaspoons of sunflower oil and vinegar dressing.

1 cup fat-free milk

Snack:

1 cup low-fat fruited yogurt

This kind of menu gives you plenty of food and nutrients without the excess calories you get from sweets and processed junk food.

(You can find more menu ideas from the USDA at www.mypyramid.gov/downloads/sample_menu.pdf.)

Guidelines Especially for Pregnant Women

The USDA also suggests these special food guidelines for pregnant women:

- Eat foods high in iron and/or consume iron-rich plant foods or iron-fortified foods with an enhancer of iron absorption, such as vitamin C–rich foods.
- Consume adequate synthetic folic acid daily (from fortified foods or supplements) in addition to food.
- Do not eat or drink raw (unpasteurized) milk or any products made from unpasteurized milk, raw or partially cooked eggs, or foods containing raw eggs, raw or undercooked meat and poultry, raw or undercooked fish or shellfish, unpasteurized juices, and raw sprouts.

HEY MOM!

You should not be on a weight-reduction diet during your pregnancy. You and your baby need a balanced diet that includes carbohydrates, protein, and fat. You should definitely stay away from a strict low-carb diet. These diets cause your body to break down muscle and become dehydrated, creating chemical compounds called ketones that can cross the placenta and seriously harm a fetus.

Dietary Supplements

Ideally, you should get all your nutrients from natural foods. But during pregnancy, when there are so many cravings, food aversions, and morning sickness, a daily vitamin and mineral supplement is a good idea. Think of it as insurance against those days when you just can't take in enough of the foods your baby needs. Most often, the supplement (usually referred to as *prenatal* vitamins) is prescribed by your doctor and contains all the nutrients you and your baby need. Women with special needs, such as those with diabetes or anemia, might need additional supplementation to meet their daily nutritional requirements.

Follow your doctor's orders regarding supplements. An excess of certain nutrients can be harmful to your developing baby. Don't get caught up in the belief that if some is good, more must be better. Take only what your doctor prescribes.

Also be cautious about any herbal supplements or over-the-counter pills you might be taking. See Chapter 16 for a discussion of supplements such as gingko biloba, echinacea, ginseng, and appetite suppressants. And talk to your doctor about any supplements you might be taking.

Water

Your body needs a steady supply of fluids, but not all drinks are created equal. Sodas and coffee are actually bad for your health (as explained in the next chapter). Fruit juices deliver fluid and nutrients, but many are very high in sugar, which you should be avoiding now. And alcoholic beverages are out during these nine months (see the next chapter to find out why). So what's left? Water!

Water is your friend during this pregnancy. It is a no-calorie thirst quencher that your body craves. Water will keep you hydrated, allowing all of your body's cells to function at their best. It will reduce problems with constipation by keeping fluid in the bowels. It can wash out toxins that accumulate in the body and cause illness. It reduces excessive swelling in feet, ankles, and fingers. And it decreases the risk of getting a urinary tract infection.

Drink fruit juices in moderation and at least eight large glasses of water each day. This isn't really as difficult as it sounds. Keep a bottle of water next to you at all times, and you'll find that with frequent sipping you'll meet this quota easily. The water in tea and coffee, however, doesn't count; in fact, it actually flushes fluid out of your body and increases your need for pure water. Increase your water intake and your body and your baby will thank you.

Tips for Vegetarians

Vegetarian diets that are not based on junk food have plenty of the nutrients needed by pregnant women. The key is to eat a wide variety of foods and avoid sweet and fatty foods (nothing new there!).

A major concern for vegetarians is that their diet might lack protein (found abundantly in meat), iron (also found in meat), and vitamin B_{12} (found only in animal products and vitamin B_{12} fortified foods). If you are a vegetarian, you have nothing to worry about if you select other foods that contain these nutrients.

Good sources of protein for vegetarians include legumes (dried peas and beans), grains, soy products (tofu and soy milk, for example), nuts and nut butters, seeds, lentils, tempeh, and dairy products (cottage cheese, milk, yogurt, cheese, and eggs). Common foods such as greens, potatoes, pasta, and corn also add to the protein count.

Some years ago, a popular theory said that it was necessary to eat certain combinations of plant proteins to get the full benefit of protein. This is no longer considered necessary; with a varied diet and adequate calorie intake, you don't have to worry about combining your proteins.

Good sources of iron are whole grains, dried beans, dark green leafy vegetables, blackstrap molasses, tofu, spinach, beet greens, bulgur, prune juice, and dried fruits.

There are a few tricks you can use to get the most iron out of these iron-rich foods:

- Be sure to include foods rich in vitamin C (such as orange juice) in your diet every day. This vitamin will help your body absorb iron.
- Cooking in a cast-iron skillet can help you get more of this mineral.
- Cut back on caffeinated drinks such as coffee, tea, and colas; they interfere with the body's ability to absorb iron.

Following the simple tips in this section will boost your iron levels.

Calcium and vitamin B_{12} are in plentiful supply in the lacto-ovo vegetarian diet. If you are a vegan vegetarian, however, these two nutrients might be lacking in your diet. To boost your intake of calcium, look for calcium-fortified products, such as orange juice and soy and rice milks. Also increase your intake of calcium-rich kale, collard greens, turnip greens, broccoli, and tofu enriched with calcium.

You might also need a calcium supplement with at least 150 to 200 milligrams of calcium. Look on the label for calcium carbonate; this is the type most easily absorbed by the body. If you're not sure whether your supplement contains carbonate, try this test: Put the supplement in a glass of vinegar. If it takes more than 10 minutes to dissolve, the supplement does not employ calcium carbonate; use another brand.

Vegan vegetarians have a particularly tough time getting enough vitamin B_{12} because it is found primarily in animal-derived foods. Still, it's vital that you find a way to keep up your supply because B_{12} is an essential nutrient for the developing fetus. Vitamin B_{12} is required by all cells that synthesize DNA, including those of the nervous system.

Food sources of B_{12} include some brands of nutritional yeast and soy milk, and B_{12}-fortified cereals, such as Grape Nuts. Your best bet is to get vitamin B_{12} through nonanimal-derived supplements. Be sure to tell your doctor that you are a vegan so he or she will know to choose a prenatal vitamin with a healthy supply of B_{12}.

HEY MOM!

Want to boost your supply of calcium? Get out in the sun (with a sunscreen, of course)! The vitamin D supplied by exposure to the sun allows more calcium to be absorbed by the body.

You've always known that a nutritious diet builds strong bones, healthy organs and nerves, and everything else you're made of. Now it's time to think about how important it is to eat the right foods if you are *creating* these body systems. Your baby is counting on you to eat good foods to give her the advantage of exceptional physical and mental health right from the start.

The Least You Need to Know

- The MyPyramid food guide illustrates which foods you should eat the most of each day and which ones you should eat moderately or not at all.
- Increase your intake of whole grains, vegetables, fruits, and milk. Decrease your intake of oils filled with saturated fats and trans fats as well as meats high in saturated fat and cholesterol.
- Avoid sweets and empty calories.
- Follow doctor's orders regarding supplements.
- Stay hydrated by drinking lots of water every day.
- Vegetarian diets that are not based on junk food are plentiful in the nutrients needed by a pregnant woman.

Chapter 15

Dietary Pitfalls

In This Chapter

- Foods to avoid that might harbor bacteria
- A warning about foods that contain toxic chemicals
- The scoop on salt and no-fat products
- The real story on the "eating for two" myth
- A close look at two drink demons: caffeine and alcohol

Are you willing to do anything to help your baby grow strong and healthy? How about giving up those sweet, empty-calorie foods? How about turning down holiday eggnog and diet soda? Are you ready to turn your back on salty snacks and fried foods? This chapter will give you the scoop on why your baby really would rather skip the junk and load up on the good stuff.

Beware Bacteria

Need we mention that salmonella or listeria poisoning for lunch would not be good for your baby? To make sure you don't take in the bacteria that hide in certain foods, stay far away from the following foods:

- Raw seafood such as oysters and clams
- Sushi and sashimi
- Nonpasteurized milk (found in some eggnogs)
- Imported soft cheeses such as Brie, Camembert, feta, or goat

- Undercooked and runny eggs
- Patés and steak tartare
- Undercooked meat and poultry (for the rest of your pregnancy, don't ever order your meat rare or even medium rare)
- Caesar salads or raw cookie dough (they contain raw eggs!)

These foods are on your forbidden-foods list. For the rest of your pregnancy, you should stay away from any raw animal product.

Junk Cravings

Have you had a craving today? Many pregnant women say they just can't get enough ice cream or chocolate. Some say they crave donuts and sweet cakes. (Unfortunately, doctors don't often hear about women craving cauliflower or apples.) Why would your body want things that aren't good for you?

DADDY ALERT!

You can help your partner turn away from junk food when you dish out the servings. Rather than ask her to go cold turkey, begin by simply giving smaller servings. How about one scoop of ice cream instead of two? Why not put some chips in a bowl rather than grab the whole bag? When she can't resist a candy bar, don't scold; encourage her to take one bite to satisfy the craving and put the rest away.

Some therapists say that cravings for junk foods are really cravings for emotional support and affection. Others say they are cravings for nutrients lacking in the diet. The answer probably lies somewhere in between. If your partner and your family give you attention and frequent hugs, and you're eating a diet based solidly on the recommendations of the MyPyramid guide (explained in Chapter 14), it's unlikely that you'll have continuous, uncontrollable junk food cravings that will jeopardize your health. If you are unable to resist junk foods (and eat an entire bag of potato chips every night and then convince yourself that this is a double serving from the vegetable group, for example), don't laugh it off as an unavoidable pregnancy thing. Talk to your doctor and ask for help in kicking the junk food habit and creating a balanced and satisfying diet.

This is a good time to start thinking creatively about the food you eat. There are lots of ways to substitute good for bad if you just think before you grab the junk food you crave.

PREGNANCY FACTS

Speaking of unusual food cravings, did you know that some pregnant women crave substances like dirt, clay, starch, ice, paraffin, and coffee grounds? This condition is called pica. These cravings are often a sign of nutritional deficiencies such as low iron, low mineral, or low-calorie intake. The cravings appear to be the body's way of making up for what it is not getting in the diet. If you have any of these "odd" cravings, don't be embarrassed to tell your doctor. Depending on the amount you eat and how long it continues, pica can be linked to complications such as preeclampsia and premature birth. Your doctor can help evaluate your diet and determine which areas need boosting. He or she might increase your iron supplementation and/or refer you to a dietitian.

When you feel like reaching for a piece of junk food that you know is not giving anything nutritionally valuable to your baby, think of something healthful you can eat instead. This way, you shouldn't feel deprived; you can eat all the "good" foods you want.

Chemical Warfare

The switch to "healthier" foods can be dangerous if you choose foods full of chemicals. The most obvious place you'll find toxins is in diet foods (especially those containing artificial sweeteners, such as aspartame), some fruits and vegetables (unfortunately), fish, preserved meats, the infamous MSG-laden Chinese food, and even some meat and dairy products.

Diet Foods

Unfortunately, it isn't any healthier to switch from regular cola to diet cola. Diet foods often contain the artificial sweetener aspartame (commercially called NutraSweet or Equal). Although there appears to be little danger of fetal damage from moderate amounts of this sweetener, it can affect your health and well-being, which is never good for the baby. Aspartame is a brain stimulant and has been reported to cause headaches and worsen feelings of anxiety (just what a pregnant woman doesn't need!). It aggravates the stress response in the brain, making you even more prone to nervousness. Overuse and long-term use can deplete amines in the brain and cause depression. To avoid the harmful effects of aspartame, stay away from "sugar-free" diet colas, diet yogurts, and foods containing sugar-free gelatin. (Aspartame is harmful to pregnant women who have the disease phenylketonuria, or PKU. This is caused by the body's inability to break down the amino acid phenylalanine.)

Definitely stay away from the artificial sweetener saccharin. Saccharin is known to cross the placenta and stay in fetal tissue for a long time. Animal studies found an increase in cancer in the offspring of mice that ate foods containing this sweetener when they were pregnant. For the most part, saccharin is no longer in use, but keep your eyes open and avoid it if you see it listed as an ingredient on a food label.

Fruits and Vegetables

The MyPyramid guide says you should have 1½ cups of fruit each day and at least 2½ cups of vegetables per day. Certainly, both fruits and vegetables are vital to good health because they contain so many necessary vitamins and minerals. Unfortunately, some also contain chemicals. Fertilizers, herbicides, fungicides, and insecticides all find their way into our produce. Some produce is also colored and waxed for better appearance. It's hard to completely avoid this problem—average Americans consume trace amounts of chemical residues in their foods amounting to 2 pounds annually. We don't know yet how high levels of these chemicals affect a fetus, so although it's best to eat plenty of fruits and vegetables, do so with caution.

There are several ways to reduce the amount of chemicals from the produce you eat:

- **Buy organic.** Organic produce is grown without the use of chemical fertilizers, herbicides, fungicides, or insecticides. It also is not processed, packaged, transported, or stored with chemicals, artificial additives, or preservatives. Although they don't always look as pretty as other produce, organically grown foods usually taste better and have superior nutritional value.

  In the past, you could find organic fruits and vegetables only at health food stores or at farmers' markets. Because organic food has become so popular lately and is required by many people with diseases of the immune system, you can probably find it right next to the produce you usually buy at the supermarket. Look carefully for a sticker that says "certified organic." This might cost you a bit more, but the peace of mind is worth it.

- **Buy produce grown only in the United States.** Imported fruits and vegetables contain highly toxic pesticides, such as DDT, which are banned for use here.
- **Wash all fresh fruits and vegetables in water.** This will remove some (but not all) of the pesticide residues on the surface. A mild solution of natural dishwashing soap and water might help remove additional surface pesticide residues.
- **Grow your own food!** If the weather is right, find a small sunny area and plant some vegetables. You don't even need garden space; you can use large pots and planters.

GREEN FROM THE START

Not all fruits and vegetables are created equal. Switching to organic foods has an immediate beneficial affect on the level of pesticides in the body. So it's never too late to make dietary changes that will reduce the concentration of industrial chemicals fed to your baby in the womb. This news comes from a study in *Environmental Health Perspectives* in which researchers tested the urine of school children before and after they ate foods from their usual diet and then again when they ate these same foods from organic sources. Within 24 hours of the diet change, the concentration of pesticides dropped dramatically.

Fish

Polluted waters make it risky to eat too much fish. Industrial and agricultural runoff has put chemicals into the water and ultimately into the food chain. A study by the U.S. Environmental Protection Agency found pesticides and mercury in 90 percent of the fish samples they tested. A variety of bacteria, viruses, parasites, and toxins can plague fish and the people who eat them.

This is not good for you or your baby. A study by Wayne State University in Michigan found that children born of mothers who had regularly eaten contaminated fish weighed less than average at birth, had smaller heads, and showed decreases in short-term memory and attention span as they matured.

Until we find a way to solve the problem of polluted water, guidelines established by the Food and Drug Administration (FDA) and the Environmental Protection Agency (EPA) advise pregnant women to follow these three recommendations.

- Do not eat shark, swordfish, king mackerel, or tilefish, because they contain high levels of mercury.
- Eat up to 12 ounces (two average meals) a week of a variety of fish and shellfish that are lower in mercury.

  Five of the most commonly eaten fish that are low in mercury are shrimp, canned light tuna, salmon, pollock, and catfish.

  Another commonly eaten fish, albacore ("white") tuna has more mercury than canned light tuna. So when choosing your two meals of fish and shellfish, you may eat up to 6 ounces (one average meal) of albacore tuna per week.
- Check local advisories about the safety of fish caught by family and friends in your local lakes, rivers, and coastal areas. If no advice is available, eat up to 6 ounces (one average meal) per week of fish you catch from local waters, but don't consume any other fish during that week.

Hot Dogs and MSG

Some preserved foods are high in food additives called nitrates (look on food labels for sodium nitrate or sodium nitrite). The link between these nitrates and cancer made big headlines a few years ago and they are still being investigated for their effects on the growing fetus. A word to the wise says, beware—it doesn't take much of these preservatives to have a negative effect. Because nitrates are present in large amounts and are water-soluble, they get into the bloodstream very easily.

The food additive monosodium glutamate (MSG) can have a toxic effect on the neurons in the brain responsible for sexual drive and behavior. When you are pregnant, it would be wise to stay away from foods containing this additive. Chinese food, for example, has long been known to contain this food additive, but many Chinese food restaurants now offer "MSG-free" dishes if you ask for them specifically. In other food products, MSG is commonly called "natural flavors" and found in most commercial salad dressings, soup bases, and meat stocks, as well as dairy products, sauces, seasoning mixtures, frozen foods, teas, and many convenience foods. Read those labels and try to avoid any with "natural flavors."

Meat and Dairy Products

Meat and dairy products (such as milk, eggs, butter, and yogurt) are filled with nutrients important to good health. However, unless you choose these products carefully, you may be getting undesirable chemicals along with your food.

On conventional farms, antibiotics are routinely given to chickens, pigs, and cows to prevent the development of intestinal infections that can reduce the animals' weight. This medication is passed on to humans through the meat and/or dairy products of these animals. Cattle are also given hormones to promote faster growth, and again, these anabolic steroids are passed on to humans in their meat and dairy products.

To skip the extra chemicals, buy organic. Organic meat and dairy products do not contain either antibiotics or hormones. With organic options now so readily available, it makes sense to make the switch when possible. When it's not possible, choose chicken, turkey, pork, lamb, or veal over steak and hamburgers. Non-red meats are not allowed to contain hormones.

HEY MOM!

Because liver contains 10,000 times the amount of vitamin A recommended for a pregnant woman, eating liver in early pregnancy may possibly be linked to birth defects. Therefore, avoiding liver is suggested for pregnant women, especially in early pregnancy. The recommended daily dose of vitamin A is 2500 IU, so it is a good idea to check your vitamin bottle to be sure that the level of daily intake of vitamin A and vitamin A foods combined does not exceed this recommended dose.

Salty Foods

The trick to staying healthy and eating salty foods is finding the middle ground. Too little salt is bad because you need the sodium in salt to help regulate the fluids in your body. Salt helps maintain the body's increased blood volume during pregnancy and is vital in hot weather when you lose salt through perspiration. Too little salt intake can reduce your appetite as well (not necessarily a good thing when you're pregnant).

Too much salt, however, isn't good at all. High salt intake can cause high blood pressure (which can lead to major complications during pregnancy) and edema (swelling), because salt causes your body to retain water.

The key is moderation. You can salt food lightly, but make sure you really need and want it before you reach for the shaker. You should also be careful of hidden sources of salt in products such as ketchup, bacon, pickles, chips, pretzels, fast foods, and soy sauce. Get in the habit of reading labels and looking for the word "sodium." This will tell you how much salt is in a food product.

Greasy Fats

In case you hadn't noticed, no-fat, low-fat, and nonfat is "in." Many breads, cakes, snacks, and dairy products boast about their reduced-fat content. This is good and bad. You should definitely watch the amount of fat you eat (no more than four servings a day), but don't be fooled by "no-fat" advertising. Eating no- or low-fat products can trick you into thinking you're safe from excess weight gain, but check out the calorie count on these products—it's still very high. If you eat one no-fat pound cake every day—you're going to get fat.

Your best bet is to avoid both high-calorie and high-fat foods. They add inches around your middle (that have nothing to do with your growing baby), they clog your veins and arteries, they raise your cholesterol levels, and they take up space in your diet that should be reserved for healthful foods.

HEY MOM!

Look out for hidden fats when you're eating out. Clues to high-fat content are words such as "creamed," "fried," "crispy," "au gratin," "hollandaise," "battered," and "buttery." Choose grilled, baked, or steamed fish, meats, and vegetables to reduce the fat content.

The four servings of fat you need each day are very easy to get; have an egg fried in butter with buttered toast on the side and you're done. If you put dressing on your salad at lunch, you've gone overboard! Because it's so easy to overindulge in fat, you need to be vigilant (without driving yourself crazy). Look for easy places to cut out fat and always look for the lesser of two evils.

Did you know …

- Regular mayonnaise has four times as much fat as the same amount of Miracle Whip dressing?
- Regular cream cheese has twice as much fat as the same amount of reduced-fat cream cheese?
- Ten whole peanuts have half the fat of four walnut halves?

You should also keep in mind that some high-fat foods are better than others. Plant-based fats in avocados; olive oil; sesame, sunflower, and pumpkin seeds; and nuts are more nutritious and better for you than animal fats such as butter, sour cream, and lamb chops.

Olestra is that magic ingredient in snacks and cakes that allows fat to slide right out of your system without being digested. It sounds like an answer to our prayers, but be cautious. Olestra is known to cause digestive distress (such as diarrhea and vomiting) in some people, and unfortunately, it's too early to know how it affects women during pregnancy. It's a good idea to avoid foods made with Olestra and choose "low-fat" instead, if you can't resist a snack.

Eating for Two

"Eating for two" is an old expression that is used to excuse the binges of pregnant women. If you have another body to feed, it's reasoned, you have to eat twice as much food. Sorry to pop your bubble, but that's just not the way it works. You need to start eating better, not more—or, rather, not much more. Surprisingly, your pregnant body needs only about 300 calories more per day; that's a mere two extra cups of milk—not much to get excited about. This puts your intake between 1,800 and 2,200 calories each day.

HEY MOM!

If you're overweight, this is the one time in your life when you should not even think about dieting. Dieting during pregnancy is not good for you or your developing baby. Many weight-loss programs forbid foods that you need for folic acid, iron, and other vitamins and minerals. If you fill your stomach with wholesome foods only, you can forget about losing weight and watch your waistline expand knowing that the weight you gain is necessary to support your baby.

You're going to be spending a lot of time looking at the scale during your pregnancy. Of course, you're supposed to get big, but if you eat too much, you'll put on excess fat that won't be easy to get rid of after the baby is born. Excess weight also increases your discomfort during pregnancy; it aggravates problems such as varicose veins, backache, leg pain, general immobility, and sleeping discomforts. Putting on too much weight during pregnancy also increases your risk of having hypertension and gestational diabetes (both are explained in Chapter 4). Excess weight is not a good thing.

On the other hand, if you eat too little, you'll deprive your baby of the nutrients he or she needs to grow. This can cause growth and birth complications. If you don't take in enough carbohydrates, for example, the body will use the calories taken in with protein foods; this robs protein from the baby, who needs it for brain and muscle development. Eating too little during pregnancy can also cause a condition called intrauterine growth restriction (IUGR); this means the baby is smaller than he should be for his age. If the baby is born underweight (less than $5\frac{1}{2}$ pounds), he will have more health problems than those born at more normal weights (over $5\frac{1}{2}$ pounds).

To help you watch your weight during pregnancy, the Institute of Medicine has published new weight-gain guidelines that are based on revised Body Mass Index (BMI) categories. Ask your health-care provider to help you set up weight-gain goals for each trimester based on these new recommendations. The weight-gain guidelines are as follows:

Prepregnancy BMI	Total Weight Gain Range
Underweight	28-40 lb.
Normal weight	25-35 lb.
Overweight	15-25 lb.
Obese	11-20 lb.

These numbers will change in special circumstances, especially if you are carrying multiples or are diabetic, but they are good guidelines for most pregnant women.

If you keep track of when you gain weight during pregnancy, you should be able to tell whether you're growing wider because your baby is developing or whether you're building new storage areas for fat. You should gain the least weight during the first trimester (only about a half pound each week) and steadily increase, gaining about a pound a week in the second trimester and about 1 to 2 pounds a week in Months 7 and 8. Many women gain very little or nothing in the ninth month. Using this as a guide, you'll know that you're taking in too many calories if you find yourself 10 pounds over your prepregnancy weight in the 10th week of pregnancy.

Cutting back on calories isn't really the answer to weight problems (bet that's a news flash) because all calories are not created equal. You would be doing your body a favor if you gave up the 100 calories in 10 potato chips, but you would take away needed nutrients if you gave up the 100 calories in a baked potato. It's empty calories you want to eliminate. The calories in chocolate bars, salty fast-food fries, cookies and chips, and sugary desserts are the ones that have to go. Drop these from your diet and you can eat all the healthy food you want.

PREGNANCY FACTS

Your baby will probably weigh between 6 and 8 pounds at birth—so why do most women gain between 25 and 30 pounds during pregnancy? Here's the breakdown:

- 2–3 pounds of increased fluids in your body
- 4–6 pounds of stored fat, protein, and other nutrients to support you and your baby
- 3–4 pounds of increased blood volume
- 2 pounds for enlarged uterus
- 1–2 pounds for enlarged breasts
- 2 pounds of amniotic fluid
- 1 pound of placenta (the organ connecting you to your baby that supplies nutrients and carries away waste)
- 6–8 pounds for the baby

Drink Demons

Your baby needs a plentiful supply of fluids every day. The fluids in water, juices, ices, and soups are all vital for good health. But there are two kinds of drinks that are just plain bad for you: caffeinated drinks and alcohol.

Caffeine

I've heard it a million times: "I can't give up coffee—I'll never be able to stay awake!" I can't argue that the caffeine in coffee doesn't give a mental and physical boost—after all, it's a central nervous stimulant that excites the brain to keep it alert and awake. That's the upside. The downside is that caffeine is an addictive drug that passes quickly to the fetal bloodstream and stays there in higher concentrations than is found in the mother. Did you know that babies have been born addicted to caffeine? It's true.

Caffeine is found not only in coffee but also in other beverages and foods. It's in tea, sodas, chocolate, and coffee ice cream. But no matter where you get it, caffeine has nothing good to offer your baby. Caffeine is known to …

- Increase your heart rate and metabolism, causing stress on the fetus.
- Be a diuretic—that means it flushes nutrients necessary for fetal development (especially fluids, calcium, potassium, magnesium, and sodium) out of the body.

- Interfere with sound sleep.
- Increase feelings of anxiousness and nervousness.
- Reduce the body's ability to absorb iron.
- Cause temporary irregular heartbeat, rapid respiration, and tremors in the newborn.

So what do you think? Maybe it's time to use good foods, plenty of rest, and exercise to give your body what it needs to stay alert. Caffeine-containing foods and drinks just don't fit into a healthy pregnancy diet.

If you give up coffee or tea, it's best to do it slowly. If you go cold turkey, you'll suffer withdrawal symptoms such as severe headaches, irritability, fatigue, and nervousness. To avoid this, you have two options. First you can reduce the amount of caffeine you take in each day (by having only two cups of coffee instead of four, for example) and then gradually cut back until you're down to none. Second, you can start cutting your coffee or tea with decaffeinated substitutes. Use half decaf and half regular for a while and then gradually build up the amount of decaf until all caffeine is gone. If you're a big cola drinker, slowly switch to caffeine-free varieties or try fruit-flavored seltzers.

If you switch to decaffeinated drinks, you should know that they're not really "caffeine-free." Decaffeinated coffees and teas are about 97 percent caffeine-free. If you drink only a moderate amount each day, they should have no bad effect on your baby.

If you're a tea drinker, you might try switching to decaffeinated or herbal teas. But be careful with herbals. Brand-name teas sold in the supermarket are generally safe for pregnant women (look for "no caffeine" on the label). But you should probably stay away from strong teas brewed with fresh herb leaves that are used for medicinal purposes. Talk to your doctor before switching to any herbal tea.

Alcohol

The great debate over whether or not moderate use of alcohol is bad for the developing fetus rages on. Some physicians still recommend an alcoholic drink to calm Braxton Hicks contractions and to "relax"; others forbid even a sip. The fact is that too much alcohol is definitely bad for the fetus. No one argues with that, but defining the line between some alcohol and too much alcohol is an ongoing subject of debate.

Consider first what we know about drinking too much alcohol during pregnancy. Women who abuse alcohol during pregnancy by drinking three or more ounces of absolute alcohol a day (eight beers, one pint of whiskey, or one bottle of wine) have a 40 percent chance of giving birth to a baby afflicted with fetal alcohol syndrome (FAS). This is a condition that causes gross malformation, growth retardation, and permanent intellectual and psychomotor defects. FAS babies wear their mother's alcohol abuse in their appearance. They have a small head circumference, underdeveloped jawbones, low-set ears, abnormalities of the eyelids, and an underdeveloped bridge of the nose. In addition to these obvious signs, the majority of these babies also have bone and joint abnormalities, abnormal creases in the palms, cardiac defects, kidney abnormalities, and female genital abnormalities. One study found that children affected by FAS had an average IQ of 65, low enough to cause learning and psychological disorders throughout their lifetime.

Birth defects that are related to the mother's intake of alcohol but are not as severe as those seen in FAS are called fetal alcohol effects (FAE). These include mental retardation and minor congenital abnormalities of the skin, heart, urinary tract, and musculoskeletal system.

DADDY ALERT!

If your partner makes the decision to give up alcohol for the sake of your baby, guess what? That's right—you should, too. Watching you unwind with an evening cocktail will not only break down your partner's determination to do what's best for the baby, but it will also paint you as a selfish, insensitive you-know-what. Parenting is a partnership. Support your partner's decision to abstain by doing the same (when you are in her presence, at the very least!).

Even moderate drinking has been connected to birth problems. Researchers tell us that women who drink during pregnancy are much more likely to have a miscarriage, a stillbirth, or babies with a low birthweight. One study found that women who consumed as little as one drink twice a week had a significantly higher rate of miscarriage. Other new research shows that drinking in the last six months of pregnancy can increase the risk of leukemia in the baby. What a tragedy for these children when all of this heartache can be prevented.

If you think you've found the perfect solution to the alcohol problem in nonalcoholic beers and wines, think again. These beverages are not alcohol-free. They all contain some level of alcohol, and that alcohol will go straight to your baby. If you are in the habit of having a drink each day, you might be able to safely "trick" your senses by drinking an alcohol-free substitute in your favorite glass at the usual time. Try a virgin Bloody Mary (without the alcohol), sparkling cider or grape juice, or a juice spritzer (half juice, half seltzer). Get creative and enjoy.

No matter how you define "heavy," "moderate," or "light" drinking, the fact is that alcohol is a drug that is toxic to the fetus. When you drink, the alcohol enters the baby's bloodstream in about the same concentrations present in your own, but the fetus doesn't have the enzymes necessary to metabolize it. So your baby gets more alcohol out of every drink than you do. Because no safe level of alcohol intake has been established for pregnant women, the surgeon general advises that pregnant women should avoid all beverages, foods, and drugs that contain alcohol. (However, you do not have to avoid foods cooked with alcohol, because the alcohol content evaporates when heated. Any alcohol left over is present in such a small amount it will not harm you or a fetus.)

HEY MOM!

Alcohol use is the major cause of mental retardation and a leading cause of birth defects in the United States. If you have a problem giving up alcohol during your pregnancy, talk to your health-care provider right away. Now is a very good time to get the help you need.

Creating a healthful pregnancy diet that stays away from empty calories and foods that contain chemicals and drugs could be the best thing that ever happens to you. Not only will it make you feel good about giving your baby only the best, but it might also change your eating habits for the better forever.

The Least You Need to Know

- Do not eat any raw or undercooked animal product.
- If you're a junk food junkie, it's time to learn how to substitute healthful foods for empty calories.
- A lot of produce, fish, diet products, preserved foods, and "natural flavors" contain toxic chemicals that should be limited during a pregnancy.
- It's a good idea to substitute no- and low-fat products for high-fat foods, but don't get carried away and think these products don't contain calories that can also pack on the pounds.
- You are not eating for two. Approximately 300 additional calories a day is all you need to build a healthy baby.
- Give it up—caffeinated coffee, tea, colas, and candy, as well as alcohol, are all bad for you and your baby.

Chapter 16

Supplements and Medications

In This Chapter

- The value of vitamin and mineral supplements during pregnancy
- The risks and benefits of natural herbal remedies
- A look at the safety of over-the-counter medications for colds, flu, allergies, morning sickness, digestive problems, and sleep problems
- Information on prescription medications, specifically antibiotics, asthma medications, and tranquilizers

Your immune system is not as strong as usual during pregnancy. This can make you prone to more ailments, diseases, and physical discomfort during these nine months. This means you might be tempted to take more medication than usual during your pregnancy—but be careful. Everything you take, your baby takes, too. Although most medications are just fine for you, they might be harmful to a developing fetus. Throughout the pregnancy, you should try to stay away from any kind of medication; when you need drug therapy, take only what is recommended by your doctor (one who knows you are pregnant) and only when it's absolutely necessary.

In this chapter, you'll get the facts on vitamin and mineral supplements; natural herbal remedies; over-the-counter medications for pain, colds, flu, allergies, morning sickness, digestive problems, and sleep problems; and prescription medications such as antibiotics, asthma medications, and tranquilizers.

Vitamin and Mineral Supplements

Supplements are often used as insurance against an inadequate diet. If you have morning sickness and aren't keeping down much food, a vitamin and mineral supplement will fill in the nutritional gaps. If you can't break the junk food habit and fill yourself with empty calories, a vitamin/mineral supplement can make sure your baby isn't deprived of what he or she needs to grow. If you eat the same foods every day, a supplement will supply nutrients that might not be included in your narrow diet. For these and lots of other reasons, supplements are an important part of your pregnancy regimen, but not every supplement does the job of a prenatal vitamin.

HEY MOM!

If you forget to take your prenatal vitamin one day, don't double up and take two the next day. This overload of vitamins can be dangerous. Just take the regular dose the next day and then create some kind of routine that will help you remember to take the pill on schedule.

During pregnancy, you need an extra supply of certain vitamins and minerals, particularly calcium, folic acid, and iron. But to get these extra nutrients, you cannot take just any vitamin supplement. Too much of certain vitamins can be poisonous to your baby. Large doses of vitamin A, for example, can cause birth defects. Also, the quality and source of the supplement as well as the fillers and other ingredients in each tablet are unpredictable in many over-the-counter vitamins. Some calcium tablets, for example, are made from ground limestone, which can contain arsenic, an element poisonous to the fetus. It's risky during pregnancy to take any old daily vitamin pill you happen to have in your kitchen.

Most physicians prescribe special prenatal vitamins for their patients. These supplements are made to meet the very specific nutritional needs of pregnant women. If you have a prescription for these vitamins, that's all you need. Do not take any other vitamin or mineral supplement. The idea that if one pill is good, adding another will be better just doesn't work with vitamin supplements. Take only what your doctor prescribes. If your doctor has not prescribed a daily supplement, ask for guidance in choosing an over-the-counter variety.

If you have a severe case of morning sickness, you might find it hard to keep your vitamin down. In fact, some women complain that it's the vitamin that causes them to vomit each morning. If this happens to you, talk to your doctor. She might want to prescribe a different kind of supplement, or suggest that you take your vitamin at a different time of day, or she might look over your diet to make sure you're getting the basics, even if you can't keep the supplement down right now.

The Dangers and Benefits of Natural Remedies

Many women who stop taking medication during their pregnancy turn for relief to the "natural" medicine in *herbs*. These remedies are natural because they come from nature, but that doesn't make them safe. Herbs are drugs; they affect your body and your fetus the same way any medication might. Some are very powerful and can cause great harm (even miscarriage) to a fetus. They have also been known to cause diarrhea, vomiting, and heart palpitations. Venture into the "natural" area with care.

Herbs can be even riskier than medications prescribed or bought off the shelf. They are not tested for general safety. They are not tested and labeled for use in pregnancy. They are not necessarily manufactured under quality-control conditions. They are often not uniformly packaged—some might be very weak, others extremely potent. And many contain contaminants such as insect parts, pollens, molds, and even toxic substances such as lead or arsenic.

Although herbal preparations such as gingko biloba and ginseng are commonly used, there are no studies that tell us about their safety during pregnancy. They are not routinely recommended during this time; and if you take them, it will be at your own risk.

If you've given up caffeinated coffee or tea and you're looking for an herbal tea to switch to, see Chapter 15 for ways to make your own herbal teas. Some pregnant women find certain herbal teas to have medicinal value that allows them to avoid harsh medications. For example, peppermint tea is known to calm digestive distress and relieve the buildup of gas. And chamomile tea may calm the body and mind to allow for peaceful sleep.

In all cases, you should use herbs as you would any medicine: Get an okay from your doctor and use them sparingly.

Over-the-Counter Medications

Here's the rule to remember about the medications you can buy *over the counter* (OTC) without a prescription: Just because these medications are readily available and safe for you to use, it does not mean they are safe for your baby. Some of the remedies we all take without a second thought need to be okayed by your doctor before you can take them during your pregnancy—aspirin, cold remedies, yeast infection medications, preparations for digestive problems, and sleep aids, for example. Your doctor or a good pharmacist can weigh the risks and benefits and decide what is best for both you and the baby.

Painkillers

If you pop a few pain pills every time you feel a tension headache coming on or feel the twinge of a stiff muscle, you might have to break this habit very quickly now that you're pregnant.

Full-strength aspirin is not good for pregnant women—especially in the last three months. It might increase bleeding tendencies in the mother and in the fetus (which is especially dangerous for babies born prematurely). When taken late in pregnancy, aspirin might delay the onset of labor, reduce the strength and frequency of contractions, and increase the length of labor. Aspirin can also increase the risk of hemorrhage at delivery and cause bleeding problems in the newborn. That's an awful lot of damage for such a "safe" medication.

HEY MOM!

Sometimes a doctor might okay the use of aspirin by a pregnant patient. If an expectant mother suffers from severe rheumatoid arthritis, for example, and can't bear the pain, the doctor might decide that the risk of taking aspirin is worth the benefits it gives the mother. This is the kind of call your doctor can help you make.

In addition to aspirin, there is a long list of over-the-counter pain medications that you should avoid because they contain both aspirin and caffeine (which, as explained in Chapter 15, is also bad for the fetus). Popular ones include: Anacin Analgesic Tablets, Cope, Excedrin Extra Strength, and Vanquish Analgesic Caplets.

HEY MOM!

Before you open a bottle of pills, try a few other remedies first. A neck massage and a nap are sometimes good for headaches. Body aches often ease with a massage and a warm bath. The pain of varicose veins can be relieved by putting your feet up and by wearing support hose. And many body discomforts in general can be zapped with the relaxation exercises explained in Chapter 18.

Another type of pain reliever to avoid during pregnancy is the nonsteroidal anti-inflammatory drug (NSAID). It includes ibuprofen (found in Motrin, Advil, Motrin IB, and Nuprin) and naproxen (found in Aleve, Anaprox, and Naprosyn). These drugs are relatively new on the pain-relief scene and not too much is known about their effect on pregnancy. It is thought that if used late in a pregnancy, NSAIDs can cause problems similar to the ones caused by aspirin. Unless your doctor says differently, it's best to avoid these pain relievers in the last three months of pregnancy.

Acetaminophen (the pain-relieving ingredient in products such as Tylenol and Datril) is the best choice for pain relief during pregnancy—but use it with caution. A new study suggests that pregnant women in their second and third trimesters might want to limit their use of products containing acetaminophen. In a study of more than 9,000 pregnant women, researchers found that frequent use of the painkiller acetaminophen—also known as paracetamol—after the 20th week of pregnancy might increase the risk of the babies wheezing as young children. Women who took acetaminophen daily or most days doubled the risk of their children beginning to wheeze when they were 3½ years old. Heavy use of aspirin was also associated with a higher risk of wheeze, but only in children under six months old. The researchers recommend that if painkillers are needed, expectant mothers should still take acetaminophen rather than aspirin, but they should not use it every day.

Sniffles and Sneezes

A bad head and chest cold, a seasonal allergy attack, or the flu during pregnancy can make you miserable—but be careful about taking over-the-counter remedies. Some cough syrups, antihistamines, and decongestants can be bad for the fetus (especially early in the pregnancy).

Many cold medicines contain alcohol. As explained in Chapter 15, alcohol is very bad for the developing baby. Some medications contain as much alcohol as a four-ounce glass of wine. They also might contain aspirin, which is bad for the baby, for the reasons explained earlier in this chapter.

When you're so stuffed up you can't breathe, a good nasal spray is a gift from heaven. But when you're pregnant, even a nasal spray can be a problem. Many contain oxymetazoline. This compound clears the sinuses by tightening the small blood vessels of the nasal passages. Unfortunately, it also has the potential to tighten the arteries leading to the uterus. If this happens, the flow of blood and oxygen to the fetus is reduced. Although the risk is small, it is best to stay away from these remedies. Watch out for oxymetazoline in nasal sprays such as all Afrin products, Coricidin Decongestant Nasal Mist, Dristan Long Lasting Nasal Spray, Duration 12 Hour Nasal Spray, Neo-Synephrine 12 Hour Nasal Spray, and Vicks Sinex Long-Acting Decongestant.

Over-the-counter cold and allergy medications in the same class as oxymetazoline often contain other compounds that do not tighten arteries. All of these are considered safe during pregnancy, when used in the proper dose under a physician's supervision. They include Actifed, Alka-Seltzer Plus Cold Medicine, Allerest Allergy Tablets and Sinus Pain Formula, A.R.M. Allergy Relief Medicine Caplets,

Benadryl Decongestant, Contac, Dimetapp, Doricidin, Maximum Strength Dristan, Robitussin-CF, Sudafed, Triaminic, Sinus Excedrin Analgesic, Sinutab, Tylenol Allergy Sinus Medication, Tylenol Cold Medicine, Vicks Formula 44D Decongestant, and Vicks NyQuil Nighttime Cold Medicine.

Some allergies are controlled by a series of injections of allergens (substances to which a person is allergic) to build up resistance. You should not start allergy shots during your pregnancy; there's no telling what kind of reaction you'll have initially. But if you have been getting allergy shots before your pregnancy, it is probably safe to continue them during the pregnancy under certain conditions:

- Make sure your allergist knows you are pregnant.
- The smallest amount possible of the allergen should be given in the first trimester.

As a bonus, some allergists believe that allergy injections during pregnancy can give the baby resistance to that particular allergen later in life. Talk to your prenatal doctor and your allergist about what is best for you.

Are you prone to the flu? Do you worry about getting the flu during your pregnancy? If so, ask your doctor about getting a flu vaccine (some do not advise it in the first trimester). The Centers for Disease Control recommend getting a flu shot if you'll be in your third trimester during the flu season (mid-November to mid-March). Because the vaccine can make you achy and feverish, however, you must talk to your doctor before getting the shot.

If you get the flu during your pregnancy, you'll feel miserable just like everybody else who gets the flu—maybe a little more so, because it's still not a good idea to load yourself up with symptom-relief medications. Tylenol is good for fever and body aches, but stay away from all the other stuff sold specifically for flu symptoms. Many of them contain alcohol and other ingredients that are bad for the baby.

There are many natural remedies for cold, flu, and allergy symptoms that you can try before you reach for the medicine bottle. If you're all stuffed up and/or have a sore throat, use a humidifier to add moisture to the air. Sleep with two pillows so your head is slightly raised and the excess mucus can drain down your throat. Drink hot broth to help open clogged sinuses. Rest—the simplest solution might be the most effective. Eat well; your body needs all the energy it can get to fight off a cold naturally.

Relief from Morning Sickness

When you've grazed on bland snacks for weeks and have had it with sucking on lemons and pushing on acupressure points to stop your morning sickness, all with no relief, your doctor might suggest that you try medication to calm your stomach. This is definitely a case where allowing you to dehydrate from frequent vomiting is a great deal worse than the cure. Your doctor might suggest the following remedies:

- **Vitamin B_6.** This nonprescription vitamin has a strong reputation for calming the queasy stomach of morning sickness.
- **Ginger.** Yep, the same stuff used to spice up ginger snap cookies and Asian dishes is a proven remedy for easing nausea. Talk to your doctor about adding the root to your diet or taking it as a supplement.
- **An antihistamine.** This nonprescription drug is found in many cold and sleep remedies. Popular brands include Dramamine (the motion-sickness medication) and Benadryl (often used for allergies). Both have been proven to be safe during pregnancy.

If these medications still don't calm the vomiting of morning sickness, your physician might choose to use a stronger remedy. You must not ignore extreme morning sickness, because it causes complications such as weight loss and mineral and body fluid loss.

Digestive Problems

All pregnant women quickly find out that a tiny little fetus can cause an awful lot of upset in the digestive tract. Everything from heartburn to constipation can be blamed on the body changes of pregnancy. If these troubles persist, your doctor might approve the use of certain medications that will bring relief. But not all medications for digestive problems are safe for your baby, so be sure to ask before you buy.

Heartburn and indigestion are badges of expectant motherhood; few can escape them during pregnancy. If you can live with the occasional discomfort, it's best to stay away from medications altogether. But if you're suffering week after week, talk to your doctor. He or she will recommend an antacid that's best for you—not all are safe.

Popular antacids such Maalox, Mylicon, Milk of Magnesia, Gelusil, Di-Gel, Tums, and Rolaids are all safe to take during pregnancy. (Some have the added bonus of containing compounds that will relieve excess gas.) Others, however, should be avoided: Alka-Seltzer, for example, is not recommended because it contains aspirin. Alka-Mint and Alka-Seltzer Advanced formula, however, are generally safe to use because they do not contain aspirin. Pepto-Bismol is on the "avoid" list; it contains an element closely related to aspirin and should not be used during pregnancy.

Newer antacids such as Pepsid, Zantac, and Tagamet have not been thoroughly tested for safety during pregnancy, but there does not seem to be a problem with their use and there have been no reports of fetal harm. Ask your doctor before you use one of these antacids.

If you're pregnant, you might be constipated also—for some women, the two just go together. If you haven't had a bowel movement for days and you're in pain, ask your doctor about using a stool softener or laxative. These medications will soften your stools so they pass easily and relieve the pressure on your bowel. Using a stool softener or laxative is good in an emergency, but don't get into the laxative habit. If you're not careful, you can "train" your bowels to need the laxative in order to work normally. After you get relief, keep your bowels in shape naturally: Drink lots of water; eat high-fiber foods, such as fruits and vegetables; and exercise.

When you have diarrhea, you want relief. Diarrhea ties you to your house; it tires you out, and it flushes fluids and nutrients out of your body. Relief is easily found in over-the-counter medications, such as Kaopectate or Imodium A-D. Both are safe to take when you're expecting.

Sleep Aids

In the first three months of pregnancy, a woman can sleep anywhere, anytime. How ironic that later in pregnancy, she sometimes can't sleep at all! When you're losing sleep because you are anxious about having a baby, or your legs ache, or the baby kicks and keeps you up, or because of 100 possible pregnancy-related reasons, you might be tempted to take a sleeping pill. You should think again and then talk to your doctor.

Most OTC sleeping pills contain antihistamines, which, in addition to clearing your sinuses, depress your central nervous system. These include Excedrin P.M., Sominex, Sleep-Eze, and Unisom. Only Unisom contains a type of antihistamine that is considered relatively safe to use during pregnancy. When used infrequently and in the right dose, Unisom should not affect your baby.

Whether pregnant or not, you should not use sleeping pills more than a few nights in a row. A side effect of antihistamines is a mental slowdown that can make it difficult to concentrate, focus, or drive a car the morning after. These OTC drugs are usually effective for only mild, temporary forms of insomnia. Because they work quickly but don't last very long, these products work only to help you fall asleep. They can't help with frequent nighttime awakenings. If you are plagued by insomnia during your pregnancy, talk to your doctor before you try to medicate yourself to sleep.

Prescription Drugs

During your pregnancy, your doctor will be very careful to prescribe medication only when a drug is safe for the fetus or when it is absolutely necessary for your own health. For your own knowledge, it's interesting to look at the kind of information the doctor has to consider before prescribing even the most common medications.

PREGNANCY FACTS

The United States Food and Drug Administration (FDA) has established five categories for drugs and medications based on how they affect fetal development. (You will find this category label on the package insert of all medications.)

You can find the pregnancy label for all drugs that have been assigned a category (not all drugs have this label) in a reference book (held by most public libraries): the *Physician's Desk Reference* (PDR). Your doctor is very familiar with these categories and will consider them every time he or she writes a prescription.

Antibiotics

Ailments such as urinary tract and respiratory infections, which are common in pregnancy, often require treatment with an antibiotic. Because your doctor knows that all antibiotics are not alike, choosing just the right one is important for the health of the fetus. The ones your doctor will stay away from include ...

- A class of antibiotic called aminoglycosides, which can cause damage to the auditory nerve (responsible for hearing) of the fetus.
- A class called tetracycline, which can cause discoloration of baby teeth, underdevelopment of tooth enamel, and a decrease in the growth of long bones.
- A class called chloramphenicol, which can cause a potentially fatal suppression of blood cell formation in the bone marrow.

Your doctor might be especially careful about prescribing antibiotics in view of a new study recently released that found that children exposed to infection and antibiotics while in the womb have an increased risk of developing asthma, eczema, and hay fever.

Of all the antibiotics prescribed, penicillin is one of the safest for use during pregnancy. (This also includes synthetic penicillin, such as ampicillin and amoxicillin.) Your doctor knows this and will choose the best one for you.

Asthma Medications

If you have a history of asthma, you will need a little extra attention during your pregnancy because an asthma attack can reduce the amount of oxygen the fetus receives (causing a condition called fetal hypoxia). But with close medical supervision and quick response to attacks, asthmatics can certainly expect to have a safe pregnancy and a normal delivery.

Right at the start of your pregnancy, talk to your doctor about your asthma medication. The job of asthma medications is to relax the muscles of the respiratory tract so you can breathe easily; some asthma medications also relax the muscles of the uterus, which can slow or stop the contractions necessary for labor. Some asthma medications have little effect on the fetus; others, however, affect the health of the fetus by raising the pregnant woman's blood pressure and sugar and sodium (salt) levels. Don't assume your asthma medication is just fine—some medications are definitely safer than others during pregnancy.

Most nasal sprays and inhalation aerosol sprays are rapidly effective and considered safe in moderation during pregnancy. Recommended sprays that contain corticosteroids include Beclovent, Beconase, Vancenase, and Vanceril. Safe bronchodilators contain albuterol. (Check the bottle for the active ingredients.)

HEY MOM!

If you suffer from asthma, you might notice an increase in attacks in the last trimester. This is the time when the enlarged uterus crowds into the lung area and can make breathing difficult, even for those who don't have asthma.

If nasal and inhalation sprays don't stop an acute asthmatic attack, your doctor might decide to use oral or intravenous corticosteroids. When this happens, your doctor will alert the pediatrician and newborn-care nurses to monitor your baby after delivery. Although these drugs are considered safe, they have been known, in rare instances, to cause temporary adrenal gland malfunction (this affects the kidneys) in the newborn. If necessary, all precautions will be taken to treat your baby after delivery.

Your doctor knows which asthma medications are not recommended during pregnancy. The inhaler Azmacort, for example, contains a drug called triamcinolone, which is best avoided during pregnancy. Medications containing cortisone are also not recommended.

After your doctor has approved a pill or inhaler, don't hesitate to use it when you need it. Any negative effect on the fetus from the medication is less dangerous than the effect of oxygen deprivation in the mother, caused by an untreated asthma attack.

Tranquilizers

Many women take prescription tranquilizers on a daily basis to fend off tension and anxiety. When these women become pregnant, they must tell their maternity doctor and the doctor who prescribed the drugs. Many minor tranquilizers are dangerous to the fetus, so you can imagine how much worse the stronger ones are. Benzodiapepines (such as Valium, Librium, Ativan, and Xanax), for example, should be strictly avoided. These drugs can cause major problems for the fetus.

If you're taking tranquilizers, tell your maternity doctor. It's a dangerous mistake to hide this fact even if you are worried that spilling the beans will mean you can't take these drugs. What it really means is that you can talk to someone who will tell you honestly what will happen if your baby is exposed to the tranquilizer you're taking. If your present prescription is for a drug that is bad for your baby, your maternity doctor might change it to a safer one (such as Buspar or Prozac). Isn't that better?

If you suffer from a severe mental disorder (manic-depression, for example), speak up! Tell your maternity physician exactly what you take for your problem. There are mountains of medications available for the treatment of psychiatric disorders; together the two of you can find a medication that is best for you and your baby.

You have to trust your health-care provider and build an honest relationship. He can't keep you and your baby healthy if he doesn't know what medications you take and what diseases and disorders you have. Right from the start, tell your doctor about every natural, over-the-counter, or prescription medication you take and together you can choose the ones that are the safest to use during pregnancy.

Your doctor knows exactly what prescription medications you can and cannot have during your pregnancy. You will have a problem with prescription drugs only if you receive them from someone other than the doctor handling your pregnancy. For example, if you visit your primary-care physician for a bad head cold and don't tell him that you're pregnant, he might prescribe something that could harm your baby, especially if you're in the early months of pregnancy. The growing trend to order prescription medications by mail or online is even worse. When this happens, no one is keeping track of what is bad for a pregnant woman or which medications might interact and cause negative side effects. The habit of using other people's prescriptions is worse yet. For example, if you take an unused medication prescribed for your partner, you're asking for trouble.

The key to the safe use of prescription drugs is: (1) use only drugs prescribed by a physician who knows you are pregnant, and (2) use them only when absolutely necessary.

The Least You Need to Know

- Take the vitamin and mineral supplement that your doctor prescribes; it is very important to the health and development of your baby.
- Use "natural" herbal remedies cautiously. They are unregulated and many are known to be dangerous to the fetus.
- Unless absolutely necessary, do not use over-the-counter medications to relieve simple discomforts. If necessary, talk to your doctor about medications that are safe for pregnant women.
- Prescription medications must be carefully monitored and supervised by your maternity physician. Be sure to tell him about any other medications you are taking, even if another doctor has prescribed them. Some antibiotics, asthma medications, and tranquilizers are safe for expectant mothers, others are not.

Environmental Hazards, Smoking, and Illicit Drugs

Chapter 17

In This Chapter

- Chemical pesticides that can harm your baby
- Potential harm from mosquito bites
- Good and bad household cleansers
- Advice on dealing with smoggy, dirty air
- The reasons that your microwave can't hurt you, but x-rays can
- The risks of smoking and illicit drugs

This chapter on environmental toxins and recreational drugs isn't meant to give you more things to worry about; it's here to give you information so that you don't have to worry. If you know in advance that you shouldn't be breathing in turpentine fumes, for example, you won't have to spend the rest of your pregnancy wondering whether the chemicals you used to clean the paintbrushes last week were bad for the baby. This chapter will look at some *teratogens*, household and environmental toxins that can cause birth defects. Knowing what to stay away from and what's safe will give you less to worry about.

GREEN FROM THE START

The Environmental Working Group sponsored a study of the chemicals found in the umbilical cord blood of 10 babies in U.S. hospitals. Although this is a small preliminary study, the results give us all reason to be aware and cautious of environmental toxins during pregnancy. Researchers found a total of 287 different industrial chemicals (including mercury, fire retardants, and pesticides) circulating through the body of newborns. You can see the entire report at ww.ewg.org/reports/bodyburden2/execsumm.php.

Pesticides

The word *pesticide* applies to any of 600 different chemicals used to kill insects, weeds, and fungi on plants. Almost all of them are harmful to a developing fetus when there is direct and prolonged exposure. Pesticides are known for causing birth defects, particularly limb deformities. If you work on a farm that is sprayed continually with pesticides, or if you are the person who sprays pesticides in homes, on lawns, or on fields, your baby is at risk. You should ask for reassignment or take an early leave from your job and talk to your doctor. But if you are not directly in the line of fire on a daily basis, the following information about pesticides should give you reasons to be cautious—but not to panic.

Most of us can avoid pesticides if we try. Here are a few tips:

- **Plan ahead.** Buy a nontoxic pest control product now *before* you need it. (Did you know that soapy water can kill ants on contact?)
- **If you must have your house sprayed with a pesticide, close all closets and doors to keep the spray off clothes, dishes, and foods.** Stay out of the house for at least 24 hours.
- **If you have your home sprayed routinely for bugs, stop the service.** You can use Combat-type traps to keep roaches and ants under control safely.
- **If you use pesticides on the plants in your garden, use gloves and a disposable facemask.** It's even better to switch to natural methods of pest control. Add ladybugs to your garden (they eat bad bugs) or spray a natural, biodegradable insecticidal soap on your plants. You can hand-pick bugs and drop them in a container of kerosene, as well.
- **Leave your lawn alone.** This is the year you might skip fertilizing and weed killing. Pull weeds by hand if they really bother you.
- **Wash all produce thoroughly.** Peel off apple and cucumber skins. (See Chapter 15 for information on organic produce.)

GREEN FROM THE START

The potted plants that add beauty and warmth to your home keep you and your baby healthy, too. Green plants take toxic fumes out of the air and replace them with pure oxygen. The more plants, the better!

If you breathe in pesticides by accident, don't get upset. Brief, occasional exposure is unlikely to harm your baby. The real danger is in direct exposure over a long period of time. If you have questions about the use or danger of pesticides, call the National Pesticide Information Center at 1-800-858-7378 or visit its website at www.npic.orst.edu.

Bug Bites

The Centers for Disease Control and Prevention recently reported a case of West Nile Virus transmitted from a pregnant woman to her fetus. Because West Nile Virus is spread through the bites of infected mosquitoes, you should take precautions to reduce your risk of being bit in the warm weather when mosquitoes are abundant. Here are some tips from the Centers for Disease Control:

- Apply insect repellent containing DEET (N,N-diethyl-meta-toluamide) when you're outdoors. The Environmental Protection Agency says that DEET is safe for use by pregnant women. (However, do not use DEET repellent with a sunscreen product. Sunscreens cause increased skin absorption and allow your body to take in three times as much pesticide if it is applied at the same time.)
- When possible, wear long-sleeved clothes and long pants treated with DEET, because mosquitoes can bite through thin clothing.
- Consider staying indoors at dawn and in the early evening, which are peak times when mosquitoes are around and biting.
- Install or repair window and door screens so that mosquitoes cannot get indoors.
- To avoid helping mosquitoes breed in your environment, drain standing water. Routinely empty water from flowerpots, pet bowls, clogged rain gutters, swimming pool covers, and other items that collect water.

Vitamin B and "ultrasonic" devices are *not* effective in preventing mosquito bites.

For more information about West Nile Virus and how to protect yourself, log on to the Centers for Disease Control's website at www.cdc.gov/ncidod/dvbid/westnile.

Cleaning Products

Wouldn't it be great if I were to say that you should not get on your knees and scrub anything during your pregnancy? I'd like to help you out here, but the truth is that there are now green cleaning products that really can't hurt you or your baby.

Companies such as Seventh Generation, Begley's Best, and Restore make 100 percent biodegradable cleaners that do not contain unnecessary ingredients such as artificial fragrances, antimicrobials, chlorine, coal dyes, or phosphates. These products are renewable, non-toxic, and biodegradable and are never tested on animals.

If you do use a conventional toxic cleanser, be sure to follow these cautionary guidelines:

- Wear gloves so the cleanser can't be absorbed through your skin.
- Your nose knows. If the smell of the cleanser is very strong, avoid inhaling it and open a few windows when you clean.
- Use pump spray cleaners rather than aerosol sprays; they are not so easily inhaled.
- Do not mix a product that contains ammonia with a product that is chlorine-based. This is a toxic combination that can be deadly. In other words, don't mix bleach with an ammonia cleanser, or an abrasive cleanser that contains bleach (Comet or Ajax, for example) with a tub cleaner that contains ammonia. Read labels and be very careful.
- Avoid products with toxic fumes, such as oven cleansers and some tub and tile cleaners. (At least that's a couple of jobs you won't have to do for a while.)

Using household cleansers safely requires no more than common sense. If the fumes are strong, or if they make you queasy, stay away.

GREEN FROM THE START

The Environmental Working Group tested popular cleaning supplies to evaluate the safety levels of their ingredients. You can read the results by visiting www.ewg.org and searching "green cleaning supplies."

Interior Decorating

If you get the urge to start remodeling while you're waiting for your baby, think about the chemicals you'll be working with first and use them safely.

Paint

Go ahead—paint the nursery any color you want, as long as you keep the windows open and avoid oil- and lead-based paints manufactured before 1990 and those that contain high levels of volatile organic compounds (VOCs). Until it was banned in 1990 by the Federal Drug Administration, mercury was often added to latex paints as a preservative. Some of these paints are still around, so it's best not to use old paints left in your parent's garage. Ask a knowledgeable salesperson if the paint you want to buy contains any mercury. The fetus is extremely sensitive to the fumes of mercury-laced paint. In extreme cases of mercury poisoning, effects on the newborn include mental retardation, tremors, seizures, and kidney and liver diseases.

As the green movement moves into the home decorating arena, you have more options than ever before in your choice of paints with reduced toxic emissions. Here are three types of paint now readily available:

- **Low-VOC paints.** These water-based paints eliminate petroleum-based solvents. They contain no or very low levels of heavy metals and formaldehyde.
- **VOC-free paints.** Also called zero-VOC paints, these contain 5 grams per liter or less of VOCs. They are a step better for the air quality in your baby's nursery than low-VOC paints.
- **Natural or milk paint.** Natural paints are made from natural substances such as balsam, chalk, clay, citrus, and talcum. They are petroleum-free, give off almost no smell, and are very low in VOCs. Odorless milk paints are made with milk protein or casein and lime and are colored with earth pigments.

These paints are sold in many hardware stores or online at sites such as www.safepaint.net and www.ecosorganicpaints.com.

If the label on a spray paint can says "M-butyl ketone" or "MBK," don't use it. If inhaled, this chemical can cause neurological (that is, nerve-related) damage to your baby.

You should also avoid breathing in the fumes from polyurethane paints and coatings that give such a nice shine to woodwork and hardwood floors. Definitely don't apply these materials in spray form and keep all windows open for at least 24 hours after the job is done. If you're putting a topcoat on movable pieces, such as furniture, it's best to do the job outside in the open air.

When it's time to clean paintbrushes, stay away from turpentine and liquid paint removers. The fumes are strong and toxic.

Remodeling

Feel like getting really dirty and scraping off some old paint, taking down ugly wallpaper, or even tearing down walls? You'd better check for lead paint on those walls first. Almost all houses built before 1950 have lead paint on the walls. If you start stirring it up now, you might expose yourself—and your baby—to high levels of lead dust and risk lead poisoning. Although this exposure might give you absolutely no problem, it is very bad for your baby. High levels of lead exposure throughout pregnancy have led to infant death, premature birth, low birthweights, deformities, and lower intellect. Even low levels of lead exposure during pregnancy are associated with lower IQ scores, poor memory, and poor academic achievement. Find out how old the paint is before you scrape.

Smog, Smoke, and Dirty Air

Cars, trucks, furnaces, and industrial machinery all spew poisonous carbon monoxide into the air. If you breathe in a lot of second-hand smoke from cigarettes and cigars, you're also taking in carbon monoxide. Carbon monoxide is a deadly, odorless gas that causes sudden death at high levels of concentration. Obviously, carbon monoxide is not good for your growing baby.

When carbon monoxide enters the body, it interferes with the blood's ability to bring oxygen to all body parts and organs. Without oxygen, the body soon shuts down. In the fetus, carbon monoxide crosses the placenta and reduces the amount of oxygen that is delivered and circulated. This can cause *fetal growth retardation.*

Although carbon monoxide is dangerous, it's not necessary to start holding your breath every time you walk outside. A few commonsense precautions will keep your baby perfectly healthy:

- Check your furnace for carbon monoxide leaks and get a carbon monoxide detector for your house.
- Make sure wood-burning stoves, fireplaces, gas heaters, gas stoves, and space heaters are all working properly. All of them can leak carbon monoxide.
- Check the exhaust system in your car for leaks. Don't start the car in the garage with the garage doors closed. Keep the car's air vents closed when you're in heavy traffic.
- Avoid jogging, running, walking, or cycling along roads with heavy traffic.
- Avoid smoke-filled rooms.
- Try to stay indoors on "smog alert" days.

Millions of healthy babies are born to mothers who live in smog-choked cities and who spend lots of time in smoke-filled rooms. But to be on the safe side, avoid plopping yourself in the middle of a smog-filled or smoky area.

Hair Dyes and Perms

It's hard enough to feel beautiful when you're pregnant, but then along comes the warning that hair dyes and permanents might be harmful to a fetus. This subject causes great debate among hairdressers, doctors, researchers, and expectant mothers. In the end, all we know is that not much is known about the effects of these beauty products on the fetus.

Certainly there are chemicals in hair dyes and permanent solutions that are toxic and known to cause cancer and genetic mutations. The question is, how much does it take to cause this damage? Studies on animals that show harm to the fetus have used doses 100 times higher than would ever be used on your own head. As the debate rages on, I think you can safely keep your hair dyed and permed if you use a bit of caution:

- Avoid perming or dying in the first three months of your pregnancy.
- Choose semipermanent dyes over permanent dyes. Better yet, stick with natural henna products.
- Wear gloves and open the windows if you apply the solution yourself.
- Chemicals are absorbed into the bloodstream through the scalp, not the hair itself, so it's probably safe to have your hair highlighted, frosted, painted, or streaked. These methods keep most of the dye away from the scalp.
- Choose non-toxic hair-color products that have been tested to be safe; safe products are listed in the Environmental Working Group's Skin Deep cosmetic safety database. You can access this information at www.cosmeticdatabase.com.

Radiation

There are two kinds of radiation exposure. The first is called nonionizing radiation, which comes from household appliances such as microwave ovens and TV sets. The second is ionizing radiation and it comes from x-rays.

Nonionizing Radiation

These days it is impossible to avoid the radiation that comes from common appliances and communication equipment, such as microwave ovens, radios, televisions, radar, high-voltage power lines, certain burglar alarms, long-distance telephone and telegraph transmissions, electric blankets, heated waterbeds, taxi dispatch lines, satellite communications towers, video display terminals (VDTs), automatic garage door openers, and electric toys. There's just no way to avoid most of this.

Some research on the effects of this kind of nonionizing radiation has raised a red flag on excessive exposure. High levels of nonionizing radiation in humans has been associated with (but not scientifically proven) to cause genetic damage, spontaneous abortion, and birth defects. But the tested levels have been far above what we are exposed to normally. You can sit 2 inches in front of your TV every day all day long during your pregnancy and not worry about radiation damage to your fetus. Still, better to err on the side of caution …

- Sit at least 5 feet away from the TV set when it's on.
- Stand at least 8 feet away and to the side when your microwave is running.
- Test for leaks in your microwave by putting a paper towel in the door and shutting it. You should not be able to pull the towel out of the door. If you can, the seals are worn and should be replaced.
- Avoid sitting near the back of a computer screen. Most radiation is emitted from the rear; so if your workstation puts you behind your colleague's screen, you might want to move. Keep in mind that extensive studies cannot find a definite link between working on a computer all day and birth defects.
- Although there is no evidence that copy machines are harmful to a fetus, be cautious and limit the amount of time you spend around these machines.

PREGNANCY FACTS

Indoor tanning salons darken the skin with a course of ultraviolet radiation. This radiation can cause skin cancer, premature wrinkling, sun plaques, pigment abnormalities, and eye damage, all of which are bad. If you don't mind getting any of the preceding, the good news is this: Indoor tanning will not hurt your baby!

The bottom line is this: Don't worry about radiation exposure from home appliances and communication equipment. The levels are so low, your baby will not be affected.

X-Rays

The ionizing radiation that enters the body through x-rays is the kind that is dangerous to the fetus. Permanent growth retardation, mental retardation, and birth defects are all possible if the fetus is exposed to high levels of ionizing radiation. Fortunately, x-rays are not something we are involuntarily subjected to. You know when you're getting x-rays, so you can act to avoid them or reduce the danger:

- Postpone any elective medical procedure that requires x-rays until after the birth of your baby.
- Tell all your doctors and your dentist that you are pregnant and do not want x-rays.
- If x-rays are absolutely vital, talk to the radiologist before the x-ray is taken. Explain that you are pregnant and need the most modern equipment, the lowest dose of radiation possible, the fewest number of x-rays possible, and a lead apron to protect all other areas of your body. These requests can drastically change the degree of radiation your body will be exposed to.
- If you are a medical or dental x-ray technician, radiologist, or nurse, you might need to take an early leave of absence from your job.

PREGNANCY FACTS

Flying in an airplane exposes you to high-energy cosmic radiation that is given off by the stars and sun. The amount of radiation you are exposed to depends on your location and altitude. The nearer the North or South Pole you fly and the higher you fly, the greater the level of radiation. Frequent flyers, flight attendants, and pregnant women have been warned that long, high-altitude flights (over the poles) can expose them to more radiation than the federal government currently recommends.

Toxic Arts and Crafts Supplies

Many craft, hobby, and art projects use materials that can be toxic to your baby. Sometimes you can tell they are dangerous because the package says so; because of their strong, offensive odor; or because the directions instruct you to use them only in a well-ventilated room. These are all clues that the product can be harmful. If you're not sure about a product, contact the manufacturer. Manufacturers are required to give you material safety data sheets that list the ingredients, possible hazards, and precautions to take when using a particular product. Many specifically note if the product is dangerous for pregnant women.

HEY MOM!

To check on the safety of an art supply, call the Arts, Crafts, and Theater Safety group in New York at 212-777-0062 (www.caseweb.com/acts).

In the meantime, look for safer substitutes. I warned house painters earlier to beware of wall paint in houses built before 1950; the artisan, too, has to be especially careful about lead exposure if she works with ceramics and glazes, jewelry making, print making, glassblowing, or stained glass. The fumes and fine dust from these items are easily inhaled. Whenever possible, substitute talc-free, premixed clay for clay in dry form. Use water-based, acrylic-based waterproofing products instead of ceramic glazes or copper enamels. For projects that use paint, inks, glue, and markers, substitute all with water-based products. If you are an artist, use liquid paints rather than powdered tempera colors; use oil pastels or dustless chalk rather than dusty pastels or chalks; use water-based paints rather than aerosol spray paints. Consider these changes a creative challenge and a responsible choice.

When you can't substitute a safer product, cover up to protect yourself:

- Wear protective clothing such as smocks and hats, and leave them in your work area when you're finished.
- Wear a disposable mask that covers the mouth and nose when working with powders, dusts, and fumes.
- Wear gloves to prevent chemicals from entering your bloodstream through your skin.
- Always keep a lid on powdered products and liquid solvents.
- Keep your work area clean; use a wet mop and vacuum often (don't sweep the floor or brush dust off the table).
- Keep the area well ventilated; open the windows and use ventilating fans.

Cigarettes and Illicit Drugs

Being a good parent means giving up bad habits that will harm your child. It means being totally responsible for another innocent human life. It means making sacrifices. If you are pregnant and smoke cigarettes or use illicit drugs, know you are endangering the health of your child and need to stop now.

Cigarettes

If you smoke cigarettes, you know what this section is going to say. You already know that smoking during pregnancy is not good for the baby. The message is out—everybody knows. The question is why are you still smoking? Maybe you don't really know just how bad smoking is, so here's the scoop:

When you smoke, your baby smokes—even more than you do, because his body is so small and the concentrations of smoke and nicotine are so much higher in his body than they are in yours. Here's what happens:

- Smoking removes oxygen from the bloodstream, reducing the amount your baby receives every time you smoke.
- Smoking decreases the amount of nutrients that are passed from mother to baby.
- Smoking brings carbon monoxide into the body, which further cuts down on the oxygen supply.

The result of these changes in your body can have many harmful effects on the baby. A few include …

- Fetal growth retardation.
- Low birthweight.
- Major birth problems.
- Placenta abnormalities.
- SIDS (sudden infant death syndrome).
- Long-term growth and intellectual development deficiencies.
- Behavioral problems.

Aren't these enough reasons to quit? The good news is that the smoking you've done before your pregnancy will not harm a developing fetus. The additional good news is that stopping smoking at any time during the pregnancy will benefit the baby in some way. Obviously, the best plan is to quit smoking right from the start of the pregnancy—this gives the baby the full advantage of healthy development. But even if a woman quits in her last month, the benefits to the baby and to herself are notable. Women who smoke commonly have difficult labors; getting the smoke and nicotine out of the system completely before labor begins can improve the ease of delivery. It also allows for a better oxygen supply to the baby, which is needed during delivery.

DADDY ALERT!

You don't have a choice. If you're a smoker, now is the time to stop. The second-hand smoke your partner takes in from your cigarettes or cigars can be very harmful to your baby's health. Even after the baby arrives, the smoke in the house that he or she will inhale is very damaging. If you can't quit cold turkey, smoke outside, at the very least, far away from your partner.

Nicotine is an addictive drug that is not easy to give up. Your doctor will be very happy to help you find a program that will support you in your gallant effort. To help you remember why you're giving up this habit and to help you drop the next cigarette you pick up, close your eyes and imagine this scene: Your adorable, innocent, healthy baby is in your arms smiling up at you. You take a lit cigarette, put it in her mouth and pinch her nose, forcing her to inhale. Can you imagine doing that? It sounds unimaginably cruel, but that's exactly what you'll be doing if you put a cigarette in your mouth while you're carrying your baby—you make her smoke, too.

The Marijuana Mistake

Yes, I know all about the medicinal powers of marijuana when prescribed by a physician for a preexisting condition. In this case, a pregnant woman would need to talk with her physicians about the risks and benefits of this therapy during pregnancy. The decision to continue therapeutic use of marijuana is a personal one. Unless your doctor has prescribed marijuana for a preexisting condition, however, it is not good for your developing baby. Many studies on the chief ingredient in marijuana (called tetra-hydrocannabinal, THC) in animals repeatedly find a significantly higher rate of miscarriage, stillbirth, and infant death when it is used during pregnancy. Exactly why this happens is unknown, but THC passes easily from the mother's blood to her baby's, which might cause the placenta to function abnormally. Other studies have found that marijuana affects the labor and delivery process. Some studies show a longer and more difficult labor in women who smoke marijuana; others found the drug caused quick and unexpected deliveries by increasing the strength and frequency of uterine contractions. Either way, apparently, marijuana can change the natural progress of labor and delivery.

All the consequences of cigarette smoking (listed previously), which include low birthweight and reduced intelligence, are also found in the children of women who smoke marijuana.

HEY MOM!

Take a tip from the surgeon general of the United States. He has warned that marijuana use by a pregnant woman might be hazardous to the health of her baby. (But don't worry about the joints you smoked years ago; they will have no effect on the health of your baby now!)

Narcotics: Playing with Fire

This one is simple to remember: All narcotics are harmful to the developing fetus. Every known illegal "recreational" narcotic (including crack/cocaine, heroin, methadone, LSD, and PCP) can cause catastrophic damage to a fetus.

It would take an entire book to detail the damage that all recreational narcotics can have on a developing fetus. To get an idea of how destructive they are, you can think of just about anything that can go wrong—birth defects, miscarriage, stillbirth, placenta abnormalities, fetal distress, hypertension, and low birthweight—and know that these drugs can cause it. The cells of your developing fetus cannot grow as they should when they are exposed to narcotics.

If you use illicit narcotics for occasional fun, the fun is over. You must stop during your pregnancy. If you are hooked on any of these drugs, tell your health-care provider immediately. The shame isn't in your addiction; it's in letting your baby down by keeping quiet. You can also call the National Institute on Drug Abuse (1-800-662-HELP) for information and referrals to addiction support programs.

PREGNANCY FACTS

Cocaine quickly passes from the mother's bloodstream to the fetus within minutes and it remains in the amniotic fluid up to five days. By swallowing this amniotic fluid (which all babies do, in utero), the fetus takes in additional amounts over that period. One hit for the mother feeds the fetus for almost a week! In several states, it has been proposed that women who take crack/cocaine during pregnancy be sent to jail on charges of child abuse or child endangerment. Most judges, however, prefer to send these women to drug counseling.

This chapter makes it seem like the world is a dangerous place to grow a child. It's not really—if you use caution and common sense. It just makes sense to stay away from pesticides; oven cleansers; lead paint; smoggy, dirty air; toxic art supplies; and recreational drugs such as nicotine, marijuana, and cocaine.

The Least You Need to Know

- The West Nile Virus can be transmitted from a pregnant woman to her fetus.
- Non-toxic household cleansers are perfectly safe for use by pregnant women. But all interior decorating should be done with water-based paints only. Avoid turpentine; liquid solvents; and oil-, lead-, and mercury-laced paints.
- Cars, furnaces, and cigarette smoke fill the air with carbon monoxide, which, at high levels, can be harmful to the fetus. Also, be cautious about dying or perming your hair in the first three months of pregnancy.
- At home, radiation from the television, microwave oven, radio, electric blankets, computers, and so on, is not harmful to the fetus.
- X-rays can cause problems in a pregnancy. They should be avoided or, when absolutely necessary, limited in dose and number. Many craft, hobby, and art materials also contain toxins that can be hazardous to a fetus.
- The fun is over with recreational drugs. Your baby-in-progress can be severely affected by cigarette smoking, marijuana, and narcotics such as crack/cocaine, heroin, LSD, and PCP.

Part 4

Day to Day

Although pregnancy tends to take over every aspect of daily existence, life does go on in the small moments from day to day.

Exercise is still very important. If you are already an exerciser, don't stop now. This part will tell you how to adjust your regimen for the safety and health of your baby. If you're not an exerciser, now is a great time to start—slowly. If you can get your muscles in shape in the nine months before delivery, you'll have a much easier time, and your body will snap back into shape much faster afterward.

If you're a working woman and plan to stay on the job every day, you'll need a little guidance to keep yourself feeling alert and healthy. This part will give you time-tested tips and advice that will keep you going when the pregnancy gets tough.

The simple things you often take for granted can suddenly become full of pitfalls when you're pregnant. Read on to find out how lovemaking, travel, sleeping, and bathing can bring you pleasure and relaxation, if you make a few adjustments for the little passenger inside.

Chapter 18
Exercise

In This Chapter

- The benefits of prenatal exercise
- How pregnancy changes the way you move
- The downside of exercise, things to avoid, and signs of danger
- Moves for beginning exercisers, advice for advanced exercisers, and simple exercises for all pregnant women
- Group exercise programs
- Recommended relaxation exercises

At the turn of the twentieth century, pregnancy was considered an illness. Upper-class women were ordered to rest in bed until the baby arrived. All physical activity was stopped, and good health was maintained by sitting still. Things have sure changed! Today pregnant women are encouraged to be active, to exercise, and to keep their bodies strong and healthy. No pampering for you—it's off your duff and into your workout clothes.

Why Exercise?

Your body is under a lot of strain during pregnancy. The bones, muscles, joints, and organs are all struggling to keep up with the demands of your growing baby. Your body could sure use some help. That's where exercise comes in. It gives you all the benefits it gives to any exerciser, and then some because you're pregnant.

We know that exercising during pregnancy offers you the same benefits as exercising at any time, including …

- Improved muscle strength
- Improved blood circulation
- Reduced fatigue, more energy
- Improved mood and emotional well-being
- Less weight gain

When you exercise during pregnancy, you get even more, including ...

- Increased muscle strength and tone to help you carry the extra weight of your baby
- Less swelling of legs, feet, hands, and face
- Relief from constipation
- Less physical discomfort from achy legs and back
- Increased strength and stamina to get through the demands of labor and delivery (the average labor requires stamina equal to jogging 12 miles!)
- An easier time getting back into physical shape after delivery

For all these reasons, this is a great time to get off the couch and exercise!

HEY MOM!

The American College of Obstetricians and Gynecologists has revised its guidelines about exercise for pregnant women and new moms. Among other things, the new ACOG guidelines eliminated a specific heart rate and duration restriction for moms-to-be. This now allows greater exercise intensity than was previously recommended.

How Pregnancy Affects Exercise

Even if you're a seasoned athlete, your body will react differently to exercise when you are pregnant. Watch for these changes:

- Balance fails after 20 weeks as your abdomen throws off your center of gravity, making you more susceptible to falls. This is something to remember if you participate in activities such as jogging or tennis.

- As the growing uterus crowds the lungs, you'll find that you lose your breath much sooner during exercise. Working out harder and longer won't change this fact.
- Your heart naturally beats faster during pregnancy. This means you won't have to exercise as vigorously to reach your target rate. It also means you can overdo it very easily.
- Blood volume increases during pregnancy, but more blood is channeled to internal organs (such as the uterus) and less to the muscles. This can make muscles tire more quickly.
- The hormone called relaxin relaxes the pelvic joints in preparation for childbirth; it also loosens all ligaments and joints, making you more prone to sprains and falls.

Two other things that can change the way you exercise during pregnancy are increased blood flow and a higher metabolic rate. This means you'll feel warmer than usual when you exercise and might become overheated sooner than you expect. This can be dangerous. Some animal studies suggest that overheating can cause birth defects. To be on the safe side, the American College of Obstetricians and Gynecologists (ACOG) cautions against overheating through exercise, especially in the first trimester. To test yourself, take your temperature by placing a thermometer under your armpit when you finish exercising. It should not be higher than 101°F.

HEY MOM!

Some women shouldn't exercise at all during pregnancy. Be sure to talk to your doctor before beginning any exercise program.

To keep from overheating, the American College of Sports Medicine makes the following recommendations:

- Drink about 16 ounces of water or a sports drink two hours before you begin exercising.
- During your workout, drink 5 to 12 ounces every 15 to 20 minutes.
- Weigh yourself before and after exercise and drink two more glasses of water for every pound you've lost.

You can see that exercise during pregnancy is not the same as before. Because your body reacts differently to physical exertion now, you have to be more mindful of how exercise affects not only you, but your baby as well.

The Downside of Exercise, Things to Avoid, and Signs of Danger

Some activities are just plain dangerous for pregnant women. Your body doesn't react to physical stress the way it used to before you were pregnant. This is especially true of exercise that involves any kind of abdominal trauma. Avoid jumping, jarring motions, or rapid changes in direction; they might cause joint instability and injury.

Because some kinds of exercise can harm the fetus, it is recommended that you stay away from the following activities:

- **Scuba diving.** Decompression might harm the fetus.
- **Skiing.** Water or downhill skiing risks violent falls and collisions. Cross-country skiing is relatively safe at elevations below 10,000 feet. If you ski any higher than that, you risk depriving the fetus of needed oxygen.
- **Surfing.** Hard falls are risky. Don't even think about it.
- **Horseback riding.** This sport is too risky because of the danger of severe falls.
- **Contact sports.** Football, wrestling, hockey, and basketball will have to wait until after you've delivered your baby.
- **Jogging.** This poses risks of overheating and jarring joints. It is okay only for seasoned runners in the first and second trimesters.

This is only a partial list of obvious dangers. Whatever sport you're considering, use common sense (the word on skydiving in your ninth month, for example, should be a no-brainer), and talk to your doctor about any sport you'd like to participate in.

Even when you follow all the do's and don'ts of safe exercise, you should look out for signs of possible danger. The American College of Obstetricians and Gynecologists recommends that you call your doctor if you have any of the following symptoms while exercising:

- Vaginal bleeding
- Dizziness or lightheadedness
- Shortness of breath
- Severe pain (anywhere, but especially in your chest)
- Headache
- Muscle weakness
- Calf pain or swelling
- Decreased fetal movement
- Amniotic fluid leakage

Any of these symptoms might be a sign that you need to slow down, or they might be a danger signal that you need medical attention. Either way, your doctor needs to know that your exercise program has caused this reaction. The "no pain no gain" mentality doesn't cut it during pregnancy.

The Do's and Don'ts of Exercise During Pregnancy

Even safe sports and exercise programs need to be closely monitored during pregnancy. This list of do's and don'ts will help you make informed decisions about your workout regimen:

Don'ts:

- Don't begin a new exercise program without explicit permission from your doctor if you …

  Have toxemia

  Have high blood pressure

  Have kidney or heart disease

  Have a history of miscarriage or premature birth

  Are excessively overweight

  Have placenta previa or bleeding during pregnancy

  Have asthma

  Are carrying multiples

PREGNANCY FACTS

In the past, pregnant women with diabetes were told not to exercise for fear of disturbing the blood-sugar levels that could affect their fetus. But more recent research has moved many doctors to change their minds. Mild to moderate exercise for diabetic women appears to have no negative effect on a pregnancy and, in fact, is beneficial for the mother and baby. Of course, pregnant diabetic women should only exercise with the permission and supervision of their doctors.

- Don't overdo it. If an exercise hurts, skip it. If you feel fatigued, stop. Don't push through to exhaustion. If you can't speak comfortably, you've passed the safe point. Listen to your body and exercise only as long as it feels good.
- After the first trimester, don't do exercises (sit-ups, for example) while lying flat on your back. This position causes the weight of the baby to press on a vein leading to the heart. This can decrease the blood flow to the fetus.
- Don't do exercises that involve excessive stretching. Your joints and ligaments are lax and prone to injury.

Do's:

When you begin a prenatal physical fitness program, there are a few things to keep in mind so that you and your baby get the most benefit from your efforts:

- Talk to your health-care provider before you begin any exercise regimen. Explain what you've done prepregnancy, what you want to do now, and how much and how often you want to exercise. Together you'll come up with a program that gives you all the benefits of exercise without any of the risks.
- Warm up your muscles before you exercise. Walk slowly or ride a stationary bike for at least five minutes before your exercise session.
- Cool down after your exercise period. Walk around slowly until your breathing and heart rate have returned to normal. Stopping exercise suddenly can cause dizziness.
- Rise slowly. When you get up from the floor too quickly, you can get dizzy or even faint because your heart is working so hard to pump blood to all your exercised muscles that it might not get a full supply to the brain.
- Drink lots of water before, during, and after exercising.

- Keep cool. It's important that you don't overheat, especially in the first trimester. Be sure to wear loose clothing and drink plenty of fluids, before, during, and after your workout. Avoid strenuous workouts outdoors on hot, humid days.
- Keep up your calorie intake. Even if the only exercise you get is lifting the TV remote, you need 300 additional calories to feed your baby each day. When you exercise, you'll need more to replace the lost calories. Do not exercise to lose weight during pregnancy.
- Schedule a definite exercise time each day. Life is hectic and things that aren't scheduled don't get done. Set aside about 20 to 30 minutes at least three days a week for exercising.

Beginning Exercisers

If the most exercise you've gotten in the last year has been standing up and sitting down again, you can certainly use some getting-into-shape exercises now. But this is not the time to jump in gung-ho and overdo it. The first thing you should do is talk to your doctor and make sure you're fit to begin exercising. Then with his okay, you should start slowly and work your way up. Start by stretching, walking, swimming, or riding a stationary bike.

Advanced Exercisers

If you have been an active exerciser, don't stop now because you're pregnant. Healthy, well-conditioned women who exercise before pregnancy can continue throughout pregnancy without compromising the baby's health or development—with a few adjustments:

- Don't let yourself get overheated, especially in the first trimester. The heat from your body can be transferred to the placenta and on to the fetus. Because the fetus cannot sweat (in order to cool down), overheating can be very harmful at a time when most of the fetus's vital organs and body parts are being formed.
- You'll have less available oxygen for aerobic activity (baby-making takes the larger share). Generally, you should not exceed 60 percent of your maximum heart rate (about 140 beats per minute).

- Stop before you're exhausted. In the past, you might have pushed yourself to the edge before calling it quits. Now you can endanger the health of your fetus if you push too hard or too long. When your muscles call for an extra load of oxygen and nutrients, it is delivered at the expense of your baby's needs. In an extreme case, this can cause fetal distress.
- Usually, mild to moderate exercise has little effect on sugar levels in the blood because energy comes from fat or carbohydrates. But during pregnancy, blood sugar is the primary source of fuel for exercise, especially during prolonged or intense workouts. Running down blood-sugar levels can have significant side effects on the fetus.
- Limit the strenuous portion of your workout to 15 or 20 minutes only. This will reduce the risk of increased body temperature and musculoskeletal injuries.

You should also consider the risk/benefit ratio of your favorite activity. If your passion is speed bicycling, you have to consider the danger of a fall, especially after the fourth month, when trauma to the abdomen can mean big trouble. The same goes for sports such as surfing, horseback riding, and skiing. Even tennis can be dangerous when your center of balance shifts after the 20th week of pregnancy. At the same time, the softening of the ligaments in your joints can make you more susceptible to injury if you fall.

If you have been strength training with weights, you can continue through your pregnancy if you remember the following guidelines:

- Don't stand in one place for long periods while you train with weights (this can decrease blood flow to the fetus). Keep moving; step back and forth; change positions.
- Don't lie flat on your back while you lift weights.
- Be very careful with free weights to avoid any trauma to your abdomen, and don't use the Valsalva maneuver (forceful exhalation without actually releasing air).
- To lessen the risk of damaging your joints (now that the ligaments have softened), use lighter weights with more repetitions.

Entering pregnancy in good physical shape has given you an advantage that you don't want to lose by getting lazy now. Keep up your exercise program, but be sure to make the adjustments necessary to protect your baby.

For All Exercisers

Whether you're a beginner or a pro, here are a few exercises that are especially geared to strengthen muscles that are strained by pregnancy.

Kegels

Here's an exercise for all pregnant women that gives the muscles of the vagina a workout! It's simple and easy, but so important to tone the muscles that will work so hard to deliver your baby. Called *kegels*, this exercise is one you can do anywhere, anytime, without special equipment, clothing, or training.

Imagine that you have to urinate really badly, but must hold it in until you get to the bathroom. Pull those vaginal muscles tight. That's it! That's a kegel. To practice this exercise, tense the muscles around your vagina and anus for as long as you can (working up to 10 seconds). Then relax the muscles. Do this at least 25 times by the end of each day. Strengthening these muscles will prepare them for labor and also help them recover their strength after delivery.

Abdominal Exercises

Abdominal exercises relieve pressure on the thighs and lower back and help you carry your baby more comfortably. There are many simple abdominal exercises you can do without overstraining yourself. Try these:

- During the first four months, when it's safe to exercise on your back, lie down with your legs straight. Lift your head and try to touch your chin to your chest. Hold for three seconds and then relax. Do this five times twice a day. If you're doing it correctly, you'll feel your stomach muscles tighten when you lift your head.
- Whether standing, sitting, or lying in bed, you can strengthen your abdominal muscles by pulling in on the muscles in your stomach. Squeeze these muscles for the count of three and then relax. Do this five times twice a day.
- This exercise, called the pelvic tilt, is great for your abdominal muscles. During the first four months, you can do it lying on the floor with your knees bent. After the fourth month, continue the exercise, but do it standing flat against a wall. It's simple: Just relax and push the small of your back flat against the floor or wall. Feel the abdomen muscles tighten? Hold it there to the count of three and then relax. Do this five times twice a day.

Leg Exercises

Leg exercises improve circulation and reduce swelling and cramping in the ankles and calves. Give these simple ones a try:

- Lie on your side with your head on a pillow. Bend the lower leg at the knee and keep the top leg straight. Stretch your top leg with toes pointed as you lift it off the floor as high as you feel comfortable. Lower it back to the floor. Do this four times and then turn on the other side and repeat.
- This is a good one for your thighs: Sit on the floor with your legs stretched out in front of you. Cross your left ankle over your right knee. Use your right hand to pull the left thigh toward the right side. Feel that stretch? Hold for one minute and then repeat on the other side. Do this just once a day and be careful not to stretch beyond your comfort level.

Stretches

During pregnancy, your joints and ligaments are soft, making them prone to injury. You can help strengthen the muscles around these weak areas with gentle stretches every day.

1. Lift your arms up over your head and stretch.
2. Bend at the waist and rotate in big circles.
3. Drop your chin to your chest and roll your head around in a big circle.
4. Shrug your shoulders up, back, and down, making circles.
5. Point your foot and then rotate your foot at the ankle 10 times (repeat with other foot). Point your foot and then pull it back up toward your knee 10 times (repeat with other foot). If you feel a muscle spasm starting, stop this exercise.
6. Clasp your hands behind your back. Lift your arms up as high as you can. Hold a few seconds and then relax.

These few exercises will get you started, but don't stop here. There are several very good books and videos on the market today that will help you plan a healthy prenatal exercise program. Talk about your plans with your doctor and then do yourself and your baby a favor and get to work.

Join the Group

Exercising alone can get boring. It can also sabotage your good intentions. Without other people to encourage you to keep up the good work, it's too easy to quit. Call your local fitness club, gym, hospital, or adult education or community center and ask about prenatal exercise classes.

DADDY ALERT!

If your partner is making an effort to exercise for the sake of your baby's health, give her your support. Show an interest: Encourage and praise her. Better yet—join in. As her exercise partner, you will keep her motivated and improve your own health at the same time.

Relaxation Exercises

"Relaxation" and "exercise" might sound like two opposites, but relaxation exercises are a fabulous, no-sweat way to work out your body and mind. These exercises help you deal with the emotional and mental stresses of pregnancy and at the same time teach you how to deal with the pain of birth mentally and physically. The trick is to practice them over and over again when you're calm so that they work when you're tense, or in labor. After all, you wouldn't decide to practice the piano for the first time in front of an audience at a concert hall, or practice driving a car for the first time on a highway. The same principle is behind the practice of these exercises. If you practice relaxation techniques while you are completely calm, you will be able to use them effectively when your mind is distracted later by stress or pain.

To start with, try the basic relaxation exercises described in the following section.

Deep Breathing

Because the body needs oxygen to fuel its response to stress, you can reduce or short-circuit the stress you feel by maintaining control of your breathing. Athletes often do this just before a race begins or when they are about to get up to bat. Follow these instructions to stop the shallow, rapid breathing that accompanies a stress response:

1. Put your hand on your stomach at the level of your belly button.
2. Take a deep breath from the bottom of your diaphragm. The hand should rise slightly if the air is getting to the bottom of the lungs.

3. Breathe in as you count to five silently.
4. Feel your lungs fill with warm air.
5. Feel your hand rise with your stomach muscles.
6. Exhale. Don't push the air out. Release it gently to the count of five.
7. When you let out the air, smile.
8. Do this sequence twice.
9. Then breathe regularly (rhythmically and comfortably).
10. Breathe deeply again after you have let a minute or two go by.
11. Repeat this deep-breathing/regular-breathing cycle two or three times.

Deep breathing is a relaxation technique you can use anywhere. No one around needs to know you're practicing stress reduction. Use it whenever you feel your body tensing from stress.

Meditation

Meditation can be used along with deep-breathing exercises to help you block out stress and focus on the present moment. The process is both physically and emotionally healing. The physical benefits come from the relaxation response, tuning down the body's stress. Emotionally, meditation decreases anxiety and calms the mind.

Whether you use meditation for relaxation, spiritual enlightenment, or healing, it requires a quiet, comfortable setting, as well as a conscious effort to relax the muscles, regulate the breathing, and calm the mind. A point of focus is needed: You can use a special word, called a mantra or focal point; it can be the word *calm* or *peace* or even a meaningless sound. You can direct your mind toward a calming mental image or to the soothing rhythm of your own breathing, as well.

Many different kinds of meditation are available, but to sample a basic meditative style, follow these instructions:

> Sit comfortably in a quiet place, free of distractions. Close your eyes and breathe freely for a few seconds to focus your mind on relaxation. Then to begin your meditation, exhale a deep breath and focus on your mantra; say this word silently to yourself. As you breathe in, your mind might be focused, still, on a stressful thought, but as you breathe out, switch your attention to

your mantra. Do this for about 15 to 30 minutes. With practice, you'll be able to breathe and meditate without being bothered by stressful thoughts. This stress-free, relaxed time will give your body an opportunity to rejuvenate and calm itself.

Progressive Muscle Relaxation

Stress causes muscles to tense, which also makes it difficult to relax. To counter muscle tension, practice this exercise: Find a comfortable place to lie down. Focus your attention on your right hand. Clench it into a fist, squeezing it as hard as you can for about five seconds. Open the fist and allow your muscles to relax. Repeat the exercise with the left hand, and the muscles in your arms, neck, shoulders, abdomen, buttocks, thighs, calves, and feet. Finally, squeeze and relax your facial muscles, including your eyes and forehead. By pairing tension with relaxation, you are conditioning your body intentionally to do the same thing naturally the next time your muscles tense.

Guided Visual Imagery

Because we all daydream and dream at night, we know there is an internal world we can experience in both positive and negative ways. Guided imagery requires you to go to that inner world and construct a place where you'll feel safe and relaxed whenever you imagine yourself being there. The core of the guided imagery approach to stress reduction lies in imagining a positive experience in order to stop, interrupt, or prevent a physical stress reaction.

To do this, create a positive image in your mind that represents a safe and relaxing environment. Practice visiting this imaginary place over and over again. Then when you're stressed, you can go there and benefit from the relaxed feeling you get, even from a brief visit. For example, you might find this image soothing:

> I am stretched out on a soft ocean beach. The sun feels warm on my body. When it gets too hot or sunny, I have an umbrella for protection. I feel the warmth of the sand on my fingertips. I see waves gently lapping the shore. I can smell the salt of the ocean, and I can taste the sea air. On my beach, there is just the right number of people—I'm not crowded or lonely. I feel just wonderful. It's an ideal place that I can visit with all my senses any time I want to. Even when I'm in the middle of a crowd with my eyes wide open, I can go to my beach.

This safe place happens to be a beach—yours can be anywhere. It can be in your family room by the fireplace, the woods by a stream, the park down the street. Wherever it is, keep these points in mind:

- Make the place real. When you're stressed or in pain, you won't be able to relate to an alien planet.
- Involve all of your senses. Pick smells, touches, tastes, sounds, and sights that are pleasing to you.
- Go to this place often. The more you practice and increase the vividness of your image, the more reliable it will be when you need it.

You can also use guided visual imagery to ease any pain and discomfort you might feel during pregnancy. You can visualize the pain disappearing. You can imagine feeling pain-free. This mental picture can dissuade the brain from transmitting pain temporarily.

These are the two kinds of exercise that can help you through your pregnancy. To stay physically healthy, your body needs to move and stay active. To stay mentally healthy, your mind needs to learn how to relax. Practice them both each day and you'll be able to sidestep the annoying aches, pains, and stressful tensions that often sabotage a happy pregnancy.

The Least You Need to Know

- Although exercise is wonderful for pregnant women, before beginning an exercise program, you must talk to your doctor and know your limitations.
- Beginning exercisers should progress slowly. Ideal exercises include walking, swimming, and using a stationary bicycle.
- Advanced exercisers should continue their regimens, with a few adjustments to keep the fetus safe.
- All pregnant women should practice kegel and stretching exercises every day.
- Relaxation exercises are a valuable part of any exercise program. They help your mind learn how to deal with the tension and stress of pregnancy and delivery.

Chapter 19

On the Job

In This Chapter

- Breaking the news: Whom to tell and when
- How to plan maternity leave
- The laws protecting pregnant women at work
- A look at some dangerous jobs
- Tips for staying healthy and comfortable at work

Working while you're pregnant isn't always easy, but it does have its benefits. It keeps the money coming in, it might give you medical benefits, and it might provide personal and professional satisfaction. For all these reasons, a national association of working women called 9to5 has estimated that more than 80 percent of employed, pregnant women have full-time jobs, and 84 percent of moms-to-be work into their last month of pregnancy. Obviously, you're not the first or the last to be pregnant on the job.

But don't kid yourself that working during pregnancy will be any different than working any other time. There are a number of things you have to do to protect yourself, your job, and your baby during this time. But if you plan ahead, know your rights, and give yourself some slack during your pregnancy, you'll find that working keeps your mind and body busy and healthy as you prepare for the new arrival.

Breaking the News to the Boss

Of course, you'll want to tell everyone your good news, but there's a pecking order to consider. The professional thing to do is tell your boss or supervisor first. This is the person who will be most directly affected by your "condition." It can be bad for your career if he or she finds out through the office grapevine. It puts you in an awkward position if the boss calls you into her office and confronts you with news she should have heard from you first. Keep your pregnancy a secret until you're ready to tell your boss.

When to Tell

Deciding when to break the news requires the strategic planning of an elaborate military operation. If you make your announcement too soon or too late, you might put yourself in a bad position. But when is just right?

Consider two things:

- If your work or environment might be hazardous to your baby, speak up immediately. For example, if you handle chemicals, lift heavy objects, stand for many hours, or work with x-rays, you can't put off your announcement. A healthy first trimester is critical to your baby's well-being, and that means that you might need to be transferred to another department or switch your responsibilities with those of another employee.
- If you have no reason to change your job in the first trimester, you might want to keep your pregnancy a secret until after the third month. This puts you safely at the point in the pregnancy when the risk of miscarriage is greatly reduced. (A miscarriage is difficult enough without having to share the news with all your colleagues.) Also, it brings you to the time when your condition is beginning to be obvious and secrets are no longer possible.

You might consider the work calendar when choosing a date to break the news as well. Is there any "downtime" coming up? Can you wait until the big sales meeting is over? Is there an especially stressful season in your industry that you can wait out? Have you made any promises that should be met before you mention a change in your condition? You can't expect your boss to be thrilled if you announce your pregnancy on a day when stress levels are skyrocketing and everything is going wrong. Look for a relaxed time when things are going right.

Think Before You Speak

Before you breathe a word of your exciting news at work, you should think carefully about the consequences and repercussions that might follow this announcement. Although the law is on your side, not all employers greet the news with open arms, so be prepared with a plan of action that explains the steps you'll take to keep up your workload, any changes you'll need to institute, when you plan to leave, and when you expect to return. Having a plan is good for your company and good for you. You'll be perceived as more of a professional, and you'll put yourself in a better position to negotiate, if necessary. Before you open your mouth, have answers to these questions ready:

1. When is your due date and when will you leave work?

   Before you can suggest a leave date, consider your personal and medical needs as well as the demands of your job. If you work in a toxic environment (in a computer chip factory, a tollbooth, or a printing shop, for example), you might want to leave immediately. If your work is very physical, you might need to leave after your sixth month; if you have a relatively nonstressful desk job, you might be able to work right to the end. Your medical condition has to be considered as well. If you have a high-risk pregnancy (see Chapter 2 for the details), you might be required to leave work very early in the pregnancy. Because of all these variables, you should always begin your statement about your leave date with the words, "Assuming no unusual medical conditions arise."

HEY MOM!

When making a decision about when to leave work, keep in mind that you'll feel the most discomfort and fatigue during the first three and the last three months. Many women feel full of energy during the second trimester.

2. How will you help train a new person?

   It's always a good idea to show that you've thought about the company's needs. Present a plan for how your job can be handled during your absence and how you might be able to train the person who will take on your responsibilities. Will you train someone already in the company? Will you come back a few days after your leave begins to help out a new person? Will you be able to do any work from home? Offering a training plan makes you a valuable team player.

3. What special considerations will you need?

   Working while pregnant is not going to be exactly the same as working before pregnancy. Don't try to be a superhero and pretend that nothing will change and nothing will get in the way of your job. You might have morning sickness (all day long). You might get tired and distracted easily. You might need to leave work for various prenatal tests or medical appointments.

   Although you don't want to scare your boss with all these possibilities right off the bat, you should mention the possibility of needing occasional time off. Bringing this up right in the beginning gives you the opportunity to be professional, be above board, and offer assurances that you will always get your work done. You might say something like, "Certainly, we both realize that I will miss work from time to time, due to medical needs. I want you to know that if that should happen, I will let you know in advance, if possible, and make sure the work gets done when I return."

Negotiating Maternity Leave

If you expect to return to work after the birth of your baby, the length and conditions of your *maternity leave* are major issues. (Remember: This leave might be paid or unpaid, depending on company policy.) The details depend on your personal wishes, your finances, your company's leave policy, and the law (see details later in this chapter). And remember that the specifics of your leave might change if you have a difficult delivery or if your child has a medical complication.

DADDY ALERT!

If financial concerns make you worried about your partner's need to take time off after the baby is born, think again about what you're really losing. Expenses associated with working can really cut into expected income. Child care alone can cost about $700 a month. Add to that a work wardrobe, lunches out, commuting, take-out dinners, and the higher tax bracket the additional income boosts you into, and suddenly the second income can look awfully small.

After you tell your boss that you're pregnant, don't make any commitment to a maternity leave plan. If he or she says something like, "Well, of course you're entitled to four weeks maternity leave. Will you be taking it?" don't jump in with an answer.

Explain that you'd like to gather more information to help you decide what to do about your maternity leave and you'd like to talk about the subject at a later time. This gives you a chance to do a little investigating. You'll need to find out what the company policy is on maternity leave. What have other women been given in the past? What is the maximum number of days allowed? Is the time extended if you have a cesarean delivery? Is the leave paid or unpaid? Are medical benefits continued during the leave? The answers to these questions will tell you what's best for you.

These are the facts you'll need:

- Make sure you know the law and how it applies to your company.
- Talk to someone from the human resources or personnel department to find out your company policy and your eligibility. (If you work for a very small company, the person to talk to might be your boss.)
- Talk to other women in your company who have left on a maternity leave and find out what terms and conditions they were given.
- Be sure to tap into the grapevine. Women who were able to negotiate cushy perks into their maternity leave might not be open about sharing their good luck, but people around them probably know the scoop.
- Find out whether you can add vacation or sick time to maternity leave.
- Gather information about your rights as a pregnant employee by consulting 1) your company's personnel handbook, 2) your union (if applicable), 3) state laws, and 4) other working parents in your company.

When you have the facts, put together your own plan. Know exactly what you are entitled to and then consider asking for a bit more. Many women have negotiated extra time off because they are valuable to the company. Because it can take several months to hire and train a full-time employee, your boss might be willing to give you an extra month rather than risk having you quit.

If you know you'd like to extend your maternity leave or return to work on a reduced schedule, plan to discuss some options. There's no harm in asking for things such as …

- Job sharing with another employee, splitting hours and benefits
- Part-time work
- Split work locations: part-time on the job, part-time at home

- *Telecommuting*, so you can work from home using the high-tech advantages of computers, phones, and faxes
- Flexible hours: putting in a 40-hour week on your own schedule (going in early and leaving early, for example)

GREEN FROM THE START

Preserving the health of the world's resources for your child's future can begin in the workplace. Turn the lights off before you leave the office; lighting represents 29 percent of energy use in an office. If you use a computer, set it to revert to standby mode after 30 minutes of inactivity. The U.S. Department of Energy says that sleep mode cuts computer energy use by 90 percent.

Ideally, these details should be worked out long before your due date. An employer is more likely to be open to a well-thought-out plan (that you've proposed in advance) than one you've put together hurriedly as you walk out the door.

The Law

It wasn't so long ago that there were no laws to protect pregnant women on the job. If an employer didn't want a pregnant woman at work, he or she could fire her. If a woman wanted to come back to work after delivering her child, there was no guarantee the job would still be there for her. Today, things have changed for the better, and there are a number of federal and state laws that will protect you during your pregnancy. But unfortunately, *discrimination* against pregnant workers still exists. If you don't know what the law is, it certainly is possible that you can miss out on rights that are legally yours. The two most notable laws protecting pregnant women are the Pregnancy Discrimination Act and the Family and Medical Leave Act.

The Pregnancy Discrimination Act

The Pregnancy Discrimination Act, which was passed in 1978, gives pregnant women the same rights as others with "medical conditions" by prohibiting job discrimination. This law, which applies to companies employing 15 or more people, says …

- Your employer cannot fire you because you are pregnant.
- Your employer cannot force you to take mandatory maternity leave.

- You must be granted the same health, disability, and sickness-leave benefits as any other employee who has a medical condition.
- You must be given modified tasks, alternate assignments, disability leave, or leave without pay (depending on company policy).
- You are allowed to work as long as you can perform your job.
- You are guaranteed job security during your leave.
- During your leave, you continue to accrue seniority and remain eligible for pay increases and benefits.

This is a discrimination law that protects you from being treated differently than other employees. On the one hand, this is good, but it also means that if your company doesn't provide job security or benefits to other employees, it doesn't have to provide them to you.

The Family and Medical Leave Act (FMLA)

The Family and Medical Leave Act, which was passed in 1993, applies to companies that employ 50 or more people within a 75-mile radius of the workplace. It says that if you have been employed for at least one year by the company you now work for, and work at least 25 hours a week, you can take up to 12 weeks of unpaid, job-protected leave in any 12-month period for the birth of your baby. All 12 weeks of maternity leave can be taken at the same time or they can be broken up over the course of the year before or after the birth of your baby. Under this law, you must be restored to an equivalent position with equal benefits when you return. (A loophole in this law says this doesn't apply to employees in the top 10 percent compensation bracket.) You can find more detailed information at the FMLA website (www.dol.gov/esa/whd/fmla/).

DADDY ALERT!

The Family and Medical Leave Act applies to you also. If you have worked at your present company for at least a year, you are entitled by this federal law to take up to 12 weeks of unpaid paternity leave. Ask someone in your personnel department for the details!

Federal laws set the minimum on what you must be allowed if you work for a middle- to large-size company. But your state laws or company policies might offer even more. For example, some states provide disability insurance if you have to leave work because of pregnancy or birth. Some companies offer paid maternity leaves. It's up to you to find out what you're entitled to. Consult the personnel director of your company's human resources department about company policy. And contact your state labor office for state laws regarding pregnancy.

HEY MOM!

You can obtain information about the Family Medical Leave Act from the Department of Labor at www.dol.gov/dol/compliance/comp-fmla.htm.

The laws regarding work and pregnancy have been written in response to a strong need for fairness. When you ask for a maternity leave, you are not asking for anything that you are not entitled to. So don't hesitate to take advantage of the laws that women before you have fought long and hard to enact.

Get It in Writing

After you and your boss have agreed on the terms of your maternity leave, as well as your responsibilities while you're still on the job, it's a good idea to write a letter detailing this agreement. Your boss is a busy person who might easily forget the details of a conversation; putting it in writing protects you from this lapse of memory. You might write something simple such as the following:

Dear Ms. ______________________:

As we agreed in our conversation on (date here):

- Within one week, I will be transferred to a position in which I will no longer handle chemicals containing lead or be required to lift heavy objects.
- During my pregnancy, I will be allowed to take reasonable time off for medical appointments.
- Assuming no extraordinary medical conditions arise, I will take my leave of absence beginning (date here).
- I will be on maternity leave for 12 weeks, returning on (date here).
- I will return to my present position on a part-time basis for one month. After this time, I will return to a full-time schedule and my current pay.

Thank you for your understanding and consideration.

Sincerely,

(your name)

Caution

Is your work hazardous to your baby's health? Take some time to look around your work environment and analyze the things you do during the day. (Be sure to read over Chapter 17 for a close-up look at environmental hazards.) You might be particularly concerned if your job is physically strenuous or if you work in computers, manufacturing, or the health-care industry.

Physically Strenuous or Hazardous Work

I know women are tough and they can do the work of any man, but your baby is not so tough right now. There are some jobs that can be too physically strenuous or toxic for a woman to continue throughout her pregnancy. These include …

- **Work that requires hours of standing.** Cooks, nurses, salesclerks, waiters, police officers, and others have jobs that keep them on their feet all day. This can be difficult for a pregnant woman, but it might be downright dangerous for her unborn baby. Studies have found that long hours of standing during the last half of pregnancy disrupt the flow of blood. Too much standing on the job might increase the risk of the mother developing high blood pressure, as well as the risk of premature birth. That is why women in high-risk pregnancies, who work more than four hours a day on their feet, should switch to a desk job or quit by the 24th week. Those who stand for 30 minutes out of each hour should change jobs or quit by the 32nd week. (Women who are feeling fine on the job and have no medical problems, however, should feel free to continue working.)
- **Jobs that require physical strength.** Do you have to lift, push, bend, shove, and load materials all day? If you do, many experts believe you should ask for a job reassignment or quit by the 20th week of pregnancy. If you do this kind of work less intensely or strenuously, you can wait until the 28th week.

  No matter what kind of job you have, you'll soon hear people say, "Put that down; it's too heavy for you." Heavy lifting is a concern during pregnancy, but the term *heavy lifting* is hard to define. Generally, it's agreed that pregnant women can lift items that weigh 25 pounds or less all day long without harm. Also, they can occasionally lift items that weigh up to 50 pounds with no problem. This explains why you can carry your toddler and preschooler occasionally, but not constantly. But if your job requires you to lift weights between 25 and 50 pounds or more on a regular basis, you should ask for reassignment or take your leave on the following schedule.

Leave by the 20th week of pregnancy if you're repetitively lifting weights over 50 pounds.

Leave by the 30th week if you are occasionally lifting weights over 50 pounds.

Leave by the 34th week if you are repetitively lifting weights between 25 and 50 pounds.

- **Jobs that involve toxic chemicals.** The list of jobs that involve dangerous substances is miles long. Consider the artist who works with paint and solvents all day, the dry cleaner who breathes in cleaning fumes, the agricultural or horticultural worker who works with pesticides, the photographer who uses toxic chemicals to develop pictures, the tollbooth attendant who breathes in car and truck exhaust, or the printer who works with lead substances. All these and countless other occupations cause harm to the fetus. Examine your work and substitute dangerous materials for safe ones (perhaps by using water-based rather than lead-based paints). You can avoid the toxic aspects of your work by asking for reassignment or protect yourself by wearing a facemask and using better ventilation. No matter what you do, be sure to talk to your doctor about your job and the dangers of toxic exposure.

Computer Work

In the 1980s, certain studies suggested a link between video display terminals (VDTs) and problem pregnancies. The media picked up the story, and it persists today. But since that time, many more studies have been conducted on the connection between working in front of a computer screen all day and birth defects and miscarriages. So far, there seems to be no relationship between the two. The level of radiation emitted from a computer is less than the level you receive from sunshine. Panic is certainly not called for.

But if you are still worried about radiation from your computer, you can take some steps to make yourself feel better:

- Try to reduce the amount of time you spend in front of the screen when you are not actually using the computer.
- Some people feel safer when they put a grounded electrically conductive filter over the screen.

The real danger in using a computer all day comes from the physical strain of sitting. If you work at a computer terminal, you might be prone to eye, neck, wrist, arm, and back strain, especially during pregnancy. To avoid these problems, you should take frequent breaks; find excuses to walk around every once in a while (frequent trips to the bathroom are the perfect cover). While sitting at your desk, do some stretching exercises to keep your muscles from cramping. Rotate your ankles. Shrug your shoulders up, back, and down. Roll your head forward and around. Bend forward at your waist, tense your back muscles and relax. Sit up tall and throw your shoulders back. Any of these simple moves will help you feel more comfortable.

Manufacturing

To judge your safety on the job, you need to know what chemicals you are exposed to each day. In fact, by law you have the right to this information, and your employer is obliged to tell you. The Occupational Safety and Health Administration (OSHA) lists a number of substances that pregnant women should avoid, including the following:

Aluminum	Benzenes
Dimethyl sulfoxide	Lithium
Alkylating agents	Carbon monoxide
Ethylene oxide	Organic mercury compounds
Arsenic	Chlorinated hydrocarbons
Lead	Polychlorinated biphenyls

PREGNANCY FACTS

The Supreme Court recently ruled that women of reproductive age could not be barred from working with materials that might be hazardous to a fetus. This ruling came in response to a rule formulated by a company that manufactured batteries. The rule banned all women from handling certain materials known to carry a risk of causing birth defects. Women's groups opposed the ban because they feared it would be used to exclude all women from higher-paying jobs that involve physical labor or other potential hazards to pregnancy. If you want to avoid these kinds of jobs during your pregnancy, you'll have to speak up and say so.

Your boss or union representative might be able to help you determine whether you are at risk in your present position. You can also get useful information from the National Institute of Occupational Safety and Health. Its online article "The Effects of Workplace Hazards on Female Reproductive Health," found at www.cdc.gov/niosh/ 99-104.html, is very informative. If you find that your job might endanger the health of your baby, you can either transfer to another position or take an early leave, if you can swing it financially.

HEY MOM!

Workplace safety hazards and tips can be found on the websites of the Occupational Safety and Health Administration (www.osha.gov) and the National Institute for Occupational Safety and Health (www.cdc.gov/niosh).

Health Care

Working in the health-care industry as a doctor, nurse, dentist, veterinarian, or lab or diagnostic technician puts you in constant contact with germs and diseases. Of course, this is an inevitable part of the job, which you knew from the outset, but now that you're pregnant, you need to look at your work from the point of view of your baby. Exposure to certain toxic chemicals used for sterilization of equipment, anesthesia gases that leak from tubes in the operating room (or even the exhaled breaths of recovering patients), radiation used for diagnostic and treatment purposes, as well as infections from patients with hepatitis B and AIDS can be harmful to the fetus. Take a close look at what you are exposed to each day and talk to your doctor about any safety concerns. If you're worried about the health of your baby, ask to be reassigned to a safer position or consider taking an early leave of absence.

Make It Easy on Yourself

Getting through any workday is hard enough, but doing it successfully while you're pregnant takes a bit of planning. Do yourself a favor and take the time to make yourself comfortable and at ease during your workday. These suggestions will get you started:

- If you sit on the job, keep a box or stool under your desk so you can put your feet up.
- If you stand a lot, wear support hose. These stockings help keep blood from pooling in your legs, which can cause or aggravate varicose veins.

- Wear comfortable shoes. Fluid tends to collect in the feet when you're active all day. Wearing tight, high-heeled shoes can be a form of torture you don't need right now.
- Dress comfortably. Because your metabolism is running in high gear, you might want to dress in layers you can add or take off as your body temperature changes.
- Take breaks and change position: Stand up, sit down, and walk around. Bend and stretch. This keeps the blood circulating and prevents the aches and pains common in pregnancy.
- Drink water. Keep a large bottle, pitcher, or glass of water within reach at all times. Flushing your system with water will help keep you healthy and on the job.
- Eat regularly and nutritiously. If you can't buy nutritious foods at work, bring your own. And don't skip meals to get in an extra half-hour of work. Your baby can't wait for nourishment.
- Learn to deal with stress. If you enjoy the deadlines and high drama of your job, then stress can be good for you. But if tension is upsetting you or driving you crazy, the stress hormones that your body releases are not good for the fetus. Make it a habit to practice relaxation exercises often at work. (See Chapter 18 for some samples.)
- Rest. You'll find yourself getting tired more quickly during the first and last trimesters of your pregnancy. Give yourself a break by getting as much rest as you can while at home, and if possible, find a place for a 15-minute nap at work. It will make a world of difference.

DADDY ALERT!

Your partner needs your help to make it through the next several months at work. The woman who used to work all day, then run errands, prepare dinner, and finish off the night with a load of laundry without missing a beat is now having trouble getting out of bed in the morning. She can't help feeling tired and uncomfortable, and she could sure use your help. Be sympathetic to her complaints, pitch in with the chores, and offer a much-needed back rub at the end of the day. Your understanding attitude will make it much easier for her to deal with the demands of pregnancy and work.

It's no use trying to pretend at work that you're not pregnant. You're pregnant, and you have special needs. So give yourself some slack and pamper yourself just a bit to make this time as comfortable and pleasant as possible.

The Least You Need to Know

- When you decide to break the news of your pregnancy at work, you should tell your boss first and carefully choose the right time.
- Before you discuss your pregnancy with your boss, think about the details of your maternity leave, your special needs at work, and your plans for training a replacement.
- Know the law pertaining to work and pregnancy, especially the Pregnancy Discrimination Act and the Family and Medical Leave Act.
- Be very cautious if your job involves physically strenuous work or exposes you to a toxic environment. You might ask for a reassignment or consider taking an early leave.
- Make life at work easier by pampering yourself a bit every day.

Life Goes On

Chapter 20

In This Chapter

- Making love during pregnancy
- Traveling when pregnant
- Getting a good night's sleep
- Taking baths and using hot tubs
- Finding clothes that make sense
- Staying sane when you're confined to bed

Pregnancy seems to change everything: how you feel, what you think about, the plans you make. This chapter guides you through the everyday activities of lovemaking, traveling, sleeping, bathing, and dressing. We also take a look at how time passes for women who must spend some or all of their pregnancy confined to bed.

Making Love

The moment you become pregnant, sex changes. It's hard to put into words or explain why, but changing the goal of sex from procreation to recreation changes feelings, attitudes, desires, and ultimately even lovemaking positions. The wacky thing about this is that the changes are unique to each couple. There's no telling if you'll now crave sex more, or if it will become a complete turnoff. Every woman is different in this area (and every man, too!). Only one thing is for sure: Whatever you feel about sex during pregnancy, it is perfectly normal and should not be hidden from your partner. This is one subject you both need to talk about throughout the pregnancy.

Sexy Feelings

If you suddenly can't get enough of your lover now that you're pregnant, there's a good reason or two for this. You no longer have the worry of getting pregnant or using cumbersome birth-control devices. You might also find that pregnancy has made you feel closer than ever to your husband. Many women find their blossoming bodies very sensual and the idea of carrying a new life inside very erotic. It's even true that some women experience more intense orgasms (or even their first orgasm) during pregnancy; this might happen because the increased blood flow to the pelvic area during pregnancy can heighten sensation in the genitals.

DADDY ALERT!

Your own feelings about sex might have changed now that your partner is pregnant. Some men find pregnancy highly erotic. Others see their sex drive take a dive as they struggle with the physical changes their partner is experiencing. The transformation of lover into mother can be disconcerting. Some men lose interest because they're worried about hurting the baby. Whatever your feelings, rest assured that you're not the first to go through this. Talk honestly to your partner; she, too, is probably struggling with a changing sex drive.

If you suddenly can't stand the thought of sex, there's good reason for this, too. The fatigue and nausea of the first trimester can be strong libido zappers. And feeling fat, awkward, and clumsy later in the pregnancy isn't exactly an aphrodisiac. Some women also struggle with the change of roles from "lover" to "mother." The parts of the body that used to be fun are now working in a very functional manner. Your breasts might feel sore and swollen. And the increased flow of blood to your vagina might make you feel overly sensitive in that area. Some women even experience abdominal cramps during or after intercourse. And finally, you might worry about hurting the baby. All these things make it perfectly natural to shy away from sexual intercourse.

If you find your interest in sex is changing, whether you want more or less, talk to your partner about it. Don't bottle up your feelings. They'll never be resolved unless you make an effort to get them out into the open. Being honest about your own feelings will encourage your partner to do the same. Men have changing sexual needs during pregnancy, too. You might find that this gives you both an opportunity to find new and more satisfying ways to make love.

Safety First

The fear of hurting the baby during intercourse has kept many couples apart during pregnancy. But fear not: No matter how well endowed your partner might be, the thrusting of the penis into the vagina cannot hurt your baby. The baby is safely cushioned in an amniotic fluid-filled sac and surrounded by the strong muscles of the uterus. The entrance to the womb is protected by a closed cervix, which has a mucous plug at the entrance to keep out all intruding bacteria or sperm. You might notice that the baby moves around a bit more after intercourse, but that's because of the pounding of your heart, not because he or she knows what's going on or is bothered by it.

The safety of the pregnancy is another concern for some couples. There are many myths and stories about how intercourse brings on premature labor, but the truth is you can make love day and night for all nine months and it still wouldn't have an effect on the delivery date of your baby, if your pregnancy is normal. (Anyone want to give it a try?)

However, there are circumstances in which women are advised to avoid intercourse. Every situation is unique and you should talk to your doctor before making any decisions about sexual abstinence, but generally, women in the following circumstances are advised to proceed with caution:

- Placenta previa (when the placenta covers the cervix and could be damaged)
- Unexplained vaginal bleeding or discharge
- Cramping
- An *incompetent cervix* (when the opening of the birth canal dilates, or opens, prematurely with little advance warning; signs of this dilation include bleeding, increased mucous discharge, and/or abdominal pain)

Sometimes sexual abstinence is necessary only at certain times during the pregnancy. Your doctor might advise that you abstain …

- During the first trimester if you have a history of miscarriage
- During the last two to three months if you have a history of premature birth
- During the last three months when carrying multiples

PREGNANCY FACTS

Women who have a history of premature labor are advised not to have intercourse in the last trimester of their pregnancy, for several reasons. For one, orgasms do cause the uterus to contract (that's why even masturbation and oral sex are out). Also, stimulation of a pregnant woman's nipples releases a natural chemical called oxytocin, a hormone that causes uterine contractions. And finally, semen contains prostaglandins, which can stimulate contractions. In a normal pregnancy, these uterine contractions cannot trigger labor, but if you are at risk for a premature birth, you might be told to abstain from sex as a safety precaution.

All women must abstain from sex after the water sac has broken or the mucous plug is passed. These are the protectors of the womb; after they are gone, the baby is vulnerable to infection. Also, if you notice any unusual symptoms during or following intercourse, such as pain or discharge, you should call your doctor before having sex again.

If your doctor advises you to abstain from intercourse, remember that sex is more than vaginal intercourse. It is being close, holding, hugging, and massaging. If intercourse is prohibited, but orgasm is allowed, you can enjoy oral sex and mutual masturbation. All of these things and more can keep you close to your husband and nurture your love.

Creative Positioning

In the beginning of your pregnancy, when your belly is still small, you and your partner can continue lovemaking without any change in positioning. But as the baby grows, you might find that it gets awkward and uncomfortable to lie underneath your partner during sex. If that happens, don't give up—get creative. This is a wonderful excuse to try new positions. Many pregnant couples find the following most satisfying:

- **Woman on top.** If you take the top spot, you can control how much pressure you put on your abdomen and also the depth of penetration.
- **Side by side.** Lying on your side with your partner lying behind you, his chest against your back, keeps your abdomen completely away from the action and allows for only shallow penetration, which some women prefer later in pregnancy.

- **On all fours.** If you kneel on your hands and knees, your partner can kneel behind you, spoon his body around yours, and enter your vagina from behind.
- **On the edge.** Sit near the edge of your bed, lie back, and put your feet up on the bed. Your partner can stand, kneel, or crouch in front of you.
- **Lap sitting.** As your partner sits in a chair, sit on his lap (either facing him or putting your back against his chest). With your feet on the floor, you can move yourself to control the depth of penetration.

Common Questions

Many patients ask the same questions about sexual activity. The most common ones are the following.

Q: Can orgasm start labor?

A: Theoretically, orgasm could get the ball rolling, if you are already on the verge of going into labor, but in any other circumstance, there is no need to worry. Although orgasm causes mild uterine contractions, these contractions calm down after a few minutes. Like Braxton Hicks contractions, they serve to prepare the uterus for the process of delivery. There is no danger to the baby or your pregnancy from orgasm. However, if you are at risk for premature labor, your doctor might advise against orgasm as a safety precaution.

Q: Is oral sex okay?

A: Oral sex is perfectly safe during pregnancy—with one word of caution. Make sure your partner does not blow air into the vagina. This can cause an air embolism that can obstruct a blood vessel and actually cause the death of the fetus or the mother.

DADDY ALERT!

Although oral sex is perfectly safe during pregnancy (unless orgasm is prohibited), you should know that vaginal secretions increase in volume and change in consistency, odor, and taste during pregnancy. This makes oral sex unpleasant to some men.

Q: Why do my breasts leak some kind of fluid during sex?

A: In the last trimester, your body begins to produce a substance called colostrum, a type of premilk. Sexual stimulation of the breasts can cause colostrum to leak, which is nothing to worry about. But if it bothers you or your partner, you can reduce leakage by leaving your breasts alone during sex.

Q: Does the baby know what's going on during sex?

A: Your baby feels the movement of your body and she probably enjoys the rhythmic rocking caused by the uterine contractions after orgasm, but she cannot see a thing and has no idea what's going on. You can also be sure she will have no memory of your lovemaking after birth.

Traveling During Pregnancy

In most healthy pregnancies, traveling isn't a problem during this time; in fact, if this is your first child, this is a great time to get away and savor the time alone with your partner. But there are a few precautions and considerations you should think about before you take off.

Always check your travel plans with your doctor early in the planning stage. If there is any medical reason your trip should be canceled, postponed, or shortened, you'll want to know before you buy tickets or schedule time off from work.

Consider the timing of your trip. The best travel time for pregnant women is usually in the second trimester. This is the time you have the most energy and are relatively free from the fatigue and morning sickness of the first trimester and the discomforts of the last trimester (such as backaches, hemorrhoids, and heartburn). Fears of miscarriage and premature birth are also less common during this middle period.

If you are traveling for an extended period in the last three months of your pregnancy, take extra precautions to keep yourself and your baby safe and healthy:

- Talk to your doctor about the signs of premature labor so you'll be aware of the danger signals.
- Find out whether your insurance company will cover an out-of-area delivery.
- Locate a health practitioner (or at least a hospital) in your destination city.

Air Travel

If you're traveling by plane, think ahead for your own comfort and safety. Although plane travel is generally safe during pregnancy, there are certain precautions you should think about. In fact, some airlines have restrictions on pregnant travelers. To avoid a delivery at 33,000 feet or an emergency landing, some will not carry women past their 36th week. This is important to keep in mind for the return trip. You might get out of your hometown at Week 30, but if you're planning to return very close to your due date, you might have trouble getting permission to board for the return trip.

As for the plane ride itself, pamper yourself:

- Ask for a bulkhead seat.
- Request an aisle seat.
- Bring your own snacks so you're not held hostage waiting for a bag of peanuts.
- If allowed, bring a large bottle of water. The recirculated air on a commercial jet can be extremely dry and can lead to dehydration.
- If you are prone to motion sickness, check with your doctor about using a medication such as Dramamine. Most are safe to take during pregnancy.

Because x-rays are dangerous to a developing fetus, many pregnant women are worried about passing through the airport x-ray machines used for security. Although x-rays are used to examine carry-on luggage that gets sent down the transport belt, the metal detector you walk through is harmless!

The real danger from radiation comes from flying itself. As explained in Chapter 17, flying in an airplane exposes you to high-energy cosmic radiation given off by the stars and sun. The amount of radiation depends on your location and altitude. The nearer the North or South Pole you fly and the higher you fly, the greater the level of radiation. Frequent flyers, flight attendants, and pregnant women have been warned that long, high-altitude flights over polar regions can expose them to more radiation than the federal government currently recommends. If you're taking a short domestic flight to visit your mother, don't worry at all. But if you're doing extensive, long-range flying, you should talk to your doctor about the levels of radiation you might be exposed to.

Foreign Travel

Traveling to a foreign country is always exciting and packed with adventure. But traveling abroad can also expose you to diseases that your immune system (which is weakened during pregnancy) might have a hard time fighting off. Proper immunizations will protect you from most problems; ideally you should get these vaccines several months before you become pregnant. But if you must be immunized now, talk to your doctor about which ones are safe during pregnancy.

The Centers for Disease Control and Prevention suggest the following:

- Pregnant women should not receive MMR (measles, mumps, and rubella) vaccine.
- The yellow fever or polio (OPV) vaccine should be given to pregnant women only if there is a substantial risk of exposure.
- Being vaccinated in the second or third trimester minimizes theoretical concerns over possible birth defects. (Vaccinations in the first trimester do not always offer this protection because the fetus's organs have not all been formed at that time.)

The Centers for Disease Control and Prevention also tell us that there is no convincing evidence for risk to the unborn baby from inactivated viral or bacterial vaccines. These vaccines include hepatitis A, hepatitis B, rabies, injected typhoid, meningococcal, pneumococcal, Tetanus-diphtheria toxoid, injected polio, and Japanese encephalitis.

Another problem that can ruin a trip to a foreign country is travelers' diarrhea. There are organisms in the food and water of some countries that don't bother the natives because they are used to them, but they can make you very sick. To reduce the risk of illness when visiting less-developed foreign countries, drink only bottled water, do not use ice cubes in your drinks, and avoid fresh, uncooked produce.

Getting the Sleep You Need

In the beginning of your pregnancy, sleeping won't be a problem. You'll probably find you can sleep anywhere, anytime. But as you get larger and larger, sleep can become a chore. Finding a sleeping position that is comfortable and supports that big belly takes a bit of creative maneuvering. If you can't get comfortable, try these sleep tactics:

- Sleep on your side—your left side, to be exact. This position doesn't scrunch the major blood vessels.
- Sleep on the couch or the floor if your aching back needs more support.
- Sleep with your upper body propped up if heartburn is keeping you awake at night.

- Sleep on your side with a pillow tucked between your knees and another pillow pushed up against your back.
- Buy a maternity pillow for support. This looks like two pillows fastened together (like a butterfly); when you lie in the middle, you get support on two sides!

With some creativity and persistence, you should be able to find a position that lets you slumber in peace.

Standing Tall

Some women find that chiropractic care relieves the back pain so common in later pregnancy. No wonder the back complains when the body's center of gravity changes, the baby places additional weight on the spine and pelvis, and the simple act of walking turns into a waddle. If you are new to chiropractic care, be sure to interview prospective practitioners to find one who is highly trained and experienced working with pregnant women.

Splish Splash, Taking a Bath

Sometimes the best thing in the world for tension and aches and pains is a good soak in a warm bath. There's no medical reason you can't take baths while you're pregnant if you keep the following couple of precautions in mind:

- Put a nonstick mat in the tub so you don't risk falling.
- Do not use hot water. The water cannot be over 102°F.
- Limit your bath to 10 or 15 minutes so you don't get dehydrated.
- Do not take a bath after your water has broken.

High temperatures are not good for the developing nervous system of your baby, especially in the first few months. For this reason it's smart to give up hot tubs, saunas, whirlpools, Jacuzzis, and hot baths. If you just love hot water, buy a pool thermometer and keep an eye on the water temperature. If it's above 102°F, it's too hot for your baby.

Dressing for Two

Your pregnancy is one crazy fashion opportunity. Your size changes day by day, so it's a real challenge to find clothing that looks good now and will still do the job next week. Your needs in this department depend, of course, on your life-style. If you are working, you'll need to build a wardrobe that can cover your expanding body and still look professional. If you spend more time at home than in public, you can get away with large shirts, leggings, and sweat suits for quite a long time.

When it's time to shop to cover the bulge, you might be tempted to run to the nearest maternity clothing shop. The problem with this is that maternity clothes are expensive. Consider a few alternatives that can get you through the fifth month without great expense:

- Visit your partner's closet. Your partner has shirts, shorts, sweatpants, and sweaters that might fit you just fine in the first four or five months.
- Revisit your own closet. During the first five months, you might be able to create outfits by wearing blouses on the outside and by doing some camouflage work with tunic tops, large button-down blouses, large denim shirts, classic A-line or empire dresses, large vests, and boxy blazers.
- In the beginning of your pregnancy, you can buy a great nonmaternity outfit on sale in a size or two larger than your prepregnancy size.

GREEN FROM THE START

There are several ways you can conserve the earth's resources as you build your pregnancy wardrobe. For starters, look for gently worn maternity outfits that you can borrow from friends or buy from second-hand shops. Online, you can search "rent maternity clothes" and find many shops that will "loan" you lovely outfits for the short period of time you will need them. This is a great way to save money and save the planet through the process of reuse, reduce, and recycle.

When it's time to hit the maternity shops (usually some time in the fifth or sixth month), you'll find that maternity clothes are made differently than your nonpregnancy clothes—at least they should be. When you shop, look for …

- A dress hem line that is longer in the front. This hem pulls up as your belly expands. (That's why buying nonmaternity dresses in large sizes won't work.)
- Extra room in the upper arm and bust. You will need it.

- No lining. Your body temperature is higher during pregnancy and lining can be very warm and uncomfortable.
- Clothing that can be layered to adjust to your changing body temperature.
- Clothing that can be mixed and matched to give you a varied selection without spending a fortune.
- Easy care, durable material. Maternity clothes are washed and worn about four times as often as nonmaternity clothes.

The Bed Rest Club

The ordinary activities of living day to day during pregnancy change drastically if your doctor prescribes the dreaded bed rest. This is a term that can mean many things, depending on the circumstances of your pregnancy, but basically it boils down to staying in bed. Bed rest is prescribed for certain complications of pregnancy, such as premature labor, preeclampsia (pregnancy-induced high blood pressure), premature rupturing of the membranes, fetal growth retardation, and unexplained bleeding. The amount of time you're confined to bed depends on your condition and your doctor's orders. Some women need bed rest for a week; others require it for the entire pregnancy. Bed rest allows some women to walk around occasionally, shower, and cook. For others, it means total confinement with a bedpan nearby.

If your doctor prescribes bed rest, get the details. Ask the following questions:

- Can I get up and walk around occasionally, shower, and go to the bathroom?
- Can I sit up and work with my computer or write?
- Can I exercise in bed?
- Can I get up to take care of my other children?

Bed rest is excruciatingly boring at best. It can wreak havoc with emotions that are already high-strung. Bed rest can cause marital and financial stress. It is just plain difficult. The only way to make this kind of pregnancy work is to keep your eye on the goal and make the best of the situation:

- Stay social. Invite friends over. Have pizza parties. Write letters. Get online.
- If you have to miss an important event (your brother's wedding, for example), have someone videotape it and then view it with family and friends around you.

- Think of your needs ahead of time. Ask your partner to fill a cooler with juices, water, and snacks and keep it by your bedside.
- If it's okay with your doctor, create a whole program of bed exercises. You can wiggle your toes, circle your ankles, flap your arms, rotate your head, stretch your legs, and so on. These kinds of bed exercises can be very helpful in maintaining your circulation and flexibility.
- Stay active. Take up a new hobby (or get back to one you've dropped). Knit, needlepoint, draw, write, play cards. Do something.

The nine months of pregnancy are like no others in your life. But in the midst of all the dreams and medical checkups, there are 280 days that are just like every other day in your life. Whatever your situation, remember that during your pregnancy, life does go on, so enjoy it and make the most of every minute.

The Least You Need to Know

- Pregnant couples often find their interest in sex changes during pregnancy. Some want more; others want less.
- Sex cannot hurt a fetus, but creative positions might be necessary to get around a very large abdomen.
- Women in high-risk pregnancies might need to abstain from sex.
- Traveling during pregnancy requires some forethought, precautions, and your doctor's okay.
- Beware of hot baths, hot tubs, whirlpools, and Jacuzzis that use water over 102°F.
- Women who are confined by bed rest need a positive attitude, lots of social activity, and support.

Chapter

21

Problem Pregnancies

In This Chapter

- Fetal problems: cord prolapse, intrauterine growth restriction, abruptio placenta, placenta previa, premature rupture of the membranes, and premature birth
- Maternal problems: preeclampsia and Rh incompatibility

A pregnant woman has enough to worry about without obsessing over every problem that could possibly happen. If you are experiencing a normal, healthy pregnancy, skip this chapter completely. If you are having symptoms that worry you, or if your doctor tells you there is a problem with your pregnancy, then use this chapter as a reference only. The information will help you understand the circumstances of your pregnancy more fully and clarify what your doctor has told you. Do not use the information to scare yourself. Use it to back up your doctor's explanations. His knowledge of your individual situation is more valuable; if this book gives you information that conflicts with his assessment of your needs and treatment, take his word first. Use this chapter only as support material to clarify medical terminology or get a better understanding of some of the complications of pregnancy.

Because this chapter is organized for quick reference, the various pregnancy problems are given in alphabetical order to help you find information more easily.

Cord Prolapse

In all pregnancies, the sac of amniotic fluid that surrounds the fetus will break in order to allow the baby to travel through the birth canal. But sometimes when the sac breaks, the gush of water carries the umbilical cord (which serves as the baby's lifeline for nutrients and blood supply) with it. The cord then slips through the cervix and might even hang into the vagina; this is called *cord prolapse*. This is a dangerous situation because as the baby presses down on the opening of the cervix, she can push against the cord, blocking its circulation. The baby will then be deprived of oxygen.

Cord prolapse is more likely to occur in premature births or when the baby is breech (feet or rear are positioned to be born first) because in these cases there is more room for the cord to slip through the cervix and into the vagina. Cord prolapse is diagnosed after the sac breaks. If the cord is visible in the vagina or if you can feel "something" in your vagina, do two things immediately:

1. Get on your hands and knees to take pressure off the cervix.
2. Get someone to rush you to the hospital or dial 911.

After you arrive at the hospital, your baby will be monitored for signs of distress. The cord might be tucked back in place, and if you are not in labor yet, you will be prepared for a cesarean delivery.

Hyperemesis Gravidarum

In most cases, the morning sickness of pregnancy is an annoyance more than a danger. But in some instances severe symptoms might stem from a condition other than morning sickness called *hyperemesis gravidarum.* This term literally means "excessive vomiting." If untreated, frequent vomiting can cause malnutrition, weight loss, and dehydration and can be harmful to the fetus. Call your doctor immediately if …

- You're vomiting more than three times a day.
- You cannot keep food down for 24 hours.
- You have fever and pain along with vomiting.

Sometimes hyperemesis gravidarum can be treated with rest, antacids, and antivomiting medications. But if the vomiting continues and no cause (other than pregnancy) can be found, intravenous feedings might be necessary to restore nutritional balance and allow the gastrointestinal tract to rest.

Intrauterine Growth Restriction (IUGR)

Intrauterine growth restriction (IUGR) is a medical way of saying that the fetus is smaller than he should be for his *gestational age* (the age of a fetus in the womb). This is a dangerous situation because low-weight babies are at risk for many medical complications at birth.

If a woman is getting regular medical care and the cause of IUGR is discovered and corrected early on, the baby will begin to thrive. Common reasons for IUGR include the following:

- Poor diet and inadequate weight gain
- Cigarette smoking
- Alcohol or other substance abuse
- Chronic or acute illnesses (such as diabetes, high blood pressure, anemia, or kidney disease)
- Closely spaced pregnancies
- Carrying multiples
- An improperly functioning placenta
- Severe nausea and vomiting that continues after the third month
- A deformed uterus or fetus

HEY MOM!

Carrying small doesn't necessarily mean IUGR is a problem. You can't judge from the outside if your baby is underweight. If your doctor feels the uterus is not expanding as it should, he or she can confirm this condition with an ultrasound.

As soon as IUGR is diagnosed, optimum nutrition and the elimination of other factors contributing to the problem drastically improve the chances of normal fetal growth. But if diet, medical, and life-style changes don't improve the baby's size and weight, other procedures might be necessary. These include bed rest or perhaps hospitalization where the mother can be fed a diet heavy in protein, calories, and iron (intravenously if necessary) and where medical problems can be addressed. In extreme cases, an induction or a cesarean delivery might be necessary if the baby is near term and not growing.

Placenta Problems

The placenta is your baby's lifeline to oxygen and nutrients. It also carries away the baby's waste. Any problem with the placenta is serious and needs medical care. The most common problems with the placenta are abruptio placenta and placenta previa.

Abruptio Placenta

Normally, the placenta is securely attached to the wall of the uterus. But if the placenta pulls away from the wall before the baby is born, the condition is called *abruptio placenta*. This condition requires prompt medical attention because it can deprive the baby of oxygen and cause hemorrhage (severe vaginal bleeding).

This condition is more likely to occur in older mothers who have had other children or in those who smoke, have hypertension, or have had a previous case of abruptio placenta. Sometimes a short umbilical cord or an accident that causes trauma to the uterus can also cause the placenta to separate from the uterus.

PREGNANCY FACTS

In days past, the lives of both the mother and child with abruptio placenta were in grave danger. Today, with prompt medical care, virtually all mothers and better than 90 percent of babies in this situation survive.

The most common and obvious symptom of abruptio placenta is vaginal bleeding. When the separation is slight, the bleeding will be similar to a light to heavy menstrual flow and there might also be mild abdominal cramping. Bed rest usually stops the bleeding and after a few days the mother can return to her normal activities. She will be closely watched and will stay alert to any signs of repeat bleeding.

If the separation is moderate, the bleeding will be heavier, the abdominal pain is more severe, and there might be contractions of the uterus. This condition might respond to bed rest, but often blood transfusions are necessary; and if either mother or baby show signs of distress, an emergency cesarean delivery might be necessary.

If the separation is extreme (more than 50 percent detached), the symptoms of moderate abruptio placenta increase in severity. Both mother and baby might show signs of blood loss, and prompt transfusions and immediate delivery are usually required.

Placenta Previa

Normally, the placenta is attached high up on the wall of the uterus. In a condition called *placenta previa*, the placenta is attached in the lower half of the uterus, covering the opening of the uterus and blocking the baby's exit route. In early pregnancy, placenta previa is of little concern because the placenta generally moves upward as the pregnancy progresses. But if the placenta is still blocking the opening of the uterus when the mother goes into labor, the stretching of the placenta as the cervix opens will cause bleeding, and hemorrhage is possible. In this case, vaginal delivery is impossible and an emergency cesarean will be performed.

The symptoms of placenta previa are usually not evident until the third trimester. As the cervix begins to dilate, the mother will notice bright red vaginal bleeding without any pain. This bleeding might stop and then start again and might be triggered by stress (coughing, bowel straining, or sexual intercourse, for example). Sometimes there are no symptoms at all until the onset of labor. A diagnosis is made through an ultrasound exam, which locates the low placement of the placenta.

Treatment of early pregnancy placenta previa is not necessary because the placenta might move itself. But after the 20th week, a woman with placenta previa might be required to limit her activity or rest in bed. The goal is to keep the pregnancy going as long as possible, but if bleeding becomes severe, a cesarean delivery will be performed in order to avoid a massive hemorrhage.

Preeclampsia

Preeclampsia is a medical term for high blood pressure that is caused by pregnancy (it is also called toxemia or pregnancy-induced hypertension). This condition occurs in about 7 percent of pregnant women (that's 7 out of every 100) in the second half of pregnancy. If left untreated, preeclampsia can cause permanent damage to the nervous system and blood vessels of the mother and cause growth retardation in the fetus (due to the reduced blood supply to the placenta). In extreme, untreated cases, preeclampsia can progress to a very serious condition called eclampsia, which causes maternal convulsions and even coma and death. Fortunately, with proper medical care throughout a pregnancy, cases of preeclampsia are diagnosed early and can usually be treated and controlled without major complications.

HEY MOM!

Some believe that preeclampsia can be prevented by taking one baby aspirin every day during pregnancy. If a friend or relative suggests this plan, beware. There is no solid evidence that aspirin can reduce the risk or treat preeclampsia, but there could be danger in taking aspirin during pregnancy. Do not take any aspirin without discussing it first with your doctor.

The symptoms of preeclampsia (which are looked for at every routine checkup) include swelling of hands and face, sudden excessive weight gain, high blood pressure, and protein in the urine.

In late, severe stages, these symptoms might be accompanied by blurred vision, headaches, irritability, confusion, severe gas pains, and abnormal blood platelet test results.

Treatment for preeclampsia varies according to the severity of symptoms and stage of pregnancy. In mild cases, bed rest is usually the prescription—either at home or in the hospital. The mother is cautioned to be alert to the signs of severe, late-stage preeclampsia, and her baby will be monitored regularly for fetal movement with nonstress tests and ultrasounds as needed. The outcome for a woman (and her baby) with mild preeclampsia is very good when appropriate medical care is given.

In severe cases of preeclampsia, treatment might be more aggressive. If the mother's blood pressure can't be controlled or there are signs of maternal or fetal deterioration, bed rest and medication will be abandoned in favor of immediate delivery of the baby. Most doctors feel that a preterm baby is better off in an intensive care neonatal unit than in the deteriorating environment of a uterus affected with preeclampsia. Labor might be induced for a vaginal delivery or a cesarean delivery might be performed.

A far better method of preventing preeclampsia is to fix up your diet. After surveying 109 women with preeclampsia and 259 healthy women about their nutritional habits before and during pregnancy, researchers reported that those eating less than five servings of fruits and vegetables a day for up to a year before delivery were almost twice as likely to develop preeclampsia. In addition, those with the lowest levels of vitamin C in their blood were nearly four times more likely to have this condition than those with higher levels. The researchers believe that eating vitamin C–rich foods or taking supplements during pregnancy can lower the risk for developing preeclampsia. This is one case where you have nothing to lose. Vitamin C is a known antioxidant that is good for you—so peel an orange and enjoy!

You can also protect yourself by visiting your dentist. Pregnant women are prone to sore and swollen gum tissues—a condition called gingivitis. New studies are finding that this dental condition can increase the risk of developing preeclampsia. So brush and floss carefully throughout your pregnancy. And if your gums swell or begin to bleed, be sure to see your dentist.

Premature Birth

Some babies just can't wait to be born and arrive too soon. A *premature birth* is one that occurs between Weeks 20 and 37. In 2001, more than 476,000 babies, or nearly 12 percent of live births, were born too soon in the United States. The reasons for premature births are many. At-risk mothers include those who have had a previous miscarriage, two or more abortions, a history of kidney disease, a pregnancy before age 16 or after age 34, or who have abnormal anatomy of the uterus. Some medical conditions increase the risk of premature births, including abruptio placenta, placenta previa, abnormal amounts of amniotic fluid, preeclampsia, prematurely ruptured membranes, and carrying multiples. Heavy smoking is also known to increase the risk of a premature birth. At the same time, a percentage of premature births happen without warning and for no apparent reason.

Symptoms of premature labor should be reported to your doctor immediately. They include …

- Menstrual-like cramps, which might be constant or occur on and off.
- A feeling of heaviness or pressure on the rectum.
- Lower-back pain.

- Cramps (which might be accompanied by diarrhea).
- A change in vaginal discharge. It might be heavier, watery, or blood-tinged.
- A trickle or flow of amniotic fluid from the vagina.
- Contractions.

With prompt medical care, many premature deliveries can be delayed. Every day spent in the womb drastically increases the baby's chances of survival and good health. Bed rest alone has been known to stop or delay premature labor. If signs of labor continue, drugs called tocolytic agents might be given to relax the uterus and perhaps stop contractions. But if the baby is persistent and refuses to wait any longer, he will be delivered and become one of the almost 500,000 preemies born each year in the United States. If he is born after Week 28, new procedures, equipment, medications, and a wealth of new research and knowledge will give him a survival rate greater than 95 percent.

Premature Rupture of the Membranes (PROM)

In the ninth month, women know that when their "water breaks," labor isn't far away. The water breaks when the membranes surrounding the amniotic sac rupture and the amniotic fluid gushes out. This is normal and expected at the time of labor and delivery, but when it happens prematurely, it creates a condition called *premature rupture of the membranes (PROM)*, which requires prompt medical attention.

When the membranes surrounding the amniotic fluid sac rupture, the baby is exposed to the outside environment and is vulnerable to infection. At term, delivery is expected within 24 to 48 hours of this rupture and labor might be induced if it is delayed beyond this point. But if the membranes rupture before Week 34, your doctor will have to weigh the risk of premature delivery against the risk of infant infection. In most cases, the mother will be hospitalized on bed rest and the baby will be closely monitored. Labor will be induced for an emergency delivery, either when the baby's lungs appear mature enough or when there is a sign of infant infection.

Rh Incompatibility

At your first medical visit, blood is drawn to determine your blood type and Rh factor. You are either Rh-positive (as approximately 85 percent of Caucasians and a slightly higher percentage of African Americans and Asians are) or you are Rh-negative. This is important to determine because if you are Rh-negative and your partner is Rh-positive, the fetus might have Rh-positive blood like the father. When this happens, the fetus's blood is different from the mother's, causing *Rh incompatibility.* The mother's blood might respond as if it were allergic to the fetus's blood by making antibodies against the fetus's blood. This is called sensitization. If the antibodies from the mother's blood cross the placenta into the fetus's blood, the antibodies attack, breaking down the fetus's red blood cells and causing anemia. This is a very serious condition known as erythroblastosis fetalis. It can cause serious illness or even death in the fetus or newborn.

BABY TALK!

Rh incompatibility occurs when the mother's blood is Rh-negative and the baby's blood is Rh-positive.

Fortunately, sensitization to the Rh factor can be prevented if the mother does not become sensitized in the first place. To do this, an Rh-negative woman is given Rh immunoglobulin (Rhlg) near the 28th week of pregnancy to prevent her from producing antibodies. If her baby is Rh-positive, the mother will be given another dose shortly after delivery. Repeat doses of Rhlg are given with each pregnancy and birth of an Rh-positive baby. This course of detection and prevention makes the deadly erythroblastosis fetalis completely preventable today.

Not all pregnancies are smooth sailing. If you find yourself in a problem pregnancy, be sure to get good medical care and follow your doctor's instructions. As medical science improves, more and more previously fatal or permanently damaging conditions have become controllable and even harmless. That's the good news.

The Least You Need to Know

- Not all pregnancies go smoothly. Sometimes nature interrupts our plans with problems that affect the fetus, the mother, or the delivery of a healthy newborn.
- Fetal problems such as cord prolapse, intrauterine growth restriction, abruptio placenta, and placenta previa can be detected and controlled with consistent prenatal medical care.
- Premature rupture of the membranes and premature labor are two serious situations that need immediate medical care.
- Preeclampsia and Rh incompatibility are two maternal health problems that are routinely controlled without serious results, but that can lead to both fetal and maternal death if left untreated.

Chapter

22 Pregnancy Loss

In This Chapter

- Miscarriage
- Ectopic pregnancy
- Molar pregnancy
- Stillbirth
- Coping with loss

Although most healthy women can expect to carry their pregnancies to full term and deliver healthy children, even in this age of modern medicine, some pregnancies fail. When they do, the disappointed parents often wonder what went wrong and what they could have done to save their baby. This chapter will outline the medical facts about the most common causes of pregnancy loss and direct you to support resources if you face this painful experience.

Fear of Miscarriage

Miscarriage means the delivery of a fetus before it is able to survive outside the womb (it's also called a spontaneous abortion). If you've been reading your stack of books about pregnancy, then you know that miscarriage within the first three months of pregnancy is not uncommon. If you haven't already read it, here it is: About one half to one third of all pregnancies end in early miscarriage; about three out of four of these miscarriages happen before the 10th week.

Now don't panic. We know about these miscarriages only because the ability to detect pregnancy earlier and earlier is getting better. A generation ago, many women conceived and miscarried without knowing either event had happened. Because we now can detect pregnancy when the fetus is only two weeks in the womb (or four weeks old, according to the counting system that dates from the first day of your last period), a very early spontaneous abortion becomes a distressing medical event. For this reason, some women choose to keep their pregnancy a secret until Week 12, when the high risk of a miscarriage is behind them.

If miscarriage is on your mind, talk to your doctor about it. He knows how easy it is to get very attached to your baby by even early in the pregnancy. It's very natural for the thought of a miscarriage to be upsetting.

When to Call Your Doctor

Call your doctor if you experience any of these signs. You might be experiencing a miscarriage:

- **Cramping down in the center of your lower abdomen.** Sharp, quick pains on the sides of your belly are probably from the ligaments adjusting to the stretch. But if you have continuous pain for more than one day that feels like menstrual cramps, get on your feet and call your doctor.
- **Vaginal bleeding.** Vaginal bleeding doesn't automatically mean miscarriage. Many women bleed a bit in the early months. But if the bleeding is as heavy as a menstrual period, or if light bleeding continues for more than one day, call your doctor.
- **Passing clots.** If you pass clots or grayish/pink matter from your vagina, call your doctor immediately.

Late Miscarriage

Many late miscarriages are due to problems with the placenta or the health of the mother. The placenta might separate from the uterus, be implanted abnormally, or be unable to produce the hormones necessary to maintain the pregnancy. The health of the mother might cause a late miscarriage if she suffers serious infection, uncontrolled chronic illness, severe malnutrition, or an incompetent cervix that opens prematurely. (This might happen due to DES exposure [see Chapter 4], multiple abortions, or prior cervical surgery.)

The possibility of a late-term miscarriage is usually signaled by a pink discharge for several days or a small amount of brown discharge for several weeks. The probability of an unavoidable miscarriage includes symptoms such as heavy bleeding usually accompanied by cramping.

A miscarriage after the 12th week is very rare in a low-risk pregnancy. So unless you are under the care of a perinatologist because your pregnancy is high risk, you shouldn't lose sleep over this worry.

Recurrent Miscarriage

A miscarriage is not uncommon in early pregnancy, but some women experience the double heartache of recurrent miscarriages. A *recurrent miscarriage* is defined as three or more miscarriages in a row—this is very uncommon. Here are the facts: The chance that you will have one miscarriage is 20 percent. The odds of having two miscarriages in a row are 4 percent. This means that although 1 in 5 women who become pregnant will have a miscarriage, 1 in 25 will have 2 miscarriages in a row; this is not particularly rare. But the odds of having three consecutive miscarriages drop to less than 1 percent. When this happens, it is likely that the miscarriages are not random events, but are caused by some specific medical problem.

If you cannot carry a fetus to term after repeated attempts, your doctor will perform some diagnostic tests to find out whether there is a physical reason for the miscarriages. After taking a detailed medical history, your doctor might order x-rays, a sonogram, or other procedures to examine the size, shape, and structure of your uterus. Abnormal uterine shape can cause repeat miscarriages either because of inadequate room for a fetus to grow or because the embryo implants on tissue that cannot support embryo growth, such as a fibroid.

If you miscarry late in your pregnancies, your doctor will evaluate your cervix (the entrance to the uterus). At the time of a full-term delivery, the cervix will open to allow the baby to be born, but if the cervix is weak or damaged, it might not be able to hold the weight of the baby after 20 weeks and will open too soon, causing a miscarriage. If this is the case, the cervix can be stitched closed during your next pregnancy to prevent another miscarriage.

Blood tests might also supply needed information. Your doctor might order a chromosome analysis of both you and your partner; this will evaluate any genetic reasons for the miscarriages. An antiphospholipid antibody blood test might also be ordered; these antibodies (also called the lupus anticoagulant or anticardiolipin antibodies) might cause blood clots, including blood clots in the placenta that prevent the placenta from growing and functioning normally. Your doctor might also order blood tests to check for certain disorders, such as thyroid disease or diabetes, that are sometimes associated with recurrent pregnancy loss.

Your doctor might also perform an endometrial biopsy. This procedure involves scraping a small amount of tissue from the endometrium (the lining of the uterus) shortly before menstruation is due. This test is used to determine whether you have a hormonal imbalance that prevents you from having a successful pregnancy because not enough progesterone is produced. Other hormone blood tests might also be ordered.

In many cases, when the cause of the recurrent miscarriages is found and treated, the woman can then have a successful pregnancy. But in some cases, there is no apparent reason for repeat miscarriages. This is so frustrating! To hear that nothing seems to be wrong is not good news when you can't complete a pregnancy. If a problem could be found, then it most likely could be fixed. Unfortunately, if you have had three consecutive miscarriages with no medical cause, you are considered infertile—which is not all bad news. With this diagnosis, you can begin to do something constructive to reach your dream of having a baby. If you find yourself in this situation, it's time to talk to your doctor about the various ways you can still become a mom.

Ectopic Pregnancy

After an egg is fertilized, it travels down the fallopian tube to find a comfy place in the uterus to attach and grow. Here a fetus will develop into a healthy, full-term baby. Occasionally, however, the egg implants itself outside the uterus (often in the fallopian tube). At first the body responds as if it were a normal pregnancy. Hormones are released and your pregnancy test is positive. But the egg can't grow outside the uterus, and so a full-term pregnancy and healthy baby are an impossibility in what is called an *ectopic pregnancy* (your mother might call it a tubal pregnancy).

It is important to catch an ectopic pregnancy before the cells grow too large, causing the fallopian tube to burst. This might destroy the tube's ability to carry another fertilized egg to the uterus in the future. A neglected ectopic pregnancy can also threaten the life of the mother.

The symptoms of an ectopic pregnancy are as follows:

- Crampy pain on one side of the abdomen
- Abdominal pain that worsens when straining with a bowel movement or coughing
- Light bleeding or brownish spotting
- Shoulder pain on one side

If the fallopian tube bursts, the woman will have severe internal bleeding, very sharp and steady pain, and probably signs of shock, which include a rapid, weak pulse; clammy skin; and fainting.

There are three treatment goals for an ectopic pregnancy: remove the embryo, remove the risk to the mother, and preserve her fertility.

Early diagnosis (before the fallopian tube bursts) and modern, high-tech medicine make it possible to meet all three of these goals. Diagnosis is usually made by testing the level of the hormone hCG in the mother's blood (the levels of this hormone will not rise as they should during pregnancy if the egg is implanted outside the uterus). Ultrasound is also used to locate the embryo within the uterus and fallopian tubes.

Treatment is given through a procedure called a laparoscopy. A tiny incision is made in the navel for the insertion of the laparoscope (a miniature scope that allows the physician to actually look inside you). Another incision is made in the lower abdomen, in order to get at the tube with surgical instruments. This method is favored over major abdominal surgery because it is effective and it allows for a much shorter hospital stay and more rapid recovery. In some cases, drug therapy might be used to destroy the fertilized cells. Your doctor will usually prescribe a follow-up test of hormone levels to be sure that all material has been removed.

Molar Pregnancy

The medical name for what is commonly called a *molar pregnancy* is trophoblastic disease or hydatidiform mole. (I'm giving you these terms just in case your doctor uses them.) The condition is caused by a chromosomal abnormality in the fertilized egg that prevents the placenta from forming properly; this causes the egg to deteriorate so that it never develops into a fetus. It is a rare occurrence (happening in about 1 in every 2,000 pregnancies) that seems to be more common in women over age 45.

The early symptoms of a molar pregnancy include a brownish discharge and severe morning sickness. By the start of the second trimester, the uterus might be larger than expected and there is no fetal heartbeat. A diagnosis is made when ultrasound examination shows a large placental mass but no fetal tissue in the uterus. Treatment for a molar pregnancy requires the removal of the abnormal placenta from the uterus through a procedure called dilation and curettage (D&C). In the hospital, under anesthesia, the cervix is dilated and the contents of the uterus are carefully cleaned out. Medical checkups following this procedure are very important because the tissue of some molar pregnancies might continue growing afterward and a repeat procedure or medical therapy might be necessary. It is recommended that a woman wait one year after a molar pregnancy before conceiving another child.

HEY MOM!

After the loss of a pregnancy, you might want to try again. After a molar pregnancy, it is recommended that you wait an entire year before having another pregnancy. After a miscarriage, ectopic pregnancy, or a stillbirth, you should let your body rest for two months, but can then safely try again if your doctor agrees you are ready.

Stillbirth

The most unexpected, difficult-to-understand outcome of a pregnancy is the delivery of a dead baby. This is called a *stillbirth.* After caring for a baby in utero for nine months and going through labor and delivery, there are no words to console parents who leave the hospital or birthing center empty-handed. The reasons for a stillbirth can include an accident with the umbilical cord, chromosomal abnormality, fetal infection, undiagnosed placenta abruption, or chronic maternal conditions such as diabetes. When an expectant mother is in a hospital, where the fetus can be monitored, stillbirths are very rare. They usually happen when medical help is unavailable.

If you experience a stillbirth, you will naturally grieve for the loss of your baby. Don't let anyone try to minimize your pain with comments such as, "Well, at least you never had time to get attached." This was your baby and he or she is very much a part of you. Support personnel who assist families suffering from a stillbirth often recommend the following ideas to help cope with the pain:

- Hold your baby. Don't be afraid to unwrap the blanket and admire the beautiful baby you've made. Count the fingers and toes and hold him or her close to you.
- Give your baby a name. For the rest of your life you will remember this child. Having a name makes his or her life in utero seem more real.
- Ask for a lock of hair and his or her hand- or footprints as keepsakes.
- Don't feel awkward about taking photos of the baby. They might be too painful to look at right away, but in the future, you will be glad for the memory.
- Arrange for a memorial service with family and close friends. This gives you an opportunity to gain support and share your sorrow.

Coping with the Loss

Women who experience a pregnancy loss quickly learn that our society doesn't understand the pain of this loss. Well-meaning friends might say, "It was probably defective in some way, so this is actually a blessing." Or, "You'll get pregnant again." Or even, "Lots of women miscarry; it's really not a big deal." Of course, any woman who has had a failed pregnancy knows that it *is* a big deal. Even if the fetus was malformed and even if she can get pregnant again, she still experiences the very deep pain of a shattered dream.

If you should have a failed pregnancy, it's likely that you will go through the typical stages of grief that follow the death of a loved one. These include (1) denial and isolation, (2) anger, (3) bargaining, (4) depression, and (5) acceptance. Almost all of us pass through these five stages during times of great loss, though not necessarily in any specific order and sometimes through more than one stage at the same time, or by jumping back and forth from one to another. It takes time to get over this great loss, so be patient with yourself.

Let yourself be angry and sad if that's what you need to do for a while. But don't add guilt to the mix. Many women who have unsuccessful pregnancies beat themselves up wondering what they could have done differently to save their baby. "I should not have gone to the gym so often." "I shouldn't have had that glass of wine." "If only I didn't take that long car ride." "I should have stopped working." And on and on and on. In almost all cases, the actions of the pregnant woman do not cause the death of the baby. So give yourself a break. Mourn your loss, but don't blame yourself.

When the initial shock passes, you might feel better if you sit down with your doctor and map out a strategy for preventing a loss in future pregnancies. Having a plan will help you feel less helpless. You can also find help through support groups (see Chapter 5 for details). In particular, you might want to contact a support organization called SHARE, a not-for-profit nondenominational, international organization providing support to those who have experienced the tragic death of a baby through early pregnancy loss, stillbirth, or newborn death. The SHARE website (at www.nationalshareoffice.com) states that its primary purpose is to "provide support toward positive resolution of grief experienced at the time of or following the death of a baby. The secondary purpose of SHARE is to provide information, education, and resources on the needs and rights of bereaved parents and siblings." You can also find excellent resources and links at the website of the Hygeia Foundation, at www.hygeia.org. Log on and see how these organizations might help you through this difficult time. (More contact information for SHARE and Hygeia is in Appendix B.)

DADDY ALERT!

Don't panic if you don't feel the same level of grief over the loss of the baby-to-be. Your partner might have a stronger bond to the child because she held him inside her and experienced the symptoms of pregnancy day after day. To you, the child might have been less "real" and existed more as a future promise. However, your partner needs you to understand her level of grief. It would not be a good idea to say something like, "It's okay, honey; we'll have another baby real soon." Give her support and comfort until she's ready to talk about the future.

It is perfectly natural to be heartbroken over the loss of your baby. But there is a line between normal grief and depression that you must be careful not to step over. After two or three weeks of mourning, if you find that you're not feeling any better, be aware of the signs of depression. These signs include loss of interest in usual activities, change of sleep patterns, changes in appetite or weight, increased use of drugs or alcohol, marital discord, social isolation, thoughts about death or suicide, and persistent feelings of helplessness, pessimism, guilt, bitterness, or anger. You might need some professional help to get you past these feelings. Tell your doctor how you're feeling and ask for a referral to a psychologist or psychiatrist who has experience working with women dealing with a pregnancy loss.

The pain of losing an unborn child runs deep. Give yourself time to mend and take extra care of yourself. Eat well, exercise (if your doctor says it's okay), and pamper your spiritual side with long walks, meditation, or even yoga. Give yourself time to heal and then move on with the memory of the lost child held dear in your heart.

The Least You Need to Know

- Despite the best efforts of modern medical science, sometimes a pregnancy ends unsuccessfully.
- Miscarriage, an ectopic pregnancy, molar pregnancy, and stillbirth are possible causes of pregnancy loss.
- The painful heartache of a lost pregnancy takes time and support to cope with. You should reach out to loving family and friends, as well as support organizations for comfort.
- Seek professional help if you show signs of depression after this loss.

Part 5
The Big Day

All your dreams and preparations during the nine months of pregnancy bring you to the one big day of labor and delivery. The birth of your baby is the main event!

Where you want to deliver your baby, the method of childbirth you'd like, and the type of delivery you choose will have an enormous impact on the kind of birth you and your baby experience. Give this part a careful read before you hit the big day—it will prepare you for what's in store.

There are three stages of labor to go through when your baby signals that it's time. And there are a number of standard hospital procedures you'll want to know about that dictate your care during labor and the care of your baby after delivery. If you read this part carefully, nothing will take you by surprise.

After the baby arrives and is placed in your arms, you're a new parent. That indescribable joy can be mixed with worry about what you're supposed to do now! This part will give you starter information on how to be a new parent.

Chapter 23

Preparing for Childbirth

In This Chapter

- Choosing a comfortable place to deliver
- Preparing for a safe delivery
- Knowing the facts about natural versus medicated deliveries
- Taking a look at cesarean and breech deliveries

As you plan and dream about the birth of your baby, you have some practical decisions to make. You'll need to decide where you want to deliver, what kind of childbirth you'll have, what classes you'll take to prepare for the big day, and what you can expect in an emergency.

Choosing the Spot

Where would you like to deliver your baby? You have several options to choose from, and each one has pros and cons that need to be considered. Talk with your partner and health-care provider about your options. If you're not sure which is best for you, take a careful look at each choice. Ask for a tour, get to know what is offered at each site, and then make your choice. Possible sites include your own home, a hospital, or a birth center.

Home Birth

Some women feel strongly about having their babies in their own homes where they can enjoy the comfort of family and familiar surroundings. Here they are in charge and there is little medical intervention. During labor, they can get up, walk around, have a cup of tea, and talk to friends on the phone. Anything goes, and this is reassuring to many women. But if you are considering this option, be sure you understand all that it entails. It is advised only in low-risk pregnancies where there is little probability that something will go wrong. Still, few licensed providers will assist at a home birth because emergency medical equipment will not be on hand if there are unexpected complications during the birth of the baby. Your delivery therefore will most likely be in the hands of a midwife who will guide you through a natural birth. If you want a home birth, be sure to find a licensed midwife who is affiliated with a backup physician and a nearby hospital in case anything goes wrong.

Traditional Hospital Rooms

In most hospitals all deliveries are handled routinely in four different rooms:

1. First you enter the labor room. Here, in a small hospital-type room or curtained-off area, you proceed through early labor with your partner.
2. After your cervix dilates to about 10 centimeters and the baby's head becomes visible at the opening of the vagina, your bed is wheeled into the delivery room. Picture the operating room you've seen on TV shows. This is a small room with a bed surrounded by lots of lights and medical equipment. This is where you will give birth to your baby.
3. After delivery, you are wheeled into the recovery room. Here nurses monitor you for an hour or so to make sure that you have no need of immediate medical attention.
4. Finally, you are wheeled into the *postpartum* room for recuperation. This room (which might be private or shared with other women) is like any other hospital room. It has a bed, a night table, and a small bathroom with a shower.

Many hospitals across the country are moving away from this kind of birth setting to a more relaxing one, as is described in the following section.

The Birthing Room

Some hospitals and all freestanding birthing centers have birthing rooms (sometimes called LDRs for labor-delivery-recovery rooms). One of the advantages of a birthing room is that labor and delivery occur in the same place rather than in several locations, as described in the preceding section. In addition, birthing rooms are usually cozier and look more welcoming than regular hospital rooms. They often have personal showers and a place for visitors to sit. To create this homey feeling, the rooms do not contain as much medical equipment as the average hospital room. Therefore, birthing rooms are usually an option for only low-risk, uncomplicated deliveries. If you would like this kind of room, check with your doctor to make sure it fits your criteria.

HEY MOM!

In most hospitals, birthing rooms are scarce and available on a first-come, first-served basis. If that's the case, don't set your heart on one, because you can't predict the moment of your baby's birth and make a reservation. Birthing room availability is one of the things you should find out in advance.

If you are considering a freestanding birthing center (a center not connected to a hospital), be sure you understand the medical limitations. Most are staffed by midwives only and cater to natural births. Little or no pain medication is available in a birthing center, nor can it provide for the needs of high-risk pregnancies that require the transferal of the mother and baby to a hospital if complications arise during delivery. To find a birthing center near you, log on to the website of the National Association of Childbearing Centers at www.birthcenters.org.

Childbirth Classes

As you think about where you'd like to deliver your baby, you can also choose the type of labor experience you would like to have. Although the baby will push his or her way down the birth canal and into the world whether you're ready or not, it's better to be prepared. When you look for a childbirth class, you'll find that there are many different kinds. There are classes offered by hospitals, YWCAs, health maintenance organizations (HMOs), physician medical practices, and so on. Each offers a unique approach to pregnancy and childbirth, so look around to find one that reflects your beliefs and philosophies. The most popular include classes that teach the birth methods of the International Childbirth Education Association, Lamaze, the Bradley Method, Grantly Dick-Read, and Leboyer gentle birth.

The International Childbirth Education Association (ICEA)

Classes sponsored by the ICEA do not emphasize any particular approach to childbirth. They offer general information about the process of labor and birth. They discuss natural childbirth, teach various methods of dealing with the pain of labor and birth, and present the options available for pain relief. All instructors are certified by the ICEA. You can get more information about the International Childbirth Education Association by contacting it at P.O. Box 20048, Minneapolis, MN 55420; 952-854-8660; or www.icea.org.

Lamaze

Lamaze is probably the most widely used method of birth in the United States. It was first introduced in France in 1951 by the French obstetrician Fernand Lamaze. You can get more information about the Lamaze method of childbirth from Lamaze, International at 2025 M Street, NW, Suite 800, Washington, D.C., 20036; 1-800-368-4404; or www.lamaze.org.

The method emphasizes natural birth and offers a variety of relaxation methods to deal with pain (although an overview of anesthesia and pain relief is included for women who prefer this). Visualization, guided imagery, massage, and coaching from a partner are all part of this program. Lamaze is best known for its patterned breathing routine that teaches a woman to focus on certain breathing patterns and a concentration point (such as a mark on a nearby wall). This technique makes it possible to block pain messages to the brain. If practiced throughout the pregnancy, a woman's conditioned response to contractions becomes a relaxed method of breathing rather than muscle tension and fear. Official Lamaze classes are taught by teachers who are certified by the American Society for Psychoprophylaxis in Obstetrics (ASPO/Lamaze) and use the initials ACCE (ASPO-certified childbirth educator) after their names.

Bradley Method

The Bradley Method emphasizes natural childbirth with the parents working as a team. Diet and exercise are practiced throughout the pregnancy to prepare the body for the rigors of birth. Bradley students are taught deep abdominal breathing and an understanding of the labor and delivery process. Rather than offering a method to try to block out pain, the Bradley Method encourages concentrated awareness that works through the pain. There is much emphasis on the education and training of the woman's labor and birth coach.

You can ask for more information about the Bradley Method of childbirth by contacting: American Academy of Husband-Coached Childbirth, P.O. Box 5224, Sherman Oaks, CA 91413; 1-800-4ABIRTH; or www.bradleybirth.com.

It was the Bradley Method that first introduced the idea of husband coaches in the delivery room. Before this method became popular, expectant dads stayed out of the way, paced the floor in the waiting room, and worried. Some men say they like it better that way, but many appreciate the fact that they can now participate in the birth of their child, support their partner, and be present the moment their baby greets the world.

Grantly Dick-Read

Grantly Dick-Read was an English obstetrician in the 1920s when the management of birth pain was handled by knocking the women unconscious with chloroform. After watching a woman refuse chloroform and deliver her baby without trauma or pain, Dick-Read came to believe that fear and tension were the cause of labor pains. He noticed that no other animal species experienced suffering, pain, or agony during the birth process and hypothesized that a woman's fear of labor pains caused blood to be filtered away from the uterus, so it could be used by the muscles that the woman would use to flee if the fear were caused by a dangerous situation (sometimes called the fight-or-flight response). As a result, the uterus did not have the oxygen supply it needed to perform efficiently or without pain. He believed that by eliminating the fear, women could return the uterus to its normal function—without pain. In 1933, Dick-Read put his ideas into a book called *Natural Childbirth*, which was not well received by the British medical community.

Dick-Read died in 1959, but his theory remains the basis of many of today's childbirth classes. His ideas are still quoted in books and papers by many of the world's most notable childbirth educators. He believed that education about the birth process and relaxation exercises during labor were the keys to reducing labor pains. Today, few disagree with this insight. Although it is out of print, Dr. Dick-Read's book *Childbirth Without Fear* is still available through various online booksellers such as Amazon.com. You might also enjoy reading *Post-War Mothers: Childbirth Letters to Grantly Dick-Read* by Mary Thomas (University of Rochester Press, 1998).

Leboyer Gentle Birth

A hospital delivery room is not the most inviting place for a newborn. The lights are bright, the noise level can be high, and until a few years ago the newcomer was welcomed by being hoisted aloft by his ankles and slapped on the buttocks. A French obstetrician named Frederick Leboyer wrote a book in 1974, *Birth Without Violence*, calling for a more sensitive and gentle approach to birth. His recommendations have evolved into the Leboyer method, which advocates low lights and soothing music in the delivery room. The newborn is immediately placed on his or her mother's abdomen, postponing umbilical cord cutting and suctioning. The baby is then placed in a warm bath to enjoy a return to the weightlessness of the womb. This method of childbirth is gaining in popularity. The birthing rooms are now often well designed with adjustable lighting and with medical equipment available nearby, but out of sight.

Types of Delivery

Sometimes you have a choice about how your baby will enter the world; other times (due to medical necessity or emergency), you do not. As you wait out your pregnancy, it's a good idea to learn about possible types of delivery so that you can make an educated choice when you have an option. The basic methods of delivery are (1) natural, (2) medicated, and (3) cesarean.

Natural Childbirth

Natural childbirth is any delivery without powerful pain medications. Whether your child is born naturally after careful preparation in natural childbirth classes or born on the way to the hospital in the back of your car without benefit of medication or medical assistance, it is a natural birth.

Today, there are many natural childbirth methods, programs, and classes to help you prepare to give birth without pain or medication. If a natural birth is something you would like to experience, make sure you take the time to prepare well in advance of your due date. With proper training, a natural birth can be very rewarding and personally satisfying. Without advance preparation, however, it can be a painful and traumatic experience.

Medicated Childbirth

Not all women care for the idea of natural childbirth. They prefer to use medication to dull or completely eliminate the pain of labor and delivery. Choosing a medicated delivery is neither a good nor bad decision; it's simply another option for women today.

If you're interested in a medicated delivery (or even if you plan a natural birth, but want to know all the options), consider the various kinds of pain relief available. Then talk to your doctor. His or her experience and expertise can help you understand the possibilities. You'll find that most doctors have the option of a variety of choices, depending on your specific needs. Most likely, your doctor will choose the best pain relief for you from a number of analgesics, tranquilizers, and anesthetics. General anesthesia might also be necessary in a complicated case.

Analgesics

You're familiar with *analgesics* such as aspirin and Tylenol. These are drugs that relieve pain. During childbirth, stronger analgesics such as Demerol are frequently used. These drugs are usually given intravenously, through an IV drip. In this case, the medication is "dripped" slowly through a needle that has been inserted in one of your veins or muscles (the buttocks, for example) after labor is well under way. Medication is fed to the needle through a tube connected to a plastic bag.

The effect of analgesics on the newborn depends on the dosage and how close to delivery the drug is administered. Some infants are born sleepy and unable to suck; others might have trouble breathing and need oxygen. These side effects are not dangerous and quickly wear off.

Anesthetics

Drugs that produce a loss of sensation are called *anesthetics.* These medications interrupt the pathway of nerves that carry sensations of pain to the brain. In effect, they "block" pain messages and are commonly called "nerve blocks." During delivery, your doctor can choose a nerve block that will completely numb you from the waist down or one that numbs a smaller vaginal area.

The most frequently used blocks are the epidural, pudendal, spinal, and caudal. Let's look at each in turn:

- The epidural block affects only the sensory nerves to numb you from the waist down, leaving you with full muscle movement. It can be given before the cervix is fully dilated and it provides excellent anesthesia during the entire active phase of labor, vaginal delivery, *forceps delivery,* or cesarean delivery. The medication is administered by inserting a long, fine needle into the space between the vertebrae of the lower back. A small plastic tube is threaded and left in the space right before the spinal cord. With the tube in place, medication can be administered throughout labor as needed. Initially, it can take up to 30 minutes to feel the effect. The epidural is rapidly becoming the most widely used type of nerve block for relief of pain during labor.

BABY TALK!

A **forceps delivery** is one that uses an obstetrical instrument that resembles a pair of tongs to gently grab hold of and pull the infant's head out of the birth canal.

- The pudendal block is administered through a needle inserted in the vaginal area. The numbness is localized and reduces pain in that area, but does not reduce the pain caused by uterine contractions. The pudendal block is frequently combined with a tranquilizer for added pain relief.

- A spinal block is administered at the end of labor, immediately before delivery. A full spinal block affects the sensory and motor nerves; it instantly numbs the body from the waist down and causes loss of voluntary leg movement and the inability to use abdominal muscles. It is usually used for cesarean deliveries. Because the spinal block numbs feeling in the part of your body that comes in contact with a saddle, if you were riding a horse, it has become known as a "saddle block." It is often used for forceps-assisted delivery. Because it interferes with the normal movement of the baby's head into the birth canal, a saddle block is not usually administered until the cervix is completely dilated and the baby's head is deep in the pelvis. The spinal block is administered by inserting a long, fine needle into a space between the vertebrae of the lower back.
- A caudal block was once a very popular method of relieving pain during labor and delivery. Today, it is less popular than the epidural, for a number of reasons. The caudal does not cover as wide an area as the epidural. It requires a larger dosage, and it is difficult to administer correctly. In addition, the increased pelvic and abdominal muscle relaxation produced by this technique might slow the progress of the second stage of labor. Like the spinal block, the caudal block is administered by inserting a long, fine needle into a space between the vertebrae of the lower back.

General Anesthesia

If you'd really like to be completely knocked out during your labor and delivery, you're not alone. Lots of women would be very happy to miss the birth, wake up, and jump right into motherhood. In years past, you might have gotten your wish. But today, general anesthesia (causing unconsciousness) is reserved in obstetrics for only a few dire cases.

General anesthesia is used only in special cases because …

- It rapidly crosses the placenta and enters fetal circulation, making the baby likely to be groggy at birth.
- Women under general anesthesia are usually unable to assist in the birth of the baby and therefore forceps are required for a vaginal birth.
- You'll miss the most joyous moment in life: the first sight of your child at birth.

- You'll also miss the first opportunity to bond with your child because you'll be unconscious.
- There is a risk that you will vomit while under general anesthesia, which can block the airway and cause complications and even death.

Convinced? Unless general anesthesia is absolutely necessary, you will be awake during your delivery. The state of "absolutely necessary" occurs when a nerve block is not an option. This includes …

- When the mother has had previous low-back surgery or a history of a herniated disk.
- When the mother has a blood clotting disorder or low platelet count.

General anesthesia is also considered when …

- Fetal distress is extreme and immediate delivery becomes urgent. In this circumstance, nerve blocks take too long to take effect.
- The vaginal delivery of a breech baby requires intense manipulation of the baby's body and head.
- An emergency cesarean is necessary and there is not time to administer a regional nerve block.

You should discuss medication options with your doctor or midwife before your delivery so you have an idea of what will happen when you go into labor. After that, you have to trust your doctor or midwife to make the right decisions based on your immediate needs at the time of delivery.

Cesarean Birth

Cesarean birth (also called a C-section) is childbirth through an incision in the mother's abdomen and uterus. This is major surgery and carries its own potential for complications. But when a cesarean is necessary, it is the safest form of delivery for the baby. Many healthy babies who are born through a C-section would not have survived a vaginal delivery.

The reasons for a C-section birth are many and the final decision is up to the doctor. Although some women ask for a cesarean in hopes of avoiding the pain of a vaginal birth, it is not an elective operation. C-sections are performed for very specific, medically sound reasons, such as …

- **Failure to progress in labor.** If a woman is in labor but her cervix stops dilating and the baby stops moving down the birth canal, the physician might decide a C-section is necessary to avoid fetal distress.
- **A very large baby.** If a baby weighs over 10 pounds, there is a risk of maternal and infant injury during a vaginal birth.
- **A breech position.** When the baby is presenting feet or buttocks first, a C-section might be the safest way to deliver the child.
- **Premature babies.** Babies born before Week 35 are more likely to be delivered by C-section. These babies often are in a breech position and show signs of fetal stress during labor.
- **Previous cesarean birth.** Although it is still common to do a C-section after a woman has had a previous C-section birth, many physicians are cautious when recommending that women try to have a vaginal birth with their next baby. This is called a VBAC (vaginal birth after a cesarean). It is a personal choice that every woman with a previous C-section has to make. But a VBAC is offered with the knowledge that there are risks to the baby and the mom. There is danger of uterine rupture, which would lead to a lack of blood to the baby, oxygen deprivation, and possibly death. If the uterus can't be repaired, the woman would have to have it removed (a hysterectomy). This is very rare, but it happens. In recent years, there have been more repeat elective C-sections than VBACs.

Cesarean delivery is a last resort. It is avoided if possible because it can cause complications that affect both infant and mother. It is major surgery and therefore causes greater blood loss and higher anesthetic risk. It also requires a longer, more expensive hospital stay; a greater need for blood transfusions; and a prolonged recovery period. But if your doctor knows in advance that you might need a cesarean, you should feel gratified that this medical option is available to give your baby the best chance of a healthy delivery. If you expect to have a vaginal delivery, you probably will, but you should also know what a C-section is so that if a medical emergency during labor makes a cesarean necessary, you'll know what's going on.

The Breech Delivery

Throughout your pregnancy, your baby has moved around inside you like a gymnast doing aerial flips. But somewhere between Weeks 32 and 36, most babies move into the birth position (head down) and stay there until birth. From this position, the head is the first part of the baby to enter the world. All babies move into this position except the 3 to 4 percent who present their buttocks for delivery. This is called a *breech* position.

A breech presentation increases the risk of complications during delivery. Sometimes the buttocks do not push against the cervix with enough force to move labor along and even when they do, delivering the head (which is the largest body part) last can cause problems. The position can be determined in the ninth month by the experienced hands of your doctor. Generally, he can feel the spine, the buttocks, and the head. He can locate the heartbeat and determine whether the heart is high or low in the uterus. If there is any question about the baby's position, a sonogram will give a clear picture.

Breech babies keep you guessing. They might turn around immediately before birth, but then again, they might not. While you wait, you and your doctor can do some persuading. After 37 weeks, the doctor might try to move the baby into position manually with ultrasound guidance (this is called a *version*). By firmly, but gently, pressing on the head and hips, the doctor will carefully attempt to rotate the baby. When this is successful, the chances of a normal, vaginal birth are high, but keep in mind that some babies push themselves right back into the breech position.

Although not scientifically proven, some mothers say they have been able to move their babies into position with a few "tricks." You might try frequently shining a flashlight low on your abdomen to encourage the baby to move toward the light. Some play soft music against this low point. Others try to move the baby through this exercise: Lie on your back with knees bent and feet flat on the floor. Put several pillows under your buttocks to raise them 9 to 12 inches. Stay in that position for 10 or 15 minutes three times a day. I can't promise results, but so many swear by it, it's worth a try.

If the baby has not turned by your due date, your doctor has a decision to make. Based on her experience and personal belief, she might try a vaginal delivery. Another doctor might schedule a cesarean delivery automatically. This is why you should talk to your doctor and trust her judgment before you go into labor.

The Least You Need to Know

- You can choose to deliver your baby in your own home, a hospital, or a birthing center.
- To prepare for childbirth you should take classes such as those that teach the methods advocated by the International Childbirth Education Association, Lamaze, the Bradley Method, Grantly Dick-Read, and Leboyer.
- Your baby might be delivered through a natural, medicated, or cesarean childbirth.
- Some deliveries are complicated if the baby is in a breech position, meaning the buttocks instead of the head are positioned to come into the world first.

Chapter 24
Labor and Delivery

In This Chapter

- Rehearsing the big moment: prelabor, false labor, and real labor
- What labor is really like
- Instrument-assisted birth: forceps and vacuum extraction
- Why inducing labor sometimes makes sense

You have nine months to plan, dream, think, and prepare for the birth of your baby. Then one day (or night), you'll go into labor and it'll be time for the big event—whether you're ready or not. Labor isn't something you can delay or put off, and it rarely happens when it's convenient or when you feel ready. It just happens.

You're more likely to stay calm and focused if you understand what's happening to you and your baby throughout the stages of labor and delivery. So in this quiet moment, take some time to sit back and read what it might be like when your baby says, "It's time."

A Review of Labor

In Chapter 13, you were introduced to three kinds of labor: prelabor, false labor, and real labor. All of these stages help the cervix to efface (thin out) and dilate (open). Eventually the opening of the cervix will be wide enough—about 10 centimeters—for the baby to pass through it. The following page gives a quick summary of all three kinds of labor.

Prelabor

Prelabor is the getting-ready-for-labor stage. Here's what you can expect:

- Lightening—the baby's head drops down into the pelvis
- An increase in vaginal discharge and/or brownish or blood-tinged mucous discharge
- An increase in the number and intensity of Braxton Hicks contractions (see Chapter 11 for a description of these practice contractions)
- A nesting instinct that makes you start cleaning closets and organizing your kitchen

False Labor

You are in false labor if you answer yes to these four questions:

- Are the contractions staying the same in intensity (not getting worse)?
- Are the contractions coming in uneven intervals (two minutes apart, then seven minutes apart, then four minutes apart, for example)?
- Is the pain in your lower abdomen rather than in your lower back?
- Do the contractions stop when you move around or change position?

If you answered yes, you're not in real labor yet.

Real Labor

You will know that real labor has begun if you answer yes to any of these three questions:

- Are the contractions occurring at regular intervals that are coming closer and closer together and getting more intense? (You will call your doctor when your contractions last about a minute and come five minutes apart for at least one hour.)
- Do I have lower-back pain (which might be accompanied by a crampy, menstrual feeling)?
- Has my water broken? (This might not necessarily happen before you get to the hospital.)

When real labor contractions begin you will find that you cannot walk or talk through them. This is a good time to start packing.

Real Labor

What is real labor like? Ask 50 women and you'll get 50 different stories. It's a unique, wonderful, terrifying, thrilling, difficult, easy, fast, unforgettable experience that will bring your baby into the world one way or another. Although no one can predict the details of your labor and delivery, the stages of delivery are the same for most women. Knowing where you are in the labor process should help you feel more in control and therefore less anxious during the birthing process.

HEY MOM!

When a woman tells you she was in labor for 40 hours, you can bet she's counting from the earliest stages of labor—not hard labor. Don't let tales like this one worry you.

Stage One Labor

The first stage of labor brings you from the first twinge of a contraction to the serious business of getting ready for birth. This first stage can be long—up to three days sometimes. That's why it's important to know what's going on so you don't rush to the hospital or birthing center only to sit around for hours or be sent home because it's still too early.

In the very early stage, you might not even know you're in labor. You might feel some menstrual-like cramps, a bloated, constipated feeling, or a pain that starts in the back and moves across to your abdomen. Gradually the discomfort will grow into sharp pains that become more regular and intense.

During this early stage, you might (or might not) have two signs of progressing labor:

- You might pass the blood-tinged mucous plug that had been sealing off your cervix. This will come out of your vagina and will show on your underwear or in the toilet.
- You might "break water." This refers to a rupture of the membranes of the amniotic sac. When this happens, amniotic fluid will leak from your vagina and make it look as if you have wet your pants. If this happens and you haven't begun labor contractions yet, this is a sign that you might begin within 24 to 48 hours. It is very important to keep the vaginal area very clean at this point, because the baby is now unprotected from germs. Do not take a bath, have sexual intercourse, or use a tampon to stop the flow.

This early stage of labor can last hours (or even days), so don't get too excited and do things that will get you tired out. It's not necessary at this point to do any breathing exercises, for example, and forget about putting the last touches on the baby's bedroom. The best thing to do is get some rest. You have a physically challenging job ahead of you—rest up.

DADDY ALERT!

Your job in the first stage of labor is to keep your partner (and yourself) calm. Try relaxation exercises and a massage. Play board games or go for a short walk together. Do whatever you have to do to stay calm and distract your partner.

If your early labor drags on, you're bound to get hungry, but watch what you eat. During labor, your stomach and intestines slow down, so you don't want to burden your sluggish digestive tract. Eat light foods that will give you energy. Toast, crackers with jelly or honey, hot cereal, and soup are all good choices. Above all, drink lots of water and juice to keep yourself from dehydrating.

The early stage of labor ends when contractions are about five minutes apart for an hour. Your doctor will tell you to let her know when your contractions reach a certain frequency and intensity. She'll also tell you not to worry too much about accidentally delivering your baby on the living room floor. Despite all the anxiety, most new mothers manage to arrive at their birthing place when it's not too soon and not too late. If you pay attention to your body, you will hear the body signals that say, "It's time to go!"

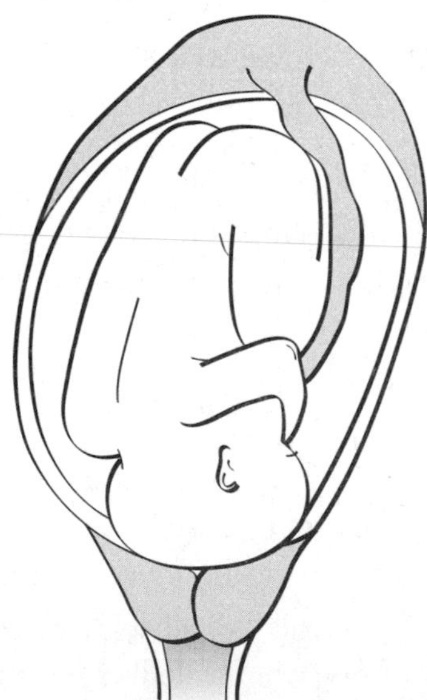

During the first stage of labor, the tough cervix begins to soften and stretch to prepare to let the baby's head pass through during delivery. This is called effacement.

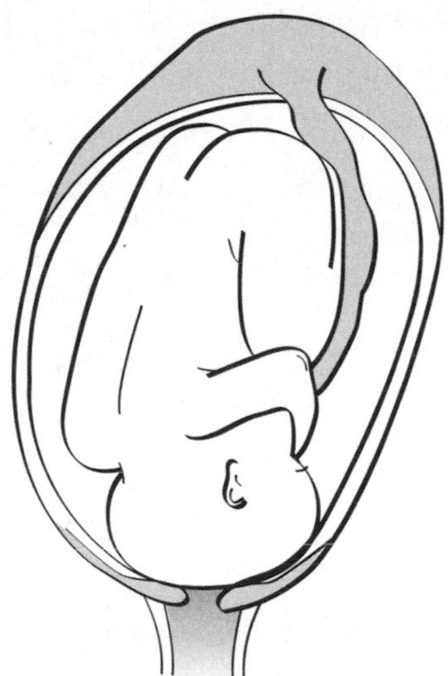

As the first stage of labor continues, the cervix begins to dilate (about 1 to 1½ centimeters per hour). When the cervix dilates to 10 centimeters, delivery of the baby begins.

Stage Two Labor

Stage two labor is more intense than early labor. You might not be able to talk or walk through these contractions. In this stage, you should not eat anything (if an anesthetic is administered when the stomach is full, severe nausea might occur and complicate delivery). You may sip some fluids or eat hard candy or ice chips if you like.

Now is the time to use the breathing and relaxation exercises you were taught if you went to childbirth classes. These will help you relax and tolerate the pain. But don't expect them to make the pain go away completely—it is very unusual for this to happen. Expecting a pain-free labor will probably leave you very disappointed and surprised. Your cervix has to dilate to 10 centimeters, and the baby has to work his or her way down the birth canal—this just hurts.

PREGNANCY FACTS

First babies usually take longer to deliver than subsequent babies, because the unused birth passage is tense and unyielding.

Now is the time to get going. In the second stage of labor, you should go to the hospital or birthing center to prepare for delivery. Ideally, you will have preregistered and won't have too many forms to fill out between contractions. When you're admitted, you will meet a nurse (or midwife, if you are delivering your baby in a birthing center) who will guide you through the rest of your labor and delivery. She will explain what's happening and will answer your questions. To prepare for the safe delivery of a baby in a hospital, you can expect the following:

- Temperature, blood pressure, pulse, and respiration will be taken frequently throughout your labor.
- The nurse will apply a fetal heart monitor. This is a machine that will indicate your baby's heart rate and the frequency and duration of your contractions. The monitor might be attached externally to your abdomen or internally to your baby's scalp.
- The doctor or nurse will perform a vaginal exam to check the dilation of your cervix to judge how far along you are in the labor process.
- You'll tell the nurse whether you want a natural or medicated birth. So much depends on how labor progresses that it is almost impossible to know, ahead of time, whether or not a woman will want or need pain medication. Regardless of what she has written in her birth plan, a laboring woman should always have the option to change her mind about pain relief.

In days long passed, it was routine to give women in labor an enema (to empty the bowel, making more room for the birth canal to expand) and to shave their pubic hair (to keep bacteria out of the vaginal area). Today, many doctors and midwives have abandoned these practices, and recent studies show they are unnecessary. Still, some continue the habit. When you write your birth plan (see Chapter 12), talk to your doctor about having an enema and shaving. If you have the option, tell the primary nurse when you enter the hospital what you and your doctor have agreed upon.

You will have a bed to lie on during labor, but that doesn't mean that lying on your back is the best labor position for you. If you are not hooked up to fetal monitors or an IV pole, ask the nurses if you can get up and move around. Try different positions during your contractions until you find one that makes you feel most comfortable. Possible labor positions include the following:

- Kneeling on your hands and knees. This is especially good if you have pain in your back.
- Walking around. This can help the labor process move along. Standing up allows gravity to work for you because being upright helps the baby move down the birth canal.

- Kneeling on the bed and holding on to your partner. If he sits on the edge of the bed and you kneel behind him, you can let gravity work for you without leaving the bed.
- Sitting in a rocking chair.
- Sitting or standing in a shower, if allowed.
- Sitting or lying on a large ball (sometimes called a birthing ball). This is not possible, however, if you have an epidural to numb pain early in your labor.

The best labor position is the one that makes you feel most comfortable. Try them all out, and move back and forth from one to another. If you're able, moving around helps labor progress.

This stage of labor can last about four to six hours as your cervix continues to dilate (about 1 to 1½ centimeters per hour). Things move along a little faster if you've previously given birth.

As your cervix becomes almost fully dilated, you'll have contractions that last for 60 to 90 seconds. You'll also have a strong urge to push out your baby. This "bearing down" is like pushing out a difficult bowel movement. You strain the vaginal muscles to push the baby down the birth canal. When you first feel this urge, the nurses might tell you not to push yet. This means you aren't dilated enough for the baby to be pushed out. (It can be hard to resist the urge but they know what they're doing!)

When you are fully dilated (at 10 centimeters) and feel the urge to push, it's time for delivery. If you are in a hospital, you might be wheeled into a delivery room, where your doctor will join you, or you might deliver right in the labor room. After a quick examination and review of your labor, you'll be relieved to hear the doctor say, "Push!" with the next contraction. This pushing stage can last anywhere from a few minutes to a few hours. This is where you might find yourself getting very tired and impatient, but the end is near.

This is also when the doctor might perform an episiotomy. This is a surgical incision that is made from your vagina toward the rectum in order to make the opening wider. An episiotomy prevents tearing, which can damage the pelvic muscles. If there is enough time to give a local anesthetic into the area, the doctor will do that. But if you've had an epidural, you won't need further anesthesia.

There is some debate over the necessity of having an episiotomy. Certainly, it's not a necessity if the baby's head has enough room to pass through. But whether or not to perform an episiotomy is a judgment call made by the physician at the last moment. I would estimate that probably over 90 percent of first-time mothers get an episiotomy. On subsequent babies, there is more room, and the necessity for an episiotomy is less likely.

Instrument-Assisted Birth

If the baby is slow coming down the birth canal, he or she might need what's called an *instrument-assisted birth.* At this point, a woman under the care of a midwife at home or at a birthing center would be transferred to the care of a physician, who would take over the delivery process. She might also be moved to her backup hospital if the physician feels this would be best. A very long labor can endanger the life of the baby, so in some cases, forceps or vacuum extraction can be lifesavers. Forceps are large, spoonlike metal tongs, the smooth blades of which are inserted into the vagina and placed on either side of the baby's head. A vacuum extraction uses a caplike device that attaches to the baby's head and uses suction to extract the baby. These instruments are used in about 10 percent of all vaginal deliveries (especially medicated ones, in which the mother is unable to push hard enough).

Induced Labor

Although it's always best to let nature take its course, sometimes labor must be induced. This means to cause labor before it begins on its own. In 2006, 22 percent of pregnancies were artificially induced in the United States. Because of this rather high statistic, the American Academy of Obstetrics and Gynecology has revised its guidelines for induction to help make the process uniform and safe for the mother and the baby.

There are many reasons a doctor or midwife might decide to induce labor (which is always done in a hospital setting). Common elective reasons include:

- The convenience of making arrangements for other family members, like other young children in the house
- To ensure that a particular physician with whom you have a special relationship is in attendance, especially if the doctor is a member of a group practice
- To schedule the baby's delivery when a particular medical specialist can be in attendance, such as a neonatologist (a doctor who specializes in newborn babies)
- To reduce anxiety if you have had a history of a poor outcome in a prior pregnancy, such as a stillbirth
- If you live far away from the hospital or if you have a history of an extremely fast prior delivery

An induction is medically necessary when the risks of continuing the pregnancy are greater for the mother or the unborn baby than the risks of an induction. Medical induction is appropriate in the following cases:

- Pregnancies complicated by preeclampsia, eclampsia, diabetes, hypertension, Rh incompatibility, or fetal growth restriction (see Chapter 21)
- A pregnancy that is post-date or one that goes beyond 41 weeks gestation
- If an infection exists in the amniotic fluid (chorioamnionitis) or if the membranes rupture prematurely (PROM)
- If the baby is projected to be larger than 8 pounds and 13 ounces
- When the testing of fetal well-being does not assure health of the unborn child or when the amniotic fluid has decreased (oligohydramnios)

Some studies suggest that elective induction can lead to an increase in risk of a cesarean delivery. If the cervix is not ripened (soft, short, and effaced) prior to an induction, this can be the case. But if the cervix is ripe, a successful induction with a vaginal delivery of a healthy baby is likely.

If an elective induction of labor is planned on a pregnancy less than 39 weeks gestation, an amniocentesis (a needle placed through the abdomen into the uterus to extract amniotic fluid) is required to check on the level of fetal lung maturity. Special tests are performed on the fluid to tell your doctor that the baby is ready to breathe on his or her own. If the lungs are not fully developed, an elective induction should wait until the baby is ready to breathe in the outside world.

There are two ways to induce labor. If the cervix is uneffaced and closed, you will be asked to go to the hospital the night before the induction to have a special medicated gel (a prostaglandin) placed on the cervix. This medication will soften the cervix and occasionally start labor without the need of any further medication. If you have had a prior cesarean delivery, you will not be offered induction in this way; the medical literature suggests that the use of prostaglandin on a woman who has had a cesarean delivery increases the risk of uterine rupture.

If the cervix is ripened (soft, effaced, or dilated), you will be admitted to the hospital in the morning of your induction. The medication oxytocin will be administered through an intravenous (IV) drip. This will cause contractions to begin. Oxytocin is administered through a needle in the arm or the back of the hand. The needle is connected by a tube to a medication bag that hangs from an IV stand. This controls dosage.

PREGNANCY FACTS

A pregnant woman releases the hormone oxytocin when her nipples are stimulated. To induce labor naturally, she might be asked to rub her nipples and stay alert for signs of uterine contractions.

Usually an induction begins slowly, with very little use of oxytocin. Then the rate of medication is increased gradually until strong contractions build in intensity and come closer together, mimicking normal labor. If labor hasn't begun after six to eight hours, the induction will be stopped, in all probability, and a second induction might be scheduled for a later time or a cesarean will be considered.

Whether the birth is natural, medicated, instrument-assisted, or induced, eventually your baby's head will "crown." This means the doctor (and you, with the help of a mirror) can see the baby's head pushing its way through the vaginal opening. After another strong contraction and a push, the head might be delivered. At this point, the doctor might tell you to stop pushing. It can be very difficult to resist the urge to push, but some doctors and midwives like to suction the baby's nose and mouth immediately, in order to remove mucus and amniotic fluid. This takes only a minute and the next push is generally the one that delivers the baby's shoulders and body. Your baby is born! Shortly afterward, the umbilical cord will be clamped and cut.

Stage Three Labor

What? There's more? After the birth of your baby, contractions will continue, at intervals of about one minute, to help deliver the placenta. The contractions help separate the placenta from the uterine wall and move it down into the vagina so you can then push it out. Your doctor might help by pressing and kneading the uterus and gently pulling on the umbilical cord.

After the placenta is delivered, your doctor or midwife will stitch up your episiotomy (if you had one) and any tears (if necessary).

Now you're finished. The labor and delivery that you looked forward to for so long is over and you are now officially a mother. At this time, the nurses will sponge-bathe the lower part of your body, give you a clean gown, and help you put on a sanitary napkin to absorb the blood you will pass. You might also put an ice pack on the perineum (crotch area) to ease the discomfort of the stretched tissues.

During this third stage of labor, your newborn baby is probably lying on your stomach (or nursing, perhaps) while you and your partner admire, praise, and gush over this new miracle of life. If you are planning to breast-feed your baby, you might start nursing right away. (This early breast milk is not high in calories, but is high in antibodies that protect the baby from infection.) If you talk softly to your baby, he might turn and look for the face that goes with the voice he has listened to for the last nine months.

The Least You Need to Know

- Become familiar with the differences between prelabor, false labor, and real labor.
- Stage one of real labor can last for hours or even days.
- Stage two of labor is the real thing. Your contractions will become more frequent and intense, and you'll make the move to your birthing place.
- In stage three labor, the placenta is delivered. The episiotomy and any tears are repaired.
- There are certain circumstances in which labor may be induced. The American Academy of Obstetrics and Gynecology has determined the guidelines that a doctor will follow when making the decision whether or not to induce labor.

Chapter 25
Recovery

In This Chapter

- Adjusting to your postpartum body: enlarged breasts, extra body weight, vaginal and rectal discomfort, and constipation
- Bonding with your newborn and the scoop on "rooming in" and visits
- Getting through postpartum with your partner
- Beating the "baby blues"

You've done it! You've nurtured your baby through the months of pregnancy and withstood the pains of labor and delivery, and now you have a newborn infant in your arms. A whole new adventure now begins. But before you jump into the next phase of your life, take some time to consider how this exceptional event will affect your relationship with your body, your baby, your partner, and yourself.

You and Your New Body

You're no longer pregnant, but your body just isn't the same as it was. You've changed, and it takes time to get back into shape. For example, your breasts are still large (whether you intend to breast-feed or not) and you're probably still padded with a layer of extra fat that your body stored in case the baby needed emergency nutrition. Your pregnancy belly is gone, but it's still not flat. Be patient with the healing process and give your body and yourself some special pampering during the postnatal period.

Breasts

Your breasts are definitely not the same as they were before you became pregnant. They are still much larger. If you plan to breast-feed, your breasts will stay enlarged for as long as you continue to nurse. Within three days after delivery, they will fill with milk and become hard, heavy, full, and maybe uncomfortable. This is the time to make sure you have a comfortable, supportive nursing bra. Your breast discomfort will be eased each time the baby sucks at the breast and relieves the pressure.

If you are not planning to breast-feed, there's no way to get the message to your body. Your breasts will still fill with milk and become hard, heavy, and full. It takes about 14 days for the glands to stop supplying milk; this is called the "drying up" period. During that time, your breasts might be painful.

Don't try to relieve the pressure by hand-expressing milk; this gives your body a signal to keep producing more, and it will be impossible for the milk supply to dry up. The discomfort is temporary, but you can make this time less distressing if you use cold compresses, wear a supportive bra 24 hours a day, and take ibuprofen pain relievers. Also, try to keep your breasts out of warm water as you shower or bathe; it stimulates more milk production. Unfortunately, there are no safe medications to dry up your milk supply. You will have to wait for Mother Nature to do the job.

Belly Size

Your pregnancy belly is gone—well, not quite gone, but it's certainly much smaller. Don't be disappointed if you can't zip up your jeans the morning after your delivery. It took nine months for your uterus to grow and expand; it will take about six weeks for it to return to its normal size. A post-pregnancy belly is especially common after the births of second and third children, or more. The muscles of the abdomen just don't bounce back like they used to.

Body Size

If your body weight after delivery is a bit heavier than your prepregnancy weight, don't get upset. Your breasts alone add extra weight; your uterus might now weigh 2 pounds instead of its usual 2 ounces. There's a bit of stored body fat that will quickly fall away now that the baby doesn't need it. Watch your diet and give yourself six weeks to return to your normal weight. (If you're breast-feeding, your body will hang on to pregnancy fat, but don't panic: This will disappear when breast-feeding ends. Those extra 5 pounds will melt away!)

If your body weight after delivery is much higher than your prepregnancy weight, that's a different story. You've added pounds that have nothing to do with pregnancy. You simply ate more than necessary and now you've got some work to do. The MyPyramid dietary guidelines offered in Chapter 14 are not just for pregnant women. Use them now to help you choose nutritious foods (in the proper serving sizes) to help you lose weight while maintaining your health and energy. You should also talk to your doctor about starting an exercise program. As soon as you are physically able, body movement will not only help you shed extra pounds, it will speed recovery by bringing more oxygen and glucose to cells that are trying to heal.

After Pains

And you thought your contractions ended with the delivery of your baby! Your uterus will continue to contract in order to shrink back to its usual size and to help push out any leftover tissue. These pains might be hardly noticeable or quite sharp (especially with the second or third child or when breast-feeding). These pains are most noticeable in the first few days after delivery. If they really bother you, ask your doctor about using a pain reliever.

HEY MOM!

Although you don't have monthly menstrual periods while you're breast-feeding, this doesn't mean you can't get pregnant again! Talk to your doctor about using contraceptives while breast-feeding.

Bleeding

If you thought one of the great advantages of pregnancy is not having to deal with your period for nine months—it's payback time. After delivery, you will bleed bright red blood that is like a heavy period. To add to the fun, you must use a sanitary pad—not a tampon. This heavy bleeding will continue for about three days. Then it will lighten up and turn a pinkish-brown. Eventually, it will turn white or yellow and then gradually taper off completely. This bleeding might end in about two weeks or it might last as long as four.

Your actual menstrual period probably won't resume until seven to nine weeks after delivery, but it would also be normal if it did not return for three or four months. There is really no such thing as "normal" here. The first period after delivery can be very erratic. It might be heavy or very light. It might start and then stop again for awhile. But within a month or two, your system will regulate itself. If you're breast-feeding, your period might stop for as long as you continue to nurse. (As your baby begins to sleep through the night and feed less often, your menstrual cycle might resume even though you're still nursing.)

Vaginal and Anal Discomfort

You might not be able to sit comfortably for about a week after your delivery, for two reasons: (1) You've had an episiotomy or a perineal tear with repair, or (2) you have hemorrhoids. Both can be a real pain.

The episiotomy is the surgical opening that is made from the vagina toward the rectum to widen the opening for birth. If your doctor used this technique, it has been stitched up, and like any cut with stitches, it will hurt at first and might itch later.

If you didn't have hemorrhoids before your delivery, you might very well have them now. The pushing and straining during labor and delivery can force them out and add to your *postpartum* discomfort.

For the discomfort of an episiotomy or hemorrhoids, you can try any of the following remedies:

- Pain medication (ask your doctor)
- Ice packs
- Warm sitz baths
- Chilled witch-hazel pads

You might also invest about $20 in a doughnut cushion. This is a pillow with a hole in the center that lets you sit down without putting pressure on your sore spots.

Bowel Battles

Pushing out your baby at delivery was good practice for your next bowel movement. During labor, bowel activity slows down, and if you used pain medication, it can make the bowel sluggish, too. If you've had a cesarean, your bowels will take even longer to recover. All this adds up to large, hard stools that can be difficult to pass. Prepare for this as soon as you're ready to eat and drink after your delivery. Go for high-fiber foods (such as fruits and whole grains) and lots of water. Ask your doctor about using a natural laxative. When you do have the urge, don't strain too much because this will worsen or cause hemorrhoids. If you do not have a bowel movement after three or four days, it's time to get your doctor's okay to use an enema in order to get your plumbing working again. You can buy a simple, packaged, and prepared enema at any pharmacy. Don't be afraid to use it—you've given birth to a baby; now you can do anything.

The C-Section Shuffle

Women who have had a cesarean delivery don't walk—they shuffle. They keep their feet flat on the floor and take tiny steps, shuffling one foot before the other. They do this because it hurts to walk! If you've had a cesarean, you will find out very quickly after your delivery that you don't recuperate from major abdominal surgery in a day or two. It can take two to three weeks just to start walking normally again. Your abdominal muscles have suffered a severe trauma, and even walking might be painful. (Sneezing or coughing is even worse.) In addition to the normal body changes after a delivery, you'll be recovering from surgery. So do yourself a favor and call in as much help as you can possibly get. Your baby will demand all your energy and your body will demand healing time. So get some help, let the dishes pile up, and don't worry about cleaning the house.

The Medical Checkup

About six weeks after delivery, your doctor will want to see you again. This visit is very important. Your doctor will check to make sure the uterus has returned to its normal size and position. She'll look to be sure vaginal stitches have dissolved and the cervix has healed. She will check your breasts for signs of uncooperative milk glands or engorgement (a painful condition that results if the breasts are not emptied of milk during each feeding). She will take time to talk to you about your weight, your feelings and emotions, and about contraception. This is a great opportunity to visit with someone who knows what you've been through and can help you get back on your feet.

Before this checkup, you should call your doctor to report any of the following symptoms:

- Fever over 100.4°F
- Heavy bleeding (soaking a sanitary napkin every hour)
- Pain and burning during urination
- Persistent pain in vaginal and anal areas
- Painful, hot breasts
- Nausea or vomiting
- The return of bright red bleeding after it had become brownish
- Severe pain in your lower abdomen

Don't wait until your postpartum checkup to tell your doctor about these symptoms. Call right away.

You and Your Baby

You now have a child to get acquainted with, care for, and love. Although this little human being is completely helpless and depends on you to make the world work, she is not very critical. She won't mind if you're not too sure how to be a mother right in the beginning. She won't tell if you put the diaper on backward. She'll give you lots of practice and lots of time to get it right. Be as patient with yourself.

DADDY ALERT!

Want to be a hero and at the same get some quiet time to bond with your baby? Offer to do some of the nighttime feedings. (If your wife is breast-feeding, use a bottle of breast milk that was expressed earlier in the day.) Sitting in the quiet of the night, just you and the baby, offers an indescribable opportunity to feel a sense of oneness.

Bonding

Bonding is a word that has been used to describe the special attachment between parents and their children. It's a myth that this attachment must happen immediately after birth in order for the child to grow up emotionally secure. Some new parents might feel an instant loving attraction to their newborn, but for many, this bond takes time. After all, most newborns don't look like the pink, cuddly cherubs on all the baby cards. And they do little more than pee, poop, cry, eat, and sleep. If you don't fall madly in love with this little person, don't beat yourself up over it. Bonding is a long, complex process that happens over time, as you both get to know each other.

Whether the first meeting with your new baby takes place in the delivery or birthing room immediately after childbirth or 24 hours later after a particularly difficult cesarean delivery, your chances of creating a strong, secure, and loving bond are the same. This attachment grows as you change diapers, give baths, feed, sing lullabies, and cuddle. Getting to know any person takes time; don't feel a need to rush this very important relationship.

If you don't feel a growing interest in your baby after a few weeks, or if you feel angry or resentful, don't be embarrassed to talk to your pediatrician about this. These feelings are not completely uncommon, and he or she can help you deal with them before they get out of hand.

GREEN FROM THE START

Bath time offers a wonderful bonding opportunity. It also gives you a chance to choose products that are kind to the baby's skin and to the planet. Check the purity of the personal care products at the Safe Cosmetics website. This site offers a product guide with a searchable database of the ingredients and safety ratings of more than 14,000 personal hygiene products. Check it out at www.cosmeticsdatabase.com.

Rooming In

If you have given birth in a hospital, you might be offered an option called "rooming in." This means that your baby will stay in the room with you at all times. This arrangement has two major advantages:

- It allows the two of you to get acquainted.
- It allows you to practice some mothering skills under the watchful eyes of the maternity nurses.

On the other hand, rooming in has one major disadvantage: It keeps you from getting the rest you need to recuperate enough to go home and take charge. Hospital stays are pitifully short these days, making it hard for new mothers to get back on their feet before being shown the door.

If you have the option of rooming in, choose what is best for you. Don't feel guilty if you'd like to sleep rather than mother right now. And don't feel inadequate or afraid if you want to give it a try right away. No one in the hospital will judge your mothering skills by the choice you make.

Visitors

If you deliver at a hospital, the visiting hours will be arranged for certain hours each day. Most hospitals allow unlimited visits for the dad, but they try to limit the hours for others. This is a good thing because you desperately need to rest. Your body has just been through a major physical trauma and it needs time to recuperate. Well-meaning family and friends steal this time and force you to shift your energy to the tasks of entertaining, talking, and staying awake. Even if you feel great, try to discourage too many people from visiting. It won't be long before you're dragging yourself around, praying for quiet and solitude.

When you get home, you will still need time to rest. Try to limit your entertaining to short visits. Don't hesitate to announce, "Thank you so much for coming, but the baby and I both need to get some rest now." This is one time when everyone should understand the lack of social enthusiasm.

The best kind of visitor is one who comes to help. If you can find a friend or relative who will visit with the baby while you take a nap, invite him or her often! If you know of someone who is good at taking charge of things such as laundry and dishes, tell him or her to come on over. Don't be shy about asking for help when people ask to visit.

You and Your Partner

You and your partner are no longer just a couple; you're a threesome (or more!). The new family member changes your relationship forever and, with a little forethought and care, for the better.

Back in the Saddle

On the very, very bottom of the list called "Things I want to do right after the delivery of my baby" are the words "have sex." Your body is in recovery, so this activity won't be moving up the list anytime soon.

It's recommended that couples wait until after the postpartum checkup (at four to six weeks after delivery) before having vaginal intercourse. (Oral sex, manual stimulation, and orgasm are fine any time you're up to it.) This waiting period gives an episiotomy time to heal. Time allows the muscles of the vagina to regain elasticity, stop the vaginal flow, and ease uterine soreness. If your doctor doesn't mention it, don't leave your postpartum checkup without asking whether your body is physically ready for sex.

Even when your body is ready, you might not feel in the mood. Don't panic: You're in good company. Many women do not feel very sexy for several months after giving birth. There are lots of reasons for this:

- As soon as the placenta is delivered, hormone levels drop and sexy feelings plummet.
- The vaginal lining thins out, making it drier and more susceptible to irritation or infection.
- Although the stitches of an episiotomy might heal, there can be soreness in the area for months.

- The exhaustion caused by round-the-clock baby care makes it very difficult to get excited about any kind of physical activity.
- Breast-feeding reduces the normal levels of the hormone estrogen, which supplies lubrication during sex. This can make intercourse painful.

No one can tell you when you're ready to have sex again. Only you know how you feel. Give yourself time and be sure to talk to your partner about your feelings. He has no way of knowing what's going on inside your body and mind unless you tell him.

DADDY ALERT!

You might need a whole new store of patience while you wait for your partner to become your lover once again. Take it easy, be romantic (but not pushy). On the other hand, if you don't feel so sexy yourself just yet, don't worry. This is a common feeling in new dads and gives both you and your partner time to get slowly reacquainted.

If you're physically healed but are afraid that sex will hurt, take it slow and take control. Use a lubricating cream (K-Y Jelly or Astroglide, for example) until your own natural lubrication system is back in working order. Ask your doctor whether it would be appropriate to use a prescribed estrogen cream to lessen the vaginal pain and tenderness. If your partner uses condoms, make sure they're the lubricated kind. Vary your sex position. Woman-on-top allows you more control of penetration and puts less pressure on your sore areas. Find time during the day to save energy you can use in bed at night: Take a nap, skip the vacuuming, use frozen vegetables instead of fresh, and hire a babysitter so you can take a relaxing bath.

Believe it or not, it won't be too long before you and your partner are lovers again and you both feel terrific. Just be patient with yourself and try not to rush the healing process.

Sharing the Baby

Mothers know best. It just seems right that you know when the baby should play, sleep, and eat. You know what's "too rough" and what's "too loud." It's an inborn sixth sense that you're given to help raise your children. But this "fact" gets many new mothers in trouble with their husbands. The new dad in your house probably already feels like a third wheel. Everyone coos over you and the baby. Everyone asks how you and the baby are doing. Life now revolves around you and the baby, and every time he tries to join the inner circle, your protective instinct might push him out.

Think about it. Have you said anything in the past day that sounds something like: "Lower your voice, you'll wake the baby." "Hold her head when you pick her up." "Don't be so rough with him." "That's not how you do it." If you have, you might need to practice the skill of sharing.

Your partner's parenting skills might be different from yours, but that doesn't necessarily mean they're wrong. If you want him to be an involved, caring dad, give him a chance to learn how to parent. Hold your breath and leave him alone when you're tempted to step in and whisk the baby away from him. Limit the number of times you tell him he's wrong each day. Make sure that he and the baby have time alone every day (and not just when she's sleeping). If he's taking a back seat, encourage him to be more involved. Ask him to feed the baby or take him for a walk. Praise his attempts. And be willing to admit your own uncertainty.

New moms and dads both experience feelings of inadequacy, anger, confusion, uncertainty, guilt, and worry. If this is your first baby, you are both learning the ropes together. If you make an effort to share your baby, you will have each other to fall back on and look to for reinforcement. This dynamic will come in handy down the road as you raise your child together.

Sharing Responsibility

Sharing the coos and smiles of a new baby is the fun part. But sharing the diapering, feeding, and caring is something else. It's not uncommon for a new mother to resent what looks like an unequal distribution of family responsibilities. While you're at home dealing with an endless cycle of crying, feeding, diapering, and washing, the baby's other parent walks out the door each morning to "freedom" in the world of adult conversations, "important" interactions, and financial rewards. You might find yourself seething with anger when he returns home with a cheery, "So how was your day?"

Before you get yourself into this corner, talk to your spouse about family responsibilities. He's busy all day; you're busy all day. So how will you divide the baby responsibilities when you're both at home? Talk, talk, talk. Make time every day to talk about your feelings and his, too. Explain your needs and create a plan that makes both of you happy. This habit of open communication will serve you well if you plan to return to work eventually. If you don't speak up now and create a system that balances the load, you'll find yourself walking in the door after a hard day at work only to find a hungry baby, a pile of laundry on the washing machine, a load of groceries in the car, and a husband contentedly watching TV. Speak up now; talk to each other about how you can both take responsibility for caring for a child who belongs equally to both of you.

You

You have looked forward to this time for so long. You've imagined the bliss of holding your baby in your arms and stroking your fingers against her soft cheek. You assumed this would be the happiest time of your life. So why are you crying? Why does the sound of the baby's cries make you so angry? Why do you snap at anyone who tries to help? It's enough to make you feel like you're going crazy. But you're not.

It's estimated that the majority of new mothers experience what's called "baby blues." For the first week or two after your baby is born, you can expect to be on an emotional roller coaster that only you can understand. Most medical experts believe that postpartum baby blues are caused by dramatic changes in hormonal levels after birth. (Levels of estrogen and progesterone drop as much as tenfold!) On top of that, it makes perfect sense for a woman to feel unhappy when she is zapped with instant body fat, constipation, hemorrhoids, abdominal pains, stitches in sensitive areas, painful breasts, bleeding from reproductive organs, and exhaustion. Then hand her a completely helpless human being to care for around the clock. You're bound to get a moody and grumpy person every time. Don't worry too much if you get the baby blues. The feeling is natural, it's very common, and in the vast majority of cases it is temporary.

For about 1 in 10 women, however, the blues turn into postpartum depression (PPD). This is a real disorder that should not be ignored or downplayed. It lasts much longer than the blues (usually from a month to a year). The emotional problems are much more severe and worsen, rather than improve, with time. Women with PPD report signs of depression, such as a sense of helplessness and gloom, loss of self-esteem, grief or sadness, anxiety or worry, irritability, suicidal thoughts, and retreat from relationships with others. A loss of appetite, energy, memory, and libido are common, too. These new moms are not failures; they are suffering the effects of changing hormone levels and stress. If your baby blues get worse instead of better, speak up and get help as soon as you suspect you might have a postpartum mood disorder. Don't ever hesitate to tell your doctor about your feelings. She knows exactly what you're talking about and can help you through it.

There are things you can do to avoid and treat postpartum depression. Most revolve around simple self-pampering. Go over this checklist every day to be sure that you're getting your daily dose of personal care:

- Take a nap.
- Take a relaxing bath.
- Ask for help.

- Eat healthful foods.
- Drink lots of fluids.
- Get fresh air.
- Ignore nonessential housework.
- Talk to a friend.
- Lower all "perfect" standards.
- Spend time giving love to your baby.

You can also help yourself get through this tough time by contacting a support group. There are many mothers out there who have been through what you're going through and are eager to talk to you. For starters, contact the organization called Postpartum Support International at 1-800-944-4773 or visit the website www.depressionafterdelivery.com. This organization offers a packet of informative materials and contact with women who have experienced baby blues and are available by telephone to support other struggling mothers.

The Least You Need to Know

- Your body will not bounce back immediately to the way it was before you had a baby.
- Bonding is a lengthy, complex process that can't be rushed.
- It's best to limit your visitors immediately after the baby's birth.
- Keep the lines of communication open between you and your partner.
- It's natural to feel down and irritable after the birth of a baby. But if the problem gets worse with time instead of better, you might have postpartum depression and need professional help.
- Do something to pamper yourself every day.

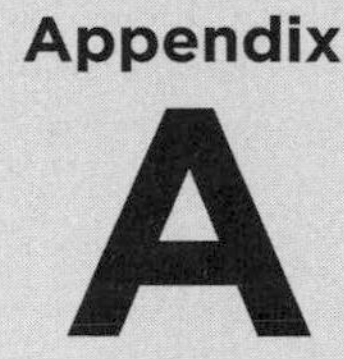

Glossary

abruptio placenta A condition in which the placenta pulls away from the uterine wall.

Alpha-fetoprotein (AFP) A screening test given between Weeks 16 and 18 that identifies a potential risk of birth defects.

American College of Obstetricians and Gynecologists (ACOG) An organization of obstetrician/gynecologists that sets universal guidelines and standards of care for doctors to follow to ensure patient safety.

amniocentesis A test for fetal maturity or defects that involves inserting a needle into the womb in order to extract a small amount of amniotic fluid for analysis.

analgesics Medications that relieve pain.

anemia A blood condition in which there is an abnormally low number of red blood cells. These cells carry oxygen from your lungs to all parts of your body in order to help it function normally.

anesthetics Medications that produce a loss of sensation.

antioxidants Substances found naturally in the body and in certain foods that battle free radicals that, if left unchallenged, damage body cells and cause a long list of diseases and ailments.

Apgar evaluation An evaluation of a newborn given at one minute and five minutes after birth. It evaluates how well the baby adapts to the outside world based on appearance, pulse rate, grimace, activity, and respiration.

bed rest Doctor's orders to stay in bed for all or a part of a pregnancy. This is often necessary to treat complications of pregnancy such as premature labor, preeclampsia, and unexplained bleeding.

blastocyst The name of the developing embryo when it first finds its nesting place in the uterus.

blood pressure The amount of pressure your blood vessels (arteries) exhibit while supplying and maintaining your body organs with enough blood.

Braxton Hicks contractions Practice contractions that prepare the muscles of the uterus to deliver a baby.

breech presentation Position of the fetus buttocks or feet down rather than head down.

cervix The entrance to the uterus, which opens during labor to let the fetus travel through the birth canal into the world.

cesarean section A surgical method of delivering a baby through an incision made in the wall of the abdomen and uterus.

chorionic villus sampling (CVS) A diagnostic test that can be given as early as the ninth week of pregnancy to identify or rule out certain genetic defects.

colostrum Premilk. Richer in protein and lower in fat and milk sugar than breast milk (which doesn't come in until three or four days after delivery), colostrum contains antibodies that may be important in protecting the baby against disease.

conception Fertilization of an egg by sperm.

contraction A strong, painful rhythmic squeezing of the uterus that pushes the baby through the birth canal.

cord prolapse A relatively rare obstetrical emergency in which the umbilical cord drops out of the uterus into the vagina before the baby. The result of early rupture of the amniotic sac, a prolapsed umbilical cord can become dangerously compressed by the weight of the baby, causing oxygen deprivation and even death of the baby.

cystitis A common bacterial bladder infection that causes painful urination, bloody urine, and fever in some cases.

dilate To open the cervix 10 centimeters. When dilation occurs, your baby is ready to be pushed through your vagina and out of your body.

doppler A hand-held device that uses ultrasound vibrations to listen to the fetal heart rate.

Down's syndrome A condition in which a child has an extra twenty-first chromosome. These babies have a distinct appearance and may have several birth defects, most commonly abnormalities of the heart and some degree of mental retardation that ranges from minimal to severe.

ectopic pregnancy A pregnancy that occurs outside the uterus, usually in the fallopian tube.

edema Swelling caused by an accumulation of fluid in the body's tissues.

efface To begin to "thin" the cervix.

embryo A medical term used to refer to the developing baby before it is 12 weeks old in the uterus.

engagement See *lightening*.

engorgement A painful condition that happens to breast-feeding moms when the breasts are not emptied during each feeding and they become overly full.

enzymes Proteins produced by the body that push all living cells into action. They are the catalysts for all bodily functions.

episiotomy A surgical incision made from the vagina toward the rectum in order to widen the vaginal opening for birth.

false labor The contractions that make you think you are in real labor when you're not. They are a false alarm.

fetal growth retardation An abnormality of fetal growth inside the womb that causes a tenfold increase in mortality.

fetus An unborn child. This term is usually used after the 12th week of pregnancy.

forceps Large, spoonlike metal tongs, the two blades of which are inserted into the vagina and placed on either side of the baby's head in an instrument-assisted birth.

genetic counselor A professional who has advanced training in the study of how genetic traits pass from one generation to the next. Genetic counselors consult couples who are at an increased risk of having a child with congenital birth defects.

gestational age The age of a fetus in the womb.

gestational diabetes A high blood sugar condition that some women get during pregnancy. It is different from other forms of diabetes because it usually goes away after the baby is born.

glucose screening A test given between Weeks 24 and 28 of pregnancy to check for gestational diabetes.

group B streptococcus Bacteria found in the vaginal or rectal areas of 10 to 35 percent of all adults. It is harmless and goes unnoticed, unless it is passed from mother to baby during labor. Women who test positive for group B strep may require antibiotics to protect their babies from picking up this potentially life-threatening infection.

hemorrhoids A mass of swollen tissue around the anus or in the rectal canal that may bleed and cause pain during bowel movements, especially after childbirth.

hormones Natural chemicals released by the body to control all aspects of sexuality. The female sex hormones, estrogen and progesterone, are released in monthly cycles throughout the reproductive years and are responsible for the monthly period. In pregnancy, the levels of estrogen and progesterone become elevated.

hyperemesis gravidarum Excessive vomiting during pregnancy.

hypertension High blood pressure.

incompetent cervix A cervix that dilates prematurely with little advance warning.

induced labor Labor that is artificially activated with the drug oxytocin.

instrument-assisted birth A birth that requires either forceps or vacuum extraction to bring the baby through the birth canal.

intrauterine growth restriction (IUGR) A condition in which the fetus is much smaller than he or she should be for his or her gestational age.

kegel An exercise that tones and strengthens the vaginal muscles in preparation for childbirth.

labor The process of childbirth, from dilation of the cervix to the delivery of the baby and the placenta.

lightening The condition that occurs when the baby's presenting part (usually the head) drops down into the pelvis as a first step in preparation for birth; also called *engagement*.

maternity leave Time off from work in which to attend to the medical and personal needs of pregnancy and childbirth. Maternity leave may be paid or unpaid, depending on company policy.

miscarriage (spontaneous abortion) The expulsion of an embryo or fetus before it is able to survive outside the womb (usually before Week 24 of gestation).

molar pregnancy A condition that prevents the placenta from forming properly; this causes the egg to deteriorate and never develop into a fetus.

narcotic A drug that dulls the senses and induces sleep. Narcotics can become addictive. A recreational, or illicit, narcotic is one that is not prescribed for medical purposes and is taken for "fun."

natural childbirth Delivery without benefit of pain medication.

newborn screening test (NBU) (heel-stick test) A test used to screen for various diseases or conditions for which early treatment can prevent death, mental retardation, or physical disability.

nonstress test A test that evaluates the fetal heart rate, and which monitors and records fetal movements.

over-the-counter (OTC) medications Medications that can be bought without a prescription.

perinatologist A medical doctor who specializes in the complications of high-risk pregnancy, labor, and delivery.

placenta The organ that develops in the uterus during pregnancy. The placenta supplies the fetus with blood and nutrients and carries away its waste products.

placenta previa A condition in which the placenta is attached in the lower half of the uterus, blocking some or all of the cervical opening.

postpartum The period after delivery.

preeclampsia A serious condition marked by high blood pressure, edema, and protein in the urine; also called *toxemia*.

prelabor The time before actual labor begins, when the body prepares for childbirth.

prenatal The period between conception and delivery—the time you're pregnant.

prostoglandin A medication that softens the cervix to help it to dilate.

recurrent miscarriage Three or more miscarriages in a row.

Rh incompatibility A condition that occurs when the mother's blood is Rh-negative and the baby's blood is Rh-positive.

stillbirth A fetal death that occurs after Week 24 of pregnancy.

sudden infant death syndrome (SIDS) A sudden, unexplained death of a baby, also known as "crib death." Typically SIDS occurs at night, when a baby stops breathing in his or her sleep and dies.

teratogen Anything in the environment that can cause birth defects in a developing baby. This includes a wide range of drugs, chemicals, infectious diseases, and radiation.

toxic Anything that is harmful, deadly, or poisonous.

toxoplasmosis A parasitic infection spread by cat feces and raw meat that can cause stillbirth or miscarriage in pregnant women and congenital defects in babies.

trimester One of three periods of your pregnancy. The first trimester of your pregnancy is months one, two, and three. The second trimester of your pregnancy is months four, five, and six. The third trimester is months seven, eight, and nine.

ultrasound A technique that uses the echoes of high-frequency sound waves to create an image, or sonogram, of the fetus on a television screen.

umbilical cord The tubelike cord that connects the placenta to the developing baby. The umbilical cord delivers nutrients and oxygenated blood to the baby through the placenta and removes waste products from the baby.

umbilical cord blood banking Saving and storing cord blood at the time of birth for its therapeutic stem cells.

umbilical vein sampling A procedure that enables doctors to extract fetal blood for analysis; also called *cordocentesis*.

vacuum extraction A process in which suction is used to assist in a birth.

vaginal suppository A hard, pill-like medicine that is inserted into the vagina, where it dissolves and is then absorbed by the body tissues.

work discrimination This occurs when an employee is treated differently than other employees due to a prejudice.

zygote The fertilized egg after conception.

Appendix

B

Resources for Further Information

American Academy of Husband-Coached Childbirth
P.O. Box 5224
Sherman Oaks, CA 91413
1-800-4-A-BIRTH
www.bradleybirth.com

American Academy of Pediatrics (AAP)
141 Northwest Point Boulevard
Elk Grove Village, IL 60009-1098
847-434-4000
www.aap.org

American Association of Birth Centers
3123 Gottshall Road
Perkiomenville, PA 18074
215-234-8068
www.birthcenters.org

American Association of Clinical Endocrinologists
245 Riverside Avenue, Suite 200
Jacksonville, FL 32202
904-353-7878
www.aace.com

American College of Nurse-Midwives (ACNM)
8403 Colesville Road, Suite 1550
Silver Spring, MD 20910
240-485-1800
www.midwife.org

American College of Obstetricians and Gynecologists (ACOG)
P.O. Box 96920
Washington, DC 20090
202-638-5577
www.acog.org

American Diabetes Association
1701 N. Beauregard Street
Alexandria, VA 22311
1-800-342-2383
www.diabetes.org

American Society for Reproductive Medicine
1209 Montgomery Highway
Birmingham, AL 35216
205-978-5000
www.asrm.org

American Society of Radiologic Technologists
15000 Central Avenue SE
Albuquerque, NM 87123
1-800-444-2778 (press 5)
www.asrt.org

Arts, Crafts, and Theater Safety
181 Thompson Street, no. 23
New York, NY 10012
212-777-0062
www.artscraftstheatersafety.org

Depression After Delivery
www.depressionafterdelivery.com

Doulas of North America (DONA)
P.O. Box 626
Jasper, IN 47547
1-888-788-DONA
www.dona.org

Drug Abuse Hotlines:
National Drug Abuse Hotline 1-800-662-HELP (1-800-662-4357)
National Institute on Drug Abuse & Alcoholism 1-888-644-6432

Hygeia Foundation, Inc.
and Institute for Perinatal Loss and Bereavement
264 Amity Road Suite 211
Woodbridge, CT 06525
1-800-893-9198
www.hygeia.org

International Childbirth Education Association (ICEA)
1500 Sunday Drive, Suite 102
Raleigh, NC 27607
1-800-624-4934
www.icea.org

March of Dimes Birth Defects Foundation
1275 Mamaroneck Avenue
White Plains, NY 10605
914-997-4488
www.marchofdimes.com

Mothers of Supertwins (MOST)
P.O. Box 306
East Islip, NY 11730
631-859-1110
www.mostonline.org

National Institute of Occupational Safety and Health
395 E Street, S.W.
Patriots Plaza Building
Washington, DC 20201
202-245-0625
www.cdc.gov/niosh

National Marrow Donor Program
3001 Broadway Street Northeast, Suite 500
Minneapolis, MN 55413
1-800-MARROW2 (1-800-627-7692)
www.nmdp.org

National Organization of Mothers of Twins Clubs
2000 Mallory Lane, Suite 130–600
Franklin, TN 37067
248-231-4480
www.nomotc.org

National Pesticide Information Center
Oregon State University
333 Weniger Hall
Corvallis, OR 97331-6502
1-800-858-7378
www.npic.orst.edu

National SHARE Office: Pregnancy and Infant Loss Support
402 Jackson Street
St. Charles, MO 63301
1-800-821-6819
www.nationalshare.org

Phoenix House: Rising Above the Addiction
1-800-DRUG-HELP
www.drughelp.org

RESOLVE: The National Infertility Association
1760 Old Meadow Road, Suite 500
McLean, VA 22102
703-556-7172
www.resolve.org

Sidelines High Risk Pregnancy Support
P.O. Box 1808
Laguna Beach, CA 92652
1-888-447-4754
www.sidelines.org

Online Resources

Online, parents-to-be can now find everything from medical advice to baby furniture to support groups and bulletin boards for sharing information and asking questions. These sites are devoted to helping expectant and new parents find information, support, and reassurance. The following sites can get you started:

www.americanbaby.com

www.babybag.com

www.babycenter.com

www.babyzone.com

www.hygeia.org (for pregnancy loss)

www.pregnancytoday.com

Green Parenting Sites

Dr. Greene: www.drgreene.com

Environmental Working Group: www.ewg.org

Healthy Child Healthy World: www.healthychild.org

Kiwi: Growing Families the Natural and Organic Way: www.kiwimagonline.com

Natural Resources Defense Council: www.nrdc.org

Organic Center: www.organic-center.org

Pesticide Action Network of North America: www.panna.org

Index

C

E

F

G

H

I

J-K

L

M

N

O

P

Q–R

S

T

X-Y-Z